THOREAU
BEYOND
BORDERS

THOREAU BEYOND BORDERS

NEW INTERNATIONAL ESSAYS ON AMERICA'S MOST FAMOUS NATURE WRITER

EDITED BY
FRANÇOIS SPECQ, LAURA DASSOW WALLS,
AND JULIEN NÈGRE

University of Massachusetts Press
Amherst and Boston

ISBN 978-1-62534-556-1 (paper); 555-4 (hardcover)

Designed by Jen Jackowitz
Set in Adobe Garamond and Trade Gothic
Printed and bound by Books International, Inc.

Cover design by Frank Gutbrod
Cover photo by Eberhard Grossgasteiger/Unsplash.com

Library of Congress Cataloging-in-Publication Data
Names: Specq, François, 1965– editor. | Walls, Laura Dassow, editor. |
Nègre, Julien, editor.
Title: Thoreau beyond borders : new international essays on America's most
famous nature writer / edited by François Specq, Laura Dassow Walls,
and Julien Nègre.
Identifiers: LCCN 2020019511 | ISBN 9781625345554 (hardcover) | ISBN
9781625345561 (paperback) | ISBN 9781613768013 (ebook) | ISBN
9781613768020 (ebook)
Subjects: LCSH: Thoreau, Henry David, 1817–1862—Criticism and
Interpretation—Congresses. | Boundaries in literature--Congresses. |
Postcolonialism in literature—Congresses.
Classification: LCC PS3054 .T55 2020 | DDC 818/.309—dc23
LC record available at https://lccn.loc.gov/2020019511

British Library Cataloguing-in-Publication Data
A catalog record for this book is available from the British Library.

CONTENTS

ACKNOWLEDGMENTS

The editors would like to thank those who had a role in organizing the conferences where these essays found their first audiences, particularly Steve Hindle, W. M. Keck Foundation Director of Research at the Huntington Library, Art Museum, and Botanical Gardens, who sponsored and helped organize West of Walden: Thoreau in the 21st Century, held at the Huntington Library in San Marino, California, on April 7–8, 2017, where several of these essays were first presented as lectures. Thanks also to those who assisted with Thoreau from Across the Pond, the international symposium held in Lyon, France, October 18–20, 2017, sponsored by the École Normale Supérieure de Lyon, the Institut d'Histoire des Représentations et des Idées dans les Modernités (IHRIM, affiliated with the Centre National de la Recherche Scientifique), and the Institut des Amériques. Many of these essays were first presented in Lyon, and this book first took shape on the banks of the Rhône and in the surrounding mountains. Laura Dassow Walls offers special thanks to the Concord Free Public Library, particularly to Leslie Perrin Wilson, curator of the William Munroe Special Collections, as well as to the Thoreau Society, which cosponsored the public lecture at which she presented "'Our True Paradise': Thoreau's Concord and the Ecstasy of the Commons" on July 14, 2017, which is published here in revised form under a new title.

Publication of this book is made possible in part by funding support from the Institute for Scholarship in the Liberal Arts, College of Arts and Letters, University of Notre Dame, and by the Institut d'Histoire des Représentations et des Idées dans les Modernités. Initial editing and formatting of the manuscript was provided by Jake McGinnis, research assistant and PhD student in the Department of English, University of Notre Dame, through the generous support of the William P. and Hazel B. White Foundation. The editors would like to thank the anonymous readers of the initial manuscript, whose helpful suggestions led to many clarifications of form and content. We would also like to thank everyone at the

University of Massachusetts Press for all their labor in turning what was once a promising pile of pages into such a beautiful book, including Brian Halley for his steadfast support and enthusiasm, Rachael DeShano for guiding us through this long process, Sally Nichols and Nancy J. Raynor for their patient editorial work, Courtney Andree for her assistance in spreading the word, our indexer Sandy Sadow for her excellent work, and Frank Gutbrod for his evocative cover design. Finally, we thank all those who participated, wherever they were, in the many events of the Thoreau Bicentennial of 2017. The conversations begun and sustained throughout the year, not only in the United States but around the world, are all reflected in these pages, which testify to the passion, commitment, enthusiasm, and generosity of the greater community of Thoreauvians beyond borders.

ABBREVIATIONS

CC   Henry David Thoreau. *Cape Cod.* Edited by Joseph J. Moldenhauer. Princeton, NJ: Princeton University Press, 1988.

Corr   Henry David Thoreau. *The Correspondence.* Edited by Robert N. Hudspeth, Elizabeth Hall Witherell, and Lihong Xie. The Writings of Henry D. Thoreau. 2 vols. to date. Princeton, NJ: Princeton University Press, 2013–.

CW   Ralph Waldo Emerson. *The Collected Works of Ralph Waldo Emerson.* Edited Joseph Slater et al. 10 vols. Cambridge, MA: Harvard University Press, 1971–2013.

EEM   Henry David Thoreau. *Early Essays and Miscellanies.* Edited by Joseph J. Moldenhauer and Edwin Moser, with Alexander Kern. Princeton, NJ: Princeton University Press, 1975.

Exc   Henry David Thoreau. *Excursions.* Edited by Joseph J. Moldenhauer. Princeton, NJ: Princeton University Press, 2007.

Faith   Henry David Thoreau. *Faith in a Seed: The Dispersion of Seeds, and Other Late Natural History Writings.* Edited by Bradley P. Dean. Washington, D.C.: Island Press, 1993.

J   Henry David Thoreau. *The Journal of Henry David Thoreau.* 14 vols. Edited by Bradford Torrey and Francis H. Allen. Boston: Houghton Mifflin, 1906. Reprint, New York: Dover, 1962. [Volumes indicated by roman numerals.]

MW   Henry David Thoreau. *The Maine Woods.* Edited by Joseph J. Moldenhauer. Princeton, NJ: Princeton University Press, 1972.

PJ   Henry David Thoreau. *Journal.* The Writings of Henry D. Thoreau. Edited by Elizabeth Hall Witherell et al. 8 vols. to date. Princeton, NJ: Princeton University Press, 1981–. [Volumes indicated by Arabic numerals.]

RP   Henry David Thoreau. *Reform Papers.* Edited by Wendell Glick. Princeton, NJ: Princeton University Press, 1973.

W   Henry David Thoreau. *Walden*. Edited by J. Lyndon Shanley.
        Princeton, NJ: Princeton University Press, 1971.
WF   Henry David Thoreau. *Wild Fruits: Thoreau's Rediscovered Last
        Manuscript*. Edited by Bradley P. Dean. New York: Norton, 2000.
Wk   Henry David Thoreau. *A Week on the Concord and Merrimack Riv-
        ers*. Edited by Carl F. Hovde, William L. Howarth, and Elizabeth
        Hall Witherell. Princeton, NJ: Princeton University Press, 1980.

THOREAU
BEYOND
BORDERS

INTRODUCTION

François Specq, Laura Dassow Walls, and Julien Nègre

The 200th birthday of Henry David Thoreau on July 12, 2017, was celebrated across the United States with conferences, panels, symposia, college courses, all-night readings of *Walden*, books, articles, essays and blogs, podcasts and radio interviews, at least one sidewalk sale (in his birthplace of Concord, Massachusetts), and a commemorative U.S. postage stamp, which, much to the delight of Thoreau fans, reads "Thoreau Forever." One would think nothing more could be said—yet this volume argues otherwise.

For Thoreau today presents us with a number of challenges. While the United States claims him as an "American" writer who defined a good part of the national narrative, his modern fame was first made not in America but in England. His principle of civil disobedience was largely ignored in the United States, but after his death it influenced Tolstoy in Russia and, thanks to Mahatma Gandhi, rocked all of India well before Martin Luther King Jr. applied it to the American civil rights movement. Thoreau was an avowed son of New England and wrote as a regionalist, yet his local thinking inspired the national park system and the American environmental movement. He is notorious as the hermit of Walden Pond, yet even as *Walden* went to press, he entered the political arena as a passionate defender of human rights for enslaved Americans. He is taught in literature courses yet made his living as a civil engineer; he is treated as an old-fashioned naturalist, yet he applied cutting-edge concepts from Alexander von Humboldt and Charles Darwin that helped found the science of ecology. He was learned in Greek and Latin but found some of his deepest insights in the languages and traditions of Native Americans; he called himself a capitalist entrepreneur yet spread ideas made famous by Karl Marx; he was steeped in history but spoke as a prophet; he was a composer and musician but never wrote a note of music; he rejected Christianity but became one of the era's most profoundly spiritual writers; he rarely traveled beyond his hometown but always imagined himself as a citizen of Planet Earth.

The problem is not his but ours: we trap Thoreau within borders. Yet he spent his life vaulting over boundaries, "as if Nature could support but one order of understandings," he grumbled in *Walden*. "I fear chiefly lest my expression may not be *extra- vagant* enough, may not wander far enough beyond the narrow limits of my daily experience, so as to be adequate to the truth of which I have been convinced. *Extra vagance!* It depends on how you are yarded" (*W* 324). Thoreau spent his life as an intellectual vagrant, jumping fences, pushing bounds, crossing borders. How, why, and to what end are the questions asked by this book. Our title deliberately echoes his famous emphasis on "living a border life" *between* the world of nature and that of the polis, for Thoreau's phrase points to the many ways he involved himself with borders and border crossings (*Exc* 217). Hence the fourteen essays in this volume all trace in various ways the import and relevance of *borders*, in the many meanings of the term. We propose "border" itself as the notion that most deeply shapes Thoreau's philosophical, aesthetic, scientific, and political outlooks, while the body of his thinking works out its multifarious implications. In particular, his work can be seen as an attempt both to acknowledge and to grow beyond the inherent tensions between polarities: national and transnational or universal, personal and political, amateur and professional, literary and scientific, transient and permanent, material and sacred. In other words, these essays take as their guiding principle the need to address the many ways Thoreau's thinking builds on distinctions and categories, while simultaneously questioning, destabilizing, or displacing their inherent boundaries to reveal new horizons.

We do not intend to carry out some predefined postmodern agenda or reveal Thoreau as a postmodernist *avant la lettre*. But we do wish to preserve a much finer sense of, and attunement to, the rich textures, nuances, and shades of Thoreau's works than has been acknowledged by critical schools relying—in Thoreau's case, among others—on hard-and-fast principles, often indebted to notions of American exceptionalism, of literary "text" versus material "context," or to a simplistic understanding of what counts as literature and what counts as science. Thus we embrace Thoreau's historical and ethnographic research, his visual design and aural sensibility, his surveys and maps, and his extensive seasonal charts alongside his better-known literary works. We hope to rejuvenate Thoreau studies by retaining the most decisive recent theoretical contributions, while standing a little aside from a wholesale adherence to postmodern theory. Why, Thoreau might ask us, are we forever "post-," perpetually on the downside of something prior? Toward what future(s) are we tending? In *Walden*, Thoreau posed as the chanticleer greeting the dawn. As we enter the sunset of the era Thoreau greeted, toward what dawn are we directing our steps?

The rich yield of the Thoreau bicentennial events and the growing worldwide enthusiasm for his writings suggest that Thoreau studies are entering a new era. Several decades of theory and philosophy have opened up more supple ways of reading, more original modes of inquiry, and new areas of thinking and have made possible a work of recovery—lifting the veil, so to speak, from a number of Thoreau's passages and artifacts (such as his maps and charts) and eliciting a thorough reexamination of overlooked texts and perspectives, allowing a revaluation of some neglected aspects of his work. We hope there is a new degree of freedom inherent in this collection. The scholars brought together here share one primary goal: the desire to interrogate texts, and to be interrogated by them, rather than to prove a point. We believe that the wide range of Thoreau's interests, his imaginative open-mindedness, his dismissal of easy polarities and attunement to multidimensionality, will never cease to stimulate and appeal to contemporary readers.

We have divided our overarching notion of borders into three major divisions: "Contact Zones"; "Crossing Boundaries"; and "Widening Circles." As distinct from a postmodern emphasis on the blurring of boundaries, which can result in some critical fuzziness, this volume foregrounds a different paradigm, one that preserves the existence and value of forms and distinctions while conceiving of boundary lines as essentially lines of force. We see Thoreau's writing and thinking as looking, or situated, across and beyond borders, rather than merely pitted against them. After all, Thoreau made his living as a professional surveyor, literally responsible for drawing lines across the landscape—abstract lines which became actual roads, fences, and boundaries. But the very fact that he drew those lines himself meant that he understood them differently, not as given but as made, divides that also joined. If we were to characterize our approach metaphorically, perhaps the notion of *symbiosis* would be most fitting. From this perspective literary texts are governed not by subversion or denial but by mediation and dialogue: the adduced lines of force are not dividing lines but lines of connection entailing complex patterns and interweavings. Our essays seek to capture and explore such interactions, drawing on methodologies that, whenever necessary, freely combine formalist and philosophical approaches with cultural and political ones—thus in their turn moving beyond disciplinary borders. In this regard we adhere to a Montaigne-like conception of literature as a site or mode, not of dissolution, but of *passage*: a trajectory that passes across, to forge new connections; that passes forward, from then to now; that passes beyond, to a horizon we cannot yet see.

The first section, "Contact Zones," addresses the ways Thoreau dealt with one of the most central conundrums in American history and culture, the intricacies of conquest and colonization. Such works as *The Maine Woods*, *Cape Cod*, and "Walking" show how Thoreau resisted a narrow Americanist perspective and disavowed any clear-cut national framework. John Kucich revisits Thoreau's perceptions of Native Americans, emphasizing how his dreams of seeing in an "Indian" manner were bound to fail in a strict sense yet nevertheless deeply nurtured his ecocultural perspective. Christa Vogelius and Michael Weisenburg examine *Cape Cod*, Thoreau's most sustained consideration of spatial and historical liminalities, pointing respectively to Thoreau's deep engagement with a maritime space that oscillated between link and barrier and his recovery of a multilayered, cosmopolitan history. Julien Nègre unpacks the multiple layers involved in Thoreau's cartographic work, using new paradigms in the field to suggest that maps and surveys are not necessarily tools of appropriation pitting diverging interests one against the other but can also be fluid links between space and text. Finally, François Specq, reading "Walking" in its full extent as a coherent whole, teases out the wonderful complexities of Thoreau's most densely packed essay and, focusing on the implications of his folding the West back upon the wild, shows how Thoreau refused to think within the limits of nationalism. Through all five essays emerges a picture of Thoreau as deeply aware of the intricate history and metaphysics of contact zones and able to engage with them fruitfully.

The second section, "Crossing Boundaries," considers the multiple ways in which Thoreau thought across intellectual boundaries, not to dissolve them but to benefit from the tension between oppositions. Henrik Otterberg opens up the formal whole of *Walden* by probing the multilayered complexities of its famous but underexamined title page, a threshold in which text and image weave multiple themes that provide a subtle overture to Thoreau's masterpiece. Rochelle Johnson decenters our common perception of Thoreau as a lone individual genius by connecting his thinking to that of his contemporary Susan Fenimore Cooper, bringing out their common entanglements of matter and meaning within a larger nineteenth-century environmental consciousness. Danielle Follett shows how Thoreau's sonic perception links aesthetics, moral philosophy, and science, resolving dissonance, even violence, into a higher harmony that anticipates some of the dilemmas posed by Darwinian evolution. Similarly, Kristen Case, tackling a body of manuscripts long known only to specialists, reveals how Thoreau's elaborate "Kalendar," composed of seasonal lists and charts, intersects with his most complex temporal meditations, resulting in a document akin to a musical score. This series of essays demonstrates Thoreau's inordinate ability to think not only wildly but also widely, across genres and disciplines.

The third section, "Widening Circles," explores the deeper forces driving Thoreau's most enduring experiments, illuminating their underlying rationale and revealing how the open and cross-cutting thought showcased in, and elicited by, his oeuvre is neither a haphazard posture nor a calculated stance but deeply embedded in, and fueled by, his worldview. That is, Thoreau's writing was driven not by a mere desire to map the knowable but was at its core cosmological. His dialogic vision not only harkens back to a time when the divisions we now assume were not yet fully established or settled but also originates in a deeply resonant intellectual engagement with the complexities of the real and its constituent interrelatedness. Daniel S. Malachuk deploys this dialogic vision toward a study of Thoreau's universalism, taking aim at ironic dismissals of Thoreau's spiritual metaphysics to recover the common, Transcendentalizing impetus behind his linked commitments to environmentalism and human rights. Benjamin Pickford explores another form of universalism, that of the capitalist economy first analyzed by Karl Marx, approaching *Cape Cod* not from geographic or historical perspectives but from Thoreau's original political economy to reveal Thoreau as a theorist of capital, giving an entirely new dimension to this supposedly straightforward excursion narrative. Sandra Harbert Petrulionis reconceptualizes Thoreau's political thinking, with all its apparent contradictions, as actually driven by a back-and-forth dialectic that may have been the only viable synthesis of his reform impulses. David M. Robinson recovers Thoreau's uneasy but nurturing dialogue with the idea of the sacred. And finally, Laura Dassow Walls pursues Thoreau's concept of "counter friction," from "Civil Disobedience" to *Walden* and beyond, as the embodied experience of the material world which binds humans and nature together into an integral ecology, a commons replacing apocalyptic millennialism with a new, *terrennial* consciousness that turns Earth into heaven below.

At a time when ancient borders are rematerializing, we hope that *Thoreau beyond Borders* helps recall our readers, in many places and of many kinds, to the task of reimagining how borders produce as well as limit possibilities. And as the vital importance of Thoreau's writings has become more broadly acknowledged both within and beyond the bounds of his native country, may this volume contribute to seeding further interest among readers, scholars, and students of literature—may it, too, like Thoreau, travel beyond borders.

PART I
CONTACT ZONES

1

AN IMPERFECT INDIAN WISDOM

THOREAU, ECOCULTURAL CONTACT, AND THE SPIRIT OF PLACE

John J. Kucich

One of the many revelations Henry Thoreau received while traveling in the Maine Woods took place at a soggy campsite at the base of Mount Kineo in 1857. Restless during the night, he awoke and found himself startled to find a faint glow emanating from a rotten log near the fire. "I saw at once it was phosphorescent wood, which I had often heard of, but never chanced to see," he writes (*MW* 179). When he asks his Penobscot guide, Joe Polis, about it the next morning, his amazement grows when Polis tells him it was, to his people, a well-known phenomenon, named *artoosoqu*. "Nature must have made a thousand revelations to them which are still secrets to us," he muses. "I let science slide, and rejoiced in that light as if it had been a fellow creature. A scientific *explanation*, as it is called, would have been altogether out of place there . . . I believed the woods were not tenantless, but choke-full of honest spirits as good as myself any day,— not an empty chamber, in which chemistry was left to work alone, but an inhabited house,—and for a few moments I enjoyed fellowship with them" (*MW* 181). Thoreau's last journey through the Maine Woods—through the Penobscot world—had just begun, but already he had had an epiphany that matched the mountaintop sublime of "Ktaadn" and the apotheosis of the pine tree in "Chesuncook."[1] This encounter with glowing wood was far less dramatic than the other two, but it stands, I suggest, as a key touch-stone in two of the great projects that occupied Thoreau's final years: his deepening commitment to science and his long fascination with Indians. This moment serves as a node in his evolving thinking that helps us weave these two projects together.

9

It is well established that Thoreau, in the years after publishing *Walden* in 1854, increasingly turned his attention to science, reading widely and systematically in a range of fields, participating in local and national scientific organizations, virtually inventing the field of river hydrology, and contributing groundbreaking work on forest succession.[2] Yet as the passage about phosphorescent wood shows, Thoreau kept aloof from a full embrace of science even as he mastered its methods and insights. He preferred to place its discourse, methods, and insights alongside other ways of seeing and knowing, a pattern that he established in his first major essay, "Natural History of Massachusetts," which ends with a call to supplement the bare facts assembled in the suite of natural history surveys that sparked this review with a more experiential, poetic knowledge of nature drawn from "direct intercourse and sympathy"—what he terms "a more perfect Indian wisdom" (*Exc* 28).

This wisdom proved elusive for Thoreau, who, despite (or perhaps because of) his long immersion in the literature about Native Americans available in the mid-nineteenth century, never fully shook free of the savagism of his time and never gained more than a long glimpse into the Penobscot world Polis opened up for him. Thoreau never learned, for example, that the fire spirits named by Polis are seen by the Penobscot as troubling omens. Frank G. Speck writes the word "*Eskudait*" and notes that "whenever it is seen, calamity is imminent."[3] Polis clearly keeps this dimension of the glowing wood to himself, and in any case, for the Penobscot people in the mid-nineteenth century, having navigated the grim effects of colonialism for generations, calamity was hardly news. Thoreau was certainly aware of this history: it informs his remarks about the degradation of Native people and their inevitable vanishing that recur throughout *The Maine Woods* and his journals. Yet Thoreau did not travel through the Penobscot world to survey the brutal dynamic of colonialism, nor did he gather his Indian Notebooks—some eleven volumes copied from dozens of sources over the course of a decade—to buttress a theory of inevitable racial succession. He sought instead a certain kind of Indian wisdom that offered a model for living in place different from the one settling over New England in his era, one that he hoped would provide an alternative to a toxic politics and an increasingly desperate economic system, one that would embody transcendental ideals and incorporate the world-changing developments in science into a broader network of lived ethics. We can glimpse the fruits of this "more perfect Indian wisdom" throughout Thoreau's work, and here I will look at two key moments. In *A Week on the Concord and Merrimack Rivers*, Thoreau examines the landscape around him through the lens of one of the most storied acts of violence on the colonial frontier. And in "Walking," a stand of pine trees suddenly grows enchanted, offering a new vision of what it means to live in place. Both of these moments, I suggest, bear the mark of Thoreau's long engagement with the Indian heritage of Musketaquid. But it is important to recognize that Thoreau's Indian project, which was never completed, never did fully engage with the struggles of Indian communities to maintain their people and culture in the face of genocidal pressure and that his project of gleaning a cultural heritage from a "vanishing" people was deeply embedded in settler colonialism. It was, in short, imperfect.

What does it mean for Thoreau—for us—to draw on Indian wisdom in an effort to complicate and deepen Western epistemology? What are the stakes, particularly when this effort is applied to understanding an environment that still bears the raw marks of conquest and colonization? And what are the limits, both ethical and ontological, of this cultural exchange? One insight, I suggest, is that whatever wisdom is gained by this exchange is necessarily imperfect, marked by the excess and unpredictability of contact. Contact between cultures, as a long tradition of criticism shows, is as fraught as it is rich; contact between any given culture and its environment, that is, its relations with the more-than-human world, is similarly marked by crossed signals, lethal misunderstandings, and sudden insight. Place these two fields together—environmental and cultural contact—and the universe grows dizzying. Points of ecocultural contact are common in the long and ongoing history of European colonization in the Americas, and although several critics have traced the environmental contexts that shaped some of these charged episodes of cultural encounter, most prioritize one field or the other, either treating the environment as a textured but passive backdrop to cultural conflict, as in most studies focused on settler colonialism or environmental justice, or relegating often brutal moments of warfare and dispossession to the background in a story focused on environmental change.[4]

Thoreau is a valuable focal point in tracing this process in the nineteenth century, as modern scientific epistemology took shape alongside the

varied forces of settler colonialism and industrialization sweeping across
the continent. Thoreau was a potent critic of these forces, even as he was
enmeshed within them. He sought to use an Indian perspective to see
a nature increasingly occluded by an emergent scientific capitalism and
to better see increasingly marginalized Native people through the prism
of the environment they shared. His efforts to gain an Indian wisdom,
imperfect as they were, carry valuable lessons in approaching his own work
and in understanding other writers who followed a similar dynamic on
the country's shifting Western frontier. All these actants came away from
such encounters transformed, largely because the usual circuits of colonial
encounter were run through the enormously complicated mesh of the
material world.

A number of scholars have traced Thoreau's effort to see the world in
its miraculous *thisness*, its hard presence and its elusive complexity, by
drawing on the critical tools of the new materialism. Jane Bennett, Laura
Dassow Walls, Rochelle Johnson, and Branka Arsić, among others, have
traced Thoreau's gradual shift from the transcendental idealism of Emerson
toward an ontology rooted in the shimmering materiality of the universe.[5]
Less clear is how this emerging transcendental materialism fits alongside
Thoreau's lasting interest in Native peoples. The nature of that interest, of
course, has been a matter of fierce debate. Was it primarily a readerly one,
culled from archives as inert as the lithics he plucked from the Concord
soil? Did it share the savagism of his sources, as Joshua Bellin and, most
recently, Richard Schneider have argued, taking part in a broader settler
colonial project?[6] Was Thoreau focused primarily on the Indian past, or
did his encounters with living Indians and, perhaps, his own long immersion in the woods and waters of Musketaquid offer him some measure of a
Native point of view? Was Thoreau more interested in Indian people or in
Indian ghosts?[7]

Thoreau's obsession with Indians was not unusual in a settler colonial
world. The manner of this obsession, however, is quite new. His effort
to ground Emersonian idealism in a metaphysics of place is very different from the dynamics of Indian vanishing in which Indian ghosts help
European settlers manage the guilt of dispossession and genocide. Thoreau
engages in such ghostly theatrics exactly once, at the very beginning of
his writing career, in the famous journal passage where he summons the
spirit of Tahattawan while standing with his brother on the bank of the

Concord River (*PJ* 1:8–9). The arrowhead he finds upon summoning this ghost is an early hint that an ontology focused on the land offers a far more complex history than an ideology of cultural succession. For Thoreau's encounters with Indian artifacts confirmed what he learned in reading Charles Lyell: an earth-centered history is one of recurring presence rather than an ordered teleology. In plucking stone tools from the earth, Thoreau confounded an orderly archaeology as much as any amateur seeking trophies, but for a different reason altogether—for him, these lithics halted the succession of time.[8] These twin currents, ordered history and timeless presence, help shape *A Week*, with episodes of colonial warfare against the Penacook and Abenaki peoples marking a genealogy of settlement, on the one hand, while stories and Indian presence help define an animate landscape, on the other.

This happens most vividly in Thoreau's retelling of Hannah Dustan's captivity and escape, a story that had long been a legend of a violent colonial past, and the one moment in *A Week* that can bear the weight of Thoreau's mourning for the loss of his brother. How does Thoreau manage this? By weaving an account of cultural contact at its most brutal into a living present rooted in the mesh of the material world. He sets the scene both the day after Dustan and her companions slew their captors and in the textual present. "Early this morning this deed was performed," he writes. "They are thinking of the dead." Then, suddenly, he draws the currents of their trauma into the web of nature: "Every withered leaf which the winter has left seems to know their story," he writes, before framing these events in the timeless return of spring in the North Woods, of breaking ice, muskrats and beavers, deer and fish hawks and geese that absorb the presence of these colonials as seamlessly as the silent frame of an empty wigwam—a primeval forest that becomes, in this moment, not a howling wilderness but a home. Hannah Dustan's family gathers again around the apple tree against which her infant's brains were dashed, eating of a fruit that becomes a sacrament of mourning, a ceremony that weaves them into the land (*Wk* 322–23). The present tense of the passage is key—Thoreau, gliding along the river and absorbing its many stories, understands that the landscape remains a home to Indian and settler alike.

This is not a moment of haunting, exactly; Dustan and her companions are not ghosts but ancestors, figures from a well-remembered history that is, for Thoreau, very much alive. Where most episodes of colonial haunting feature an accusatory or tragic Indian ghost, Thoreau's tone here is curiously neutral. He describes the Indian attack on Haverhill in oddly passive terms: Dustan "had been compelled to rise from her bed" and soon thereafter "had seen her infant's brains dashed against an apple-tree" (*Wk* 321)—a moment of horrific violence that Thoreau conspicuously does not use to justify Dustan's killing of her captors (who, it should be noted, were not the ones who raided Haverhill but a different group). This is not a moment of romanticized frontier violence à la Cooper or, indeed, the local histories on which Thoreau drew. Nor is it an effort to redress the wrongs of colonial history: Thoreau has no interest in weighing the political grievances that lead up to this brutal episode in King William's War. Instead, Thoreau diffuses the violence, portraying it as ripple in the fabric of a landscape that encompasses competing groups of humans, to be sure, but only as part of system that stretches to include the wide reaches of the more-than-human world as well. Human blood has been spilt along the Merrimack, and ice is in the river, and the beaver and muskrat have been flooded out of their dens. All this takes place beneath the "smile of the Great Spirit" (*Wk* 323), an Indian wisdom that decenters the narrative of colonial succession and widens to include the two boatmen who ponder the memory of a canoe voyage taken some hundred and forty years before. Robert Sayre argues that Dustan's act of violence, justified or not, carries a terrible price: an estrangement from nature that bears the terrible fruit of anger and revenge embodied in the apple tree.[9] But that is not quite the tone of the passage, which is less of anger or triumph than of sober memory—the apple, after all, is for Thoreau not an emblem of the fall so much as a vehicle of belonging, a seed that takes root in American soil, grows wild, and proffers a certain kind of naturalized wisdom. Thoreau's writing, of course, does not restore the Abenaki world; *A Week* contains only the barest traces of a continuing Native presence (on Thursday, they learn their campsite had been recently used by a group of Penobscot) and is more comfortable depicting Indian people in an increasingly distant past. But Thoreau clearly suggests that in order to be fully embedded in a place, one needs to fully confront this past. In tracing the river that shapes his home from the meadows of Musketaquid, the grass-ground river, to the farthest reaches of the watershed high atop Agiochook, Thoreau encompasses the whole sweep of the ecosystem and its history, weaving together the disparate points of this rapidly changing world in both time and space. Dustan's apple—a European tree growing in American soil, an emblem of renewal and fertility rooted in violence—is the fruit of this ecocultural contact.

Yet it is important to keep in mind that as he wrote this, Thoreau had had little contact with Native people. In his years at Walden Pond, Thoreau had more direct and extensive engagement with his Irish and African American neighbors. His contacts with the Penobscot during his 1845 trip to Maine were abortive, and they tended to affirm the savagist notions that permeated his reading on Indians. While Thoreau sought out Indians who lectured in the Boston area or traveled through Concord, including a Penobscot family who camped near town in November 1850 (Concord, it turns out, was an outer edge of the Penobscot world), the deeper engagement with Native people in their own homelands, captured in "Chesuncook" and "The Allegash and East Branch," would come later. Yet in the years between "Ktaadn" and his trips to Maine in the mid- and late 1850s, Thoreau's own thinking about nature, science, and indigeneity went through an evolution that helped prepare him for the revelation about glowing wood and an enchanted world that Joe Polis helped him see that rainy night camped near Mount Kineo. In the years between the publication of *A Week* and *Walden*, Thoreau began to dig deeply into science, conceived of his phenology project and *Wild Fruits*, started gathering his Indian Notebooks, and reconceived of his journal not as raw material for other projects but as a way to embed himself in the Concord environment. This shift, I suggest, is not a turn from Transcendentalism toward science, nor toward an abandoned Indian book, nor toward a parochial interest in the merely local, but instead an effort to better understand the wellspring of each, and the best place to see these strands intersect is in the essay "Walking."

"Walking" was one of the essays Thoreau revised on his deathbed with help from his sister Sophia. Initially composed in the spring of 1851, it was drawn primarily from Journal entries in the winter of 1850–51, though the final essay incorporates entries from the Journal as late as February 1852. From a loose manuscript of some hundred pages, Thoreau drew at least three lectures—"Walking," "The Wild," and "Moonlight"—separating and recombining them as the occasion required. Those occasions were many. The material was a mainstay of his lecturing until the end of his life;

he gave the lecture during one of his last appearances, before a Spiritual-ist gathering in Lowell on September 9, 1860.[10] Though the material was written just as Thoreau began filling out the Indian Notebooks in earnest, "Walking" has little to say directly about Native Americans; it does, how-ever, have a great deal to say about the inevitable movement of human his-tory from East to West, drawing heavily on Arnold Guyot's *The Earth and Man* (1849). As Richard Schneider has noted, Guyot provided a powerful intellectual foundation for savagism and Manifest Destiny, and Thoreau was clearly intrigued.[11]

Yet Thoreau pushes against this grand narrative of cultural succession. The key passage about Guyot appears late in the first half of the essay, and while Thoreau admires the Swiss geographer's paeon to the westward movement of European civilization, he notes that Guyot "goes . . . further than I am ready to follow him" (*Exc* 198). Thoreau puts a decided emphasis on the primitive vigor of America, rather than the European project of col-onizing it. The very concept of the wild, so central to the essay, undercuts any orderly structure imposed on nature; his project, revising Emerson, is "to regard man as an inhabitant, or part and parcel of Nature" (*Exc* 185). And rather than endorse the westward arc of colonization, the essay contains one of Thoreau's most powerful articulations of living in place, the fruits of what we might call a "learned indigeneity." This project has a complicated relationship with settler colonialism. Although it avoids the worst excesses of savagism, it is less interested in providing some measure of justice toward Native people than in building a deep connection to a local environment. "The farmer displaces the Indian," Thoreau writes, not as an instrument of the inevitable march of European civilization but more as a historical accident. What matters in Thoreau's calculus is not one's culture or race but one's willingness to forge a deeper connection to the wild, to "intrench himself in the land" (*Exc* 206–7). He suggests that the "wildness of the savages" is not a mark of cultural inferiority but "a faint symbol of the awful ferity with which good men and lovers meet" (*Exc* 210). What exactly is this "awful ferity"? Toward the end of the essay, we get a glimpse. As Thoreau describes walking through a pine grove at evening, his prose lifts into the register of mysticism—beings appear, emblems of an enchanted world just visible to those who have learned to dwell.

The Spaulding Farm passage has its sources in a number of Journal entries. There's the afternoon walk on October 31, 1850, when "looking through a stately pine-grove I saw the western sun falling in golden streams through its aisles—Its west side opposite to me was all lit up with golden light; but what was I to it?" (*PJ* 3:124). On November 11, "the west side of every wood & rising ground gleamed like the boundary of elysium" (*PJ* 3:138). On November 21, Thoreau finds that the sun in a pine wood "reinspires the dreams of my youth . . . it was like looking into dream land" (*PJ* 3:148). And on February 27, Thoreau muses over the pure oddness that a deed should give title to a swamp he recently surveyed "to Spaulding his Heirs & Assigns . . . at all times & forever after . . . [to] have, hold, use, occupy and enjoy the said swamp."[12] What is that absurdity, he asks, compared with "the shadow of the wings of thought" that suggest events of greater importance in the world (*PJ* 3:198–200)?

Thoreau weaves these thoughts into a vision of a reenchanted world. In the finished essay, he describes walking through a pine wood at sunset, where he half-glimpses, half-imagines a family of ethereal beings who live on the edge of the material world, amid the golden afternoon rays that illuminate a pine grove behind an ordinary farm: "I was impressed as if some ancient and altogether admirable and shining family had seated there in that part of Concord, unknown to me; to whom the sun was servant; who had not gone into society in the village; who had not been called on . . . The pines furnished them with gables as they grew. Their house was not obvious to vision; the trees grew through it. I do not know whether I heard the sounds of a suppressed hilarity or not. They seemed to recline on sunbeams. They have sons and daughters. They are quite well . . . Nothing can equal the serenity of their lives" (*Exc* 218). Thus the "shadows of the wings of thought" take form, transmuted into beings described with a warmth and wonder that make the passage a touchstone in Thoreau's growing understanding of nature. It is, first, an intuited understanding, more akin to Coleridge's conception of reason than empirical knowledge, and this moment is emblematic of Thoreau's insistence on his Transcendentalism even as he mastered the emerging practice and discourse of science. It is, second, better described not as a moment of transcendence, like Emerson's transparent eyeball passage in *Nature*, where the subject sees the world dissolve into its ideal essences, but one of immanence. Thoreau here doesn't see through or beyond the material world; he sees it spring to life, its spiritual essence suddenly made visible. And it is, finally, a vision of wholeness, of pleasure, serenity, and even suppressed hilarity, rather than terror or dissolution. This pine wood on the edge of Concord is the Holy Land to which his walks all tend—not the West of Manifest Destiny but the Westering impulse in all of humankind. Elysium is not beyond some far distant horizon but on the western side of every pine wood.

This is the great treasure of Spaulding's wood, though Spaulding himself is blind to it, and Thoreau himself can see it only by glimpses: "But I find it difficult to remember them. They fade irrevocably out of my mind even now while I speak and endeavor to recall them, and recollect myself. It is only after a long and serious effort to recollect my best thoughts that I become again aware of their cohabitancy" (*Exc* 219). This is a resonant passage, one that echoes many of the strings Thoreau touched throughout his work. The wide traveling in Concord. The wild spaces at the town's margins. The animate earth, alive, organic. The familiar world grown transcendent. The ethereal family in the pines, however, strikes a new note. Who are these beings? Not quite the fairies whose lore fascinated the young Louisa May Alcott, nor New World relatives of the Greek god Pan, survivors of the long tradition of British folklore and classical myth that Timothy Morton terms the *archelithic*.[13] Nor, exactly, are they symbols of a more formal pantheism that Thoreau invoked when bemoaning the unthinking felling of a Chesuncook pine, a spirit of nature that was, by the mid-nineteenth century, a comfortable foil for Protestant orthodoxy, with a heritage reaching back beyond the monism of Baruch Spinoza to Lucretius and the pre-Socratic Greeks.

Edward Mooney has argued that the beings of Spaulding Farm are emblems of reverie itself, an example of the sublime that draws in equal parts from Immanuel Kant and Søren Kierkegaard—a different order of perception and aura that must not yield to science.[14] In a journal entry in early November 1850, below a missing half page, Thoreau writes, "Thou art a personality so vast & universal that I have never seen one of thy features. I am suddenly very near to another land than can be bought & sold. This is not Mr Bull's swamp. This is a far faraway field on the confines of the actual Concord where nature is partially present. These farms I have myself surveyed—these lines I have run—these bounds set up—they have no chemistry to fix them they fade from the surface of the glass (the picture) this light is too strong for them" (*PJ* 3:125). The passage is followed by more missing pages—at this stage of the Journal, Thoreau cut passages to be used in lectures and essays, and it is certainly possible that the missing passages went directly into "Walking." These lines, with their direct expression of pantheism glimpsed in a moment of transcendental intuition, may have been in a register too familiar for the strangeness of the beings glimpsed at Spaulding Farm, who refuse to resolve into recognizable terms. Thoreau wanted to strike a different note in this reverie.

Mooney notes that the Spaulding Farm passage, as well as the mode of being Thoreau captures here, is inflected by his extensive reading of Hindu sacred writing and by his readings in Native American ethnography, and this last area is worth considering in more detail.[15] In those winter journals that fueled the essay, Thoreau describes his visits to a Penobscot family camping in Concord, recording a lengthy conversation on November 26 that is full of lore—on moose, caribou, hunting practices, and the uses of their hides; on spears and spear-fishing, birch-bark vessels, snowshoes, and traps (*PJ* 3:152–54). The passage reads like an entry from one of the Indian Notebooks; indeed, Thoreau seems to be validating his sources by doing his own fieldwork. Yet he appears to gain more from this encounter than a simple list of ethnographic data. The Penobscot family were not, after all, simply a repository of Native artifacts. They were living members of a Native community who may have been far from their center on Indian Island but who clearly included the banks of the Musketaquid within their territory. In talking with this family, Thoreau came face to face with the Indigenous world that still existed on the edge of Concord village. From Thoreau's record, the conversation must have been rather stiff and marked by generosity and patience on the Penobscot side. The family was likely in town to sell baskets, and if the inquisitive visitor to their tent was not interested in buying, they seemed happy to cultivate his goodwill and share details of their life in the Maine Woods. Both parties look to have sought common ground.[16]

The message is driven home two days later, when Thoreau recollects the conversation. "The Indian talked about 'our folks' & 'your folks' 'my grandfather' & 'my grandfather's cousin,' Samoset" (*PJ* 3:155). This is the heart of their exchange—a reworking of the colonial past that is relived and recalibrated. As the Wabanaki sachem Samoset's arrival in the fledgling Plymouth colony in 1622, greeting the English in their own language, showed the Pilgrims that this colonial world would be more complicated than they had imagined, this conversation jolts Thoreau out of his fixation on an Indian past. The world that Thoreau was trying to glimpse in the

Jesuit Relations was in fact alive and well on the edge of Concord, with a Penobscot teacher patiently explaining to his interlocutor what it means to be Indigenous—to know the land and to live off of its wild fruits. If there is a difference between "our folks" and "your folks," it is one that can be bridged. Thoreau, interestingly, records no talk of religion, of spirits, as there is none of politics; a discussion of hunting, trapping, and subsistence skills would have been safer common ground. But the issue was clearly on Thoreau's mind that winter, as the draft of "Walking" took shape. The Indian Notebooks from this period include a wide variety of sources, including a number that focus on Indian spirituality: two books by Ephraim Squire on Indian antiquities and an excerpt from David Cusick's *Sketches of Ancient History of the Six Nations* in Notebook 3; descriptions of Wampanoag story holes and *pneise*, or "warrior-shamans," stories collected by Henry Rowe Schoolcraft, and a discussion by Squire of the Great Serpent, Manabosho, and Earth Diver traditions in Notebook 4.[17] Notebook 5, written between September 1851 and February 1852 (toward the end of the final revision of the "Walking" manuscript) includes more oral traditions: Lenape stories gathered by John Heckewelder and Adrian Van Doren. In a later notebook, Thoreau would quote Schoolcraft again on Indian spirituality: they "live in the ancient belief of the diurgus, or Soul of the Universe, which inhabits and animates everything."[18] By the time Thoreau copied this passage in 1852, that message had long grown familiar.

The key insight of the Spaulding Farm passage is captured by the final word: "cohabitancy." It's an odd word—the *Oxford English Dictionary* includes only this one citation for this particular form. Thoreau would have been familiar with the older sense of the word, referring to people living together in a sexual relationship outside of marriage; he would have been interested to learn that biologists now use the term to describe different species who share an ecological space. Both senses are at work in Thoreau's use of the word—of different orders of beings juxtaposed almost invisibly on a certain landscape, woven together with a tinge of eros that defies any normative ordering of reproduction. To inhabit nature, as Thoreau calls for in the essay's opening sentence, is to cohabit. "Cohabitancy" is, in a word, *queer*, and that queerness undermines the order of racial succession at the heart of "Walking." The beings of Spaulding Farm defy the orderly clock of Manifest Destiny, the steady march of cultural evolution and Anglo-Saxon supremacy, the yielding of savagery to civilization, that was the bedrock assumption of its advocates. These beings of ambiguous heritage, not quite fairies, not quite the little people of the Algonquian, *pukwudgees* or *muh-keahweesug*, are better seen not as a cultural memory but as an autochthonous manifestation of place, a mark of indigeneity that defies the orderly division of time into past and future in the same way the wild force of nature defies efforts to mark a swamp with surveying tools. These beings mark an eternal present; they are the grace notes of mourning.

As Thoreau diffuses his grief into the mesh of the natural world, losing, as Arsić argues, a distinct personhood while gaining access to a living nature, Thoreau here begins to see the Indian past in Concord as not really past at all.[19] In the same way, the Hannah Dustan passage in *A Week* shifts from the historical past to a living presence. It is no accident that this sliding scale of time took shape as Thoreau conceived of the Kalendar project in the early 1850s, where phenology and succession serve at once as firmly fixed historical data and part of a long, slow cycle of change and renewal. What is true for flowers and forests is true for peoples. This was not easy to see—the beings at Spaulding Farm are only glimpsed sidelong and quickly fade from view, and this was true, too, of his views of Indians—at times fixed to the simple past tense, at times extended into the past imperfect, at moments understood in the perfect tense, with the past flowing into the present; at key moments, projected into the region's future.

Such moments were rare, however, and they never lead to the fierce sense of injustice that defined Thoreau's attacks on slavery. Thoreau never fully shook off the savagism that saturated American culture, and he failed to see a powerful example of an Indian community advancing an environmental vision in his own neighborhood. Thoreau called for national preserves in "Chesuncook" and local conservation in *Walden*, but despite making four trips to Cape Cod, he never visited the Indian town of Mashpee. There the Wampanoag community carefully managed its recently secured land base, sustainably harvesting timber and funding its needs through carefully controlled access to hunting and fishing on its ecologically intact territory—perhaps the earliest American example of sustainable ecotourism. Thoreau, however, steered clear, and his Indian Notebooks showed that he was more interested in a vanished Indian past than a more complicated Indian present. Yet it's important to keep in mind that this is not the only story. Thoreau's long immersion in writings about Indians, as Robert Sayre notes, was not so much a dead end as it was "a means of discovery, not only about America but about the natural world"; it provoked in him "a keener sense of the world, an Indian eye."[20] These studies are integral to Thoreau's great project of these years—his effort to live deeply in a specific place, learning to adopt an ethical stance that encompasses the human and more-than-human world, learning to understand the patterns and mechanisms that governed the dizzying complexity of a world he was just beginning to see. There's no perfect word for the stance he was attempting to adopt; "Native" and "Indigenous" are close but tinged indelibly with the stain of colonialism, as are Thoreau's efforts (as are our own). Yet it's important not to see the ghost of Hannah Dustan gliding down the Merrimack with her bag of Indian scalps, or the spirits of the Maine Woods, or the beings who emerge on the edge of Spaulding Farm, as merely the specters of colonial guilt. These are better seen as manifestations of place—one stained with blood, to be sure, but still very much alive. Gary Snyder describes a conversation with a Crow elder, who says, "If people stay somewhere long enough—even white people—the spirits will begin to speak to them. It's the power of the spirits coming up from the land."[21] These spirits are Thoreau's effort to get people to listen to the land before it is too late.

Notes

1. For further discussion of Thoreau's encounters with the Penobscot, see my essay "Lost in the Maine Woods: Henry Thoreau, Joseph Nicolar, and the Penobscot World," *The Concord Saunterer* 19/20 (2011–12): 22–52.

2. On Thoreau's engagement with science, see Laura Dassow Walls, *Seeing New Worlds: Thoreau and Nineteenth-Century Natural Science* (Madison: University of Wisconsin Press, 1995), and *Henry David Thoreau: A Life* (Chicago: University of Chicago Press, 2017); William Rossi, "Poetry and Progress: Thoreau, Lyell, and the Geological Principles of *A Week*," *American Literature* 66, no. 2 (June 1994): 275–300; and Robert Thorson, *The Boatman: Henry David Thoreau's River Years* (Cambridge, MA: Harvard University Press, 2017).

3. Frank G. Speck, "Penobscot Tales and Religious Beliefs," *Journal of American Folklore* 48, no. 187 (January–March 1935): 15.

4. Examples of the former might include Mark Spence, *Dispossessing the Wilderness: Indian Removal and the Making of National Parks* (London: Oxford University Press, 2001), or Deagan Miller, *This Radical Land: A Natural History of American Dissent* (Chicago: University of Chicago Press, 2018); the latter might include William Cronon, *Changes in the Land: Indians, Colonists, and the Ecology of New England* (New York: Hill and Wang, 1983). Mary Louise Pratt's *Imperial Eyes: Travel Writing and Transculturation* (New York: Routledge, 1992) is a key text in studies of the contact zone.

5. See Jane Bennett, *Thoreau's Nature: Ethics, Politics, and the Wild* (Latham, MD: Rowan and Littlefield, 2002); Walls, *Seeing New Worlds*; Rochelle Johnson, "'This Enchantment Is No Delusion': Henry David Thoreau, the New Materialisms, and Ineffable Materiality," *Interdisciplinary Studies in Literature and Environment* 21, no. 3 (Summer 2014): 606–35; Kristen Case, "Thoreau's Radical Empiricism: The Kalendar, Pragmatism, and Science," in *Thoreauvian Modernities: Transatlantic Conversations about an American Icon*, ed. François Specq, Laura Dassow Walls, and Michel Granger (Athens: University of Georgia Press, 2013), 187–99; and James Finley, "'Who Are We? Where Are We?': Contact and Literary Navigation in *The Maine Woods*," *Interdisciplinary Studies in Literature and Environment* 19, no. 2 (Spring 2012): 336–55. Branka Arsić's *Bird Relics: Grief and Vitalism in Thoreau* (Cambridge, MA: Harvard University Press, 2016) is a powerful new materialist reading of Thoreau's mourning focused primarily on *A Week on the Concord and Merrimack Rivers*, along with a detailed account of Thoreau's fascination with Huron burial rituals in the Indian Notebooks.

6. See Joshua Bellin, "In the Company of Savagists: Thoreau's Indian Books and Antebellum Ethnology," *The Concord Saunterer* 16 (2008): 1–32, and Richard Schneider, *Civilizing Thoreau: Human Ecology and the Social Sciences in the Major Works* (Rochester, NY: Camden House, 2016). For a keystone work on Native presence in New England, see Lisa Brooks, *The Common Pot: The Recovery of Native Space in the Northeast* (Minneapolis: University of Minnesota Press, 2008). The most comprehensive work on savagism in New England is Jean O'Brien, *Firsting and Lasting: Writing Indians out of Existence in New England* (Minneapolis: University of Minnesota Press, 2010).

7. Renee Bergland, *The National Uncanny: Indian Ghosts and American Subjects* (Hanover, NH: University Press of New England, 2000).

8. There has been little published work on Thoreau's archaeology to date. For a more recent overview, see Curtis Runnels, "Henry Thoreau, Archaeologist?," The Concord Saunterer 27 (2019): 42–67. See also Shirley Blanke "The Archaeology of Walden Woods" in *Thoreau's World and Ours*, ed. Edmund A. Schofield and Robert C. Barron (Golden, CO: North American Press, 1993), 242–53. My own understanding has also been shaped by unpublished work by Duncan Caldwell, "Thoreau's Prehistoric Artifact Collection: A New Examination" (Uses and Abuses of Thoreau at 200, University of Gothenburg, Sweden, May 2018).

9. Robert F. Sayre, *Thoreau and the American Indians* (Princeton, NJ: Princeton University Press, 1977), 52.

10. The manuscript of "Walking" and its composition history is detailed by Joseph Moldenhauer in "'Walking' Headnote," *Exc* 561–70. According to Bradley P. Dean and Ronald Wesley Hoag, Thoreau assembled different portions of the manuscript for multiple different lectures; see "Thoreau's Later Lectures after *Walden*," in *Studies in the American Renaissance*, ed. Joel Myerson (Charlottesville: University of Virginia Press, 1996): 127–228.

11. See Schneider, *Civilizing Thoreau*, 7–23.

12. The survey of Spaulding's swamp does not appear in the collection of Thoreau's surveying documents in the Munroe Special Collections, Concord Free Public Library, Concord, MA. Between November 1850 and February 1851, there are three surveys of woodlots and swamps belonging to Cyrus Stow. Thoreau was involved in a dispute over land in Lincoln owned by the Spaulding family, surveying a dam and testifying in court in January 1854. See *Corr* 2:191.

13. Timothy Morton, *Dark Ecology: For a Logic of Future Coexistence* (New York: Columbia University Press, 2016).

14. Edward Mooney, "'Sympathy with Intelligence': Thoreau's Reveries of Wonder, Presence and Divinities," *The Concord Saunterer* 24 (2016): 63–81.

15. Mooney, "'Sympathy with Intelligence,'" 66–69.

16. This family may be the source of the episode on selling baskets recast in "Economy" in *Walden*; the journal passage is written shortly before November 8, 1850 (*PJ* 3:130–31). Thoreau later proved more helpful to Indian visitors in Concord, at one point telling a group camped on Brister's Hill where black ash trees essential for making baskets grew in the area (*J* XIII:186–87, 192, March 8, 1960).

17. I follow Robert Sayre's dating of the Indian Notebooks, which are labeled differently in the Morgan Library & Museum collections ("Extracts relating to Indians," MA 596–606). In this essay, I have relied heavily on the transcripts of the Indian Notebooks completed in the 1930s by a number of graduate students (all women) under the direction of Arthur Christy. I am grateful to Brent Ranalli and the staff of the Morgan Library & Museum for making these transcripts available to me.

18. Henry David Thoreau, Indian Notebook ("Extracts relating to Indians," MA 600 Thoreau 48/Christy Number 5, transcribed by Louisa Pearson, 1931/Sayre 6: Feb–Oct 1852), 54. The citation is from Henry Rowe Schoolcraft, *Historical and Statistical Information regarding the History, Condition and Prospects of the Indian Tribes of the United States* (1847; Philadelphia: Lippincott, 1851), 15.

19. See Arsić, *Bird Relics*, 35–40.

20. Sayre, *Thoreau and the American Indians*, 122.

21. Gary Snyder, "Bioregional Perspectives" [excerpt from *The Practice of the Wild*], in *The Gary Snyder Reader* (Washington, D.C.: Counterpoint, 1999), 193.

2

CAPE COD'S TRANSNATIONAL BODIES

Christa Holm Vogelius

On July 24, 1850, Henry David Thoreau wrote a hurried note to Horace Greeley telling him that "If Wm E. Channing calls—will you say that I am gone to Fire-Island by cars at 9 this morn. via Thompson. with W^m. H. Channing." The two men had gone at Emerson's request to obtain "all the intelligence &, if possible, any fragments of manuscript or other property" on the site of the wreck of the *Elizabeth*, the vessel bearing Margaret Fuller, her husband, Giovanni Ossoli, and their young son, Angelino, from Italy (*Corr* 2:61–62). By the time Thoreau arrived, five days after the ship had run aground in a storm just three hundred yards off the coast of Fire Island, Fuller and Ossoli had drowned and the body of the young boy, only recently dead, had surfaced on shore. The men found some personal effects—chests of books, a desk with papers, carpetbags of clothing—but never the main object of their quest, Fuller's only manuscript copy of her history of the Italian *Risorgimento*, nor, definitively, either Fuller's or Ossoli's bodies.[1] Scavengers competed with friends and family members to recover valuables that they could resell at auction; Thoreau noted "a man with six hats on." Thoreau himself found Ossoli's coat and tore a button off to take home.[2] He visited the grave of Fuller's son and left the site of the shipwreck five days after he had arrived, not long after he saw on the beach "four or five miles west of the wreck, a portion of a human skeleton, which was found the day before, probably from the *Elizabeth*, but I have not knowledge enough of anatomy to decide confidently, as many might, whether it was that of a male or a female" (*Corr* 2:74–76). The body was buried, and in letters from the days that follow, Thoreau refers to Fuller and the search for her effects only in passing.

Nonetheless, it would be difficult to argue that the search did not affect Thoreau or his work. Around this time another shipwreck, one that anticipated the outlines of Fuller's, was also on Thoreau's mind. Only weeks before, in late May, Thoreau had been asked to deliver a lecture in Worcester based on his travelogue-in-progress, *Cape Cod*.[3] That January and February, he had delivered three lectures based on his initial October 1849 trip to Cape Cod; titled "The Shipwreck," they detailed the trip's opening day, in which he and his traveling companion, William Ellery Channing, followed a newspaper announcement to arrive at the wreck of the *St. John*, a ship ferrying Irish immigrants from Galway to Cohasset. The announcement advertised 145 passengers as dead, and bodies and wreckage scattered the beach. Only 16 adult passengers and 10 members of the crew made their way to the shore alive; a beachcomber later recovered a living infant.[4] Passersby like Thoreau joined family members, friends, and locals, as well as workers carting off the valuable seaweed also washed up by the storm. The *St. John*, like the *Elizabeth*, had wrecked less than a mile from shore. Eventually, the remains of the *Elizabeth*, too, would make their way into the revisions and expansions of *Cape Cod*, which Thoreau worked on until 1861. The text echoes the Fire Island search throughout in its fixation on the drowning dangers of the coast, its descriptions of beachcombing, and its conversations with family members of the lost at sea.

But these resonances of the shipwreck capture within them another, more literary form of haunting. *Cape Cod* is, despite its author's assertion that he is "a land animal," a text with its face turned stubbornly toward the sea. It opens with the project of "get[ting] a better view than I had yet had of the ocean" and ends with the note that on the coast of the Cape, a man may "put all America behind him" (*CC* 96, 3, 215). And the coastal setting, while it has inescapable biographical echoes with Fuller's last hours, has yet deeper echoes with the ideological project of nation-mapping that both writers undertook in earlier Transcendental travelogues. These narratives— Fuller's *Summer on the Lakes, in 1843* (1844) and Thoreau's "Walking" (1851), "Wild Apples"(1862), and even *Walden* (1854)—attempt, through both a lateral and an inward survey of the land, to map what Wai Chee Dimock calls the "deep time" of the American continent, claiming a history whose complexity rivaled that of Europe and whose evidence was to be found in the geologic layers of the soil itself.[5] *Cape Cod* undoes this exploration in its insistent focus on the ocean, whose depth is both unknowable and, where human life is concerned, utterly empty. Facing defiantly eastward, Thoreau counters the contemporary westward push of Manifest Destiny and claims land, ocean, and the meeting of the two as the subject of his study. The shore, for Thoreau, marks the site where the deep history of the American soil and the ahistorical wilderness of the ocean meet violently, often in death. Drowning in this sense functions as a way of representing the conceptual clash between history, where individual figures have great importance, and the amoral force of nature, where they have none at all. *Cape Cod* is remarkable for its aim to map this central nationalist site in ways that alternately affirm and deny ideas of nation.

In this sense, as a body of water, the ocean is also weighted much differently from other bodies of water—Walden Pond, the Concord River—that figure so centrally in Thoreau's work. While these bodies are symbolic of man's imaginative or spiritual capacities and in that sense personified, the ocean is insistently foreign and stubbornly unassimilable. In a text that centers on the founding site of American nationhood and that spends much of its time on land mapping out this history, Thoreau's insistent return to the blank and deeply foreign space of the ocean is striking. It is also, I would argue, an intentional contrast, one that presents the world as more than nation, plotting the foreign not in other countries, customs, or peoples but in the ocean, in death, in the mysteries unknowable to humans owing to their limitations as "land animal[s]."

In my focus on Thoreau's particular brand of nationalism, I follow Paul Giles's readings of Thoreau as an author of both the local and the global. As Giles writes, "Thoreau's genius involves his capacity to interweave close and distant, near and far, in a symbiotic relation where each side of the equation interpenetrates and informs its opposite, and if the 'great circle-sailing' of his writing postulates a sublimation of material into spiritual, it also involves a style of juxtaposition through which different spatial and temporal coordinates are brought productively into contact with each other."[6] But to the modes of nineteenth-century temporality that Giles identifies in *Walden*—industrial time, domestic time, non-Western time, slow time—I would add another: ahistorical time, or the voiding of temporality altogether. For Thoreau in *Cape Cod*, this is the space of the ocean, and the site it comes "productively into contact with" is the Cape itself, that most historical of early nationalist spaces.

Cape Cod is a text that, like most of Thoreau's works, depends intimately on naturalist narratives and local histories to flesh out the land that it surveys. But Thoreau's descriptions of the ocean, which are central to the text, emphasize not history but sublimity. To demonstrate this difference, I first contrast Margaret Fuller's mapping of Native settlements and European encounters with Thoreau's own. I then turn to *Cape Cod*'s preoccupation with shipwrecks, the dangers of the shoreline, and victims of drowning not merely as a morbid fixation that recalls his contemporary search for the Ossolis but as a carefully layered metaphor that sutures this personal memory to a larger idea of the "unfathomable" beyond nation or history.

Transcendental Vikings and the Traces of Men

One way of tracking Thoreau's nation-mapping in *Cape Cod* is through his discussion of the Norse settlement of the North Atlantic coast, which several prominent midcentury American writers, including Margaret Fuller, feature in their works. In focusing on the Cape, Thoreau chooses a location that has, particularly to his contemporary readers, an implied nationalist backstory. It is the site of the first British landing, in Provincetown, and of extensive early colonial settlement. But as Annette Kolodny has shown, nineteenth-century archaeological theories that proposed the area around Massachusetts Bay as the site of a medieval Viking settlement, establishing a European ancestry in America hundreds of years before Columbus, also gripped many of the New England intellectual elite in the 1830s and 1840s. Henry Wadsworth Longfellow, James Russell Lowell, and John Greenleaf Whittier all wrote poetic tributes to the idea of this pre-Colombian discovery. Oliver Wendell Holmes helped support the construction of a statue of Leif Eriksson in Boston.[7] Thoreau's own traveling companion on two of his four trips to Cape Cod, William Ellery Channing, wrote a long poem composed over several years equating contemporary Cape Cod fishermen with the Norse settlers who sailed the same waters.[8] Massachusetts was a site for several apparent Viking relics, from Dighton Rock, which some scholars argued showed markings in Old Norse, to mysterious and contested ancient skeletons. But Cape Cod held a privileged place even within the state, since prominent proponents of the Norse discovery narrative located Vinland, the settlement recorded in the Icelandic sagas as the most significant Atlantic settlement, on the Cape. There was, as Kolodny notes, an inescapable racialist motivation for these theories, particularly later in the century, when they functioned, at least in part, as an Anglo-Saxon counter to mass immigration from southern and eastern Europe.[9] But for many of the writers at that time, literary nationalism also motivated connecting the ancient sagas with America's early nineteenth-century literary hub in the Boston area.

Thoreau was not only aware of these theories of Viking settlement but also included them prominently in his text alongside other accounts of the Cape's history and exploration. His cited source for this history was the most vocal proponent of the Norse theory, the Danish historian Carl Christian Rafn, who in 1837 published the hefty two-volume set *Antiquitates Americanæ*, which argued, using saga translations, maps, sketches of artifacts, and other texts, that Norse settlers lived on modern-day Cape Cod around the turn of the first millennium and that the record of their voyage in fact inspired later explorers and colonialists such as Christopher Columbus. The text was reviewed in the American press but was too expensive for widespread private ownership; in 1838 Rafn published *America Discovered in the Tenth Century*, a briefer, more affordable, and entirely English-language version of the same theory that pointed readers toward the original documents of *Antiquitates Americanæ* for its substantiation.

Thoreau's approach to Rafn's theories, unlike that of many of his contemporaries, came with a fair dose of skepticism and humor. As Richard Schneider argues, *Cape Cod* offers Thoreau a space to "compare historical accounts of the ever-changing Cape to its current reality and question conventional historical accounts of the settling of America."[10] Thoreau touches at several points on the theories of Viking settlement of the New England coast, citing Rafn by name, and even quoting (and retranslating) the Latin translations of passages in the Icelandic sagas that appear in *Antiquitates Americanæ*. Thoreau's take on the theories of Norse settlement demonstrates his skepticism with typical Thoreauvian dissimulation, in a playful punning on his own name and a broadly noncommittal stance. Of Rafn's belief that an account by Icelandic explorer Thorfinn Karlsefni of a coastal mirage took place on the Cape, Thoreau writes, "But whether Thor-finn saw the mirage here or not, Thor-eau, one of the same family, did; and perchance it was because Leif the Lucky had, in a previous voyage, taken Thor-er and his people off the rock in the middle of the sea, that Thor-eau was born to see it" (*CC* 151). In a single witty sentence, Thoreau demonstrates his familiarity not only with the most detailed points of Rafn's theory but also with the original sagas on which it is based, which narrate the rescue of the Northman Thorer and his crew off the North American coast by Leif Eriksson, or Leif the Lucky. Remaining neutral on the question of whether the explorers actually arrived at the Cape, Thoreau also constructs an alternative genealogy in the movement from Thorfinn to Thorer to Thoreau that plays knowingly with the literalness of traditional Scandinavian family names at the same time as it pokes fun at the implicitly nationalist and racialist nineteenth-century desires to claim a Scandinavian lineage. This idea of lineage comes up again even more explicitly later on, when Thoreau writes that Thor-finn "is said to have a son born in New England, from whom Thorwaldsen the sculptor was descended" (*CC* 195). This last Thor in the lineage is the Danish Icelandic neoclassical sculptor Bertel Thorvaldsen, who himself claimed descent from the first European born in America, Snorri Thorfinnsson.

Thorvaldsen had a prominent place in Margaret Fuller's nation-mapping project, *Summer on the Lakes, in 1843*. Hailed by Evert Duyckinck, that midcentury champion of literary nationalism, as "the only genuine American book . . . published this season," Fuller's text is both a likely and an unlikely candidate for the publisher's admiration.[11] On the one hand, it checks the boxes of many traditionally nationalist concerns: it deals with distinctly American scenes in the form of rural Western landscapes, Native American settlements, and frontier camps; it comments explicitly on the supposed traits of the American character and developing nation; and it functions as an antidote to the flood of American travel writings about Europe. On the other hand, the text is haunted from its inception with transatlantic desire: the trip it recounted was an affordable alternative to the tour of Europe that Fuller had longed to take in the 1830s and early 1840s, while the dense and allusive writing continuously references the Continental figures and ideas of Fuller's classical education. In this sense, Thorvaldsen is for Fuller an ideal artistic subject. His self-assertion of his American lineage, as well as the Boston Athenæum's recent solo exhibition of his work and acquisition of one of the sculptures in his Ganymede series, balanced with his status as a central figure in European neoclassicism, neatly demonstrates the inextricability of the American and the European.

To claim this interconnection, while also arguing for the particularities of the American soil and its need to free itself from European mores not suited to the new environment, is the often paradoxical project of *Summer on the Lakes*. Thorvaldsen participates in some of these convolutions, representing both European neoclassicism and America's continued dependence on European mores. In a key nationalist moment, Fuller frames her seventeen-line poem, "Ganymede to His Eagle, Suggested by a Work of Thorwaldsen's, Composed on the Height Called the Eagle's Nest, Oregon, Rock River, July 4th, 1843," with a description of the Illinois prairie on Independence Day. Fuller's Midwest in this passage presents a stratified layering of what she frames as Indigenous past and Euro-American future. Her presentation of the landscape is infused by the presence of its inhabitants, past and future, who shape its structure. She begins the chapter in which the poem appears with a summary of Black Hawk's War in the 1830s, part of the Jacksonian push toward western removal, which she both bemoans and uses to claim a deep geologic history: "How happy the Indians must have been here! It is not long since they were driven away, and the ground, above and below is full of their traces. 'The earth is full of men.'" Following her atypically jingoistic assertion that "I think I had never felt so happy that I was born in America," she then introduces "Ganymede to His Eagle," a poem that superimposes onto the American plains this Scandinavian work about a mortal's servitude to the Classical gods, making an argument for America's cultural ties (both recent and historical) as a necessary part of the narrative of American literary nationalism.[12]

In the poem, Fuller uses Thorvaldsen, as well as her own accounts of the land's recent history, to build a sense of both the American continent's geologic stratification and its need to assert intellectual and emotional independence. Her poem centers on Ganymede, the beautiful young mortal who is abducted by Jove (in eagle form) to serve as his cupbearer in Olympus. While traditional representations of the myth focus on the violent moment of Ganymede's capture in the eagle's claws, Fuller's more static version, like Thorvaldsen's 1804 statue, imagines the moment after the boy's initial abduction, when he, with "a goblet of pure water in his hand . . . / A willing servant to sweet love's command," waits for the eagle to bring him back to Jove. Focusing on a moment of lovesickness and

abandonment that most versions of the tale elide, Fuller's poem emphasizes longing and Ganymede's wish "to wait, to wait, but not to wait too
long."[13] And the eagle, "the emblem of sovereignty of the United States,"
is not an incarnation of Jove but, like Ganymede himself, a servant to
this "Olympian king," a "fellow bondsman in a royal cause." Given the
weight of the eagle as a national symbol, its connection elsewhere to the
Native Americans whom Fuller describes as inhabiting the land, and Jove's
repeated description as a "monarch," the dominant subtext of the poem
emerges as Anglo-American nostalgia and its displacement in the American setting.[14]

By contrast, Thoreau's presentation of Cape Cod generally aligns with
his resistance to a nationalizing and Eurocentric narrative. While historical
accounts of the area center on the Cape's land, emphasizing its relics—
stones, tools, and skeletons—Thoreau's focus is instead on the ocean,
which he emphasizes from the outset as ahistorical. And although much
of the text is devoted to tracing, in some detail, historical accounts of the
land, Thoreau stresses that the sea cannot be subjected to such consider-
ations. As he writes in the context of a discussion of the Cape's history,
"We do not associate the idea of antiquity with the ocean, nor wonder how
it looked a thousand years ago, as we do of the land, for it was equally wild
and unfathomable always. The Indians have left no traces on its surface,
but it is the same to the civilized man and the savage. The aspect of the
shore only has changed" (CC 148). The text's focus on the ocean, then,
prioritizes ahistorical natural force over the stratification of history.

Thoreau's notion that the ocean is outside both antiquity and historical
time does not preclude his assertion that it is at the origin of life. The ocean
brings Thoreau to a space before nation-states, even before human history,
so the life it helps him to map is well to the side of America's history of
settlement. His framing of the sea as "wild and unfathomable," "a wilderness reaching around the globe, wilder than a Bengal jungle, and fuller
of monsters," defines the sea as prenational and insistently primordial
(CC 148). This framework is not merely poetic; it also relies closely on his
discussion some chapters earlier, in "The Beach Again," of the Swiss naturalist Édouard Desor's assertion that "the ocean is the origin of all things,"
although in terms of the evolution of the species, "progress invariably
points toward the dry land." If the ocean is an unmappable primeval pool,
land records the march of known history. But Thoreau emphasizes instead

that global origins lie in water, citing Desor's statement that "in going back through the geological ages, we come to an epoch when, according to all appearances, the dry land did not exist, and when the surface of our globe was covered entirely with water" (*CC* 100).[15]

The evolution of the world may have been, then, from water to land, but the outcome of that evolution is in active debate. On Thoreau's Cape, the boundary of land and sea is in constant, often violent negotiation. References to erosion, from discussion of the government's fruitless efforts to anchor the soil with beach grass to the locals' worries about their coastline, form the backdrop of the text. "According to the lighthouse keeper," Thoreau writes, "the Cape is wasting here on both sides . . . We calculated *from his data*, how soon the Cape would be quite worn away at this point" (*CC* 118–19). The violent winds, as well as the sea, are responsible for the shifting shoreline, as "sand is blown from the beach directly up the steep bank where it is one hundred and fifty feet high, and covers the original surface there many feet deep . . . This sand is steadily travelling westward at a rapid rate" (*CC* 120). Coastal erosion is exacerbated by the razing of trees and brush as well as the destruction of beach grass, and in what Thoreau calls Cape Cod Harbor the local government realized that "unless some measures were taken to check its progress, it would in a few years destroy both the harbor and the town." Thoreau records their (potentially futile) efforts to plant beach grass behind the town, while "the inhabitants are rolling the sand into the harbor in wheelbarrows, in order to make houselots." His passing remark that the patent office "has recently imported the seed of this grass from Holland" conjures up a genealogy of human efforts to keep the sea from flooding precarious land (*CC* 164).

If the meeting of land and sea is figured as a battle between human history and raw nature, nowhere is this played out more clearly than in the scene of the shipwreck. It is thus not surprising that shipwrecks—the one at Cohasset, Fuller's on Fire Island, and numerous others—are a fixation in *Cape Cod*. They are the sites where human culture comes up against the force of nature, and the fates almost always favor the latter. But this precarity, this narrow terrestrial existence, is also what makes the Cape, for Thoreau, such a privileged site. As he writes, "The inhabitants of all the lower Cape towns enjoy thus the prospect of two seas," meaning Massachusetts Bay and the Atlantic Ocean, the local and global bodies of water (*CC* 115). They are also, as he frequently remarks, "salted" by the winds carrying seawater. Cape Cod allows for a rare human vantage point that is nearly engulfed in water, the closest that we get in life to drowning.

The Shipwreck and the Shoreline

The opening chapter of *Cape Cod*, "The Shipwreck," begins not with a scene of the damage but with a playful figuration of the vying battle between land and sea. "Cape Cod," Thoreau writes, "is the bared and bended arm of Massachusetts; the shoulder is at Buzzard's Bay, the elbow, or the crazy bone, at Cape Mallebarre, the wrist at Truro, and the sandy fist at Provincetown." Thoreau's metaphorical mapping serves primarily to underline the constant contest between his text's two natural forces. As he continues, the Cape's "feet [are] planted on the floor of the ocean, like an athlete protecting her bay—boxing with north-east storms, and, ever and anon, heaving up her Atlantic adversary from the lap of the earth" (*CC* 4).

The scene of a wreck is, for Thoreau, a battle not just between man and nature but also between the national and the global. This emerges clearly in his discussion of the scores of drowned Irish emigrants, in which he draws a parallel between these victims and Columbus's arrival to American shores. But while this parallel between national circulations then and now would seem to emphasize the centrality of American history to daily lived experience, in fact it subverts nation to a metaphysical state. As Thoreau writes, "Why care for these dead bodies? They really have no friends but the worms or fishes. Their owners were coming to the New World, as Columbus and the Pilgrims did, they were within a mile of its shores; but, before they could reach it, they emigrated to a newer world than ever Columbus dreamed of, yet one of whose existence we believe that there is far more universal and convincing evidence—though it has not yet been discovered by science—than Columbus had of this" (*CC* 10). In his comparison of the New World with the afterlife, it is the metaphysical state that takes on greater substantiality. The pause after "there is far more . . . convincing evidence" lets us entertain the idea that there may be more evidence for the afterlife than for the new nation, not merely in Columbus's time but as a general law, well after the nation-state has taken on an apparent substantiality.

Thoreau's descriptions of mass trauma on the beach are in line with his prioritization of the "newer world." The scale of the destruction numbs sympathy, or as he writes, "On the whole, it was not so impressive a scene as I might have expected. If I had found one body cast upon the beach in some lonely place, it would have affected me more . . . It is the individual and private that demands our sympathy" (*CC* 9). The numbing effect of the scene is apparent in Thoreau's descriptions of the victims, who take on the qualities of objects: "I saw many marble feet and matted heads as the cloths were raised, and one livid, swollen and mangled body of a drowned girl—who probably had intended to go out to service in some American family—to which some rags still adhered, with a string, half concealed by the flesh, about its swollen neck; the coiled-up wreck of a human hulk, gashed by the rocks or fishes, so that the bone and muscle were exposed, but quite bloodless—merely red and white—with wide-open and staring eyes, yet lustreless, dead-lights; or, like the cabin windows of a stranded vessel, filled with sand" (*CC* 5–6). The "marble feet" of the victims are statuesque, but the would-be servant girl transforms through Thoreau's words into the ship in which she has so recently traveled, her body a "wreck," her eyes "dead-lights; or, like the cabin windows of a stranded vessel." This metaphor emphasizes the parallel between the boat parts and the human bodies strewn on the beach, both fated to be empty vessels, objects that have lost their central function of ferrying souls. Robert Pinsky calls this movement back and forth, between the generalized proclamation ("It is the individual . . . that demands our sympathy") and concrete description, "the mock-sermon, almost a parody-sermon"; Thoreau's lack of sentimentality is an aspect of the text's "startling" humor.[16] But the point of the passage is ultimately that these bodies fail not only to have an impact on Thoreau but also on the continent, in whose world they never come to participate.

Contrast this assimilation to Margaret Fuller's mapping of American immigrants, not as one step along the westward movement to a spiritual migration but as one layer in the stratification of the land, a sort of living history. In her travels through the Midwest, the Scandinavian, German, and Irish immigrants figure prominently among the frontier settlements, often in their own communities, each preserving their own traditions in the American landscape. Their assimilation into the fabric of the nation is essential to the ideal that she would later map out in her essay "American Literature," of both literature and the American people as "the fusion of the races among us."[17] This "fusion" will result in an aesthetic and a cultural continuity emerging out of difference, or as she writes near the conclusion of *Summer on the Lakes*: "Do not blame me that I have written so much about Germany and Hades, while you were looking for news of the West. Here, on the pier, I see disembarking the Germans, the Norwegians, the Swedes, the Swiss. Who knows how much of old legendary lore, of modern wonder, they have already planted amid the Wisconsin forests? Soon, soon their tales of the origin of things, and the Providence which rules them, will be so mingled with those of the Indian, that the very oak trees will not know them apart,—will not know whether itself be a Runic, a Druid, or a Winnebago oak. Some seeds of all growths that have ever been known in this world might, no doubt, already be found in these Western wilds, if we had the power to call them to life."[18] Like the Indigenous people who leave the earth "full of their traces," the newer immigrants to the continent structure the very substance of the natural landscape, infusing the trees with their particular origin stories. The "seeds" they plant, though new arrivals, bring with them the historical heritage of all the people they represent, infusing the American continent with all the depth of a global culture. Where Thoreau frames immigrant bodies as merely empty vessels and narratives of early settlement as open to question, Fuller finds cultural depth in both older and newer inhabitation.

Given these distinct conceptualizations of the immigrant and of the significance of man to nature, the description of Margaret Fuller's body, or what could have been her body, about halfway through *Cape Cod* rings as a personalized tribute to human remains that have lost all of their personality. The corpse is very clearly "one body cast upon the beach in some lonely place," while Fuller's life is the "individual and private" that carries more emotional resonance than Thoreau's earlier dehumanized "dead bodies" (CC 10). As Thoreau writes in "The Beach Again":

> Once also it was my business to go in search of the relics of a human body, mangled by sharks, which had just been cast up, a week after a wreck, having got the direction from a light-house: I should find it a mile or two distant over the sand, a dozen rods from the water, covered with a cloth, by a stick stuck up . . . Close at hand they were simply some bones with a little flesh adhering to them, in fact, only a slight inequality in the sweep of the shore. There was nothing at all remarkable about them, and they were singularly inoffensive both to the senses and the imagination. But as I stood there they grew more and more imposing. They were alone with the beach and the sea, whose hollow roar seemed addressed to them,

and I was impressed as if there was an understanding between them and the ocean which necessarily left me out, with my snivelling sympathies. That dead body had taken possession of the shore, and reigned over it as no living one could, in the name of a certain majesty which belonged to it. (*CC* 84–85)

This passage, originally drafted in Thoreau's journal at the time of the Fire Island search, is remarkable for the power it grants the almost fleshless body. While Thoreau emphasizes the grotesqueness of the drowning victims from Cohasset to underline their fundamental inhumanity and objectification, here the "relics" of a body assimilate to the natural landscape, "only a slight inequality" in the shoreline, and "singularly inoffensive." But the "majesty" of this corpse is striking. Neither an empty vessel nor a natural element, this skeleton "reigns" over nature, "tak[ing] possession of the shore," a feat that upends the hierarchy of man and nature in effect for most of this text. This stature speaks to its having passed into the "newer world" of the spirit but also, considering the far more prosaic treatment of corpses that introduces *Cape Cod*, the particular characteristics of its former owner.

While Thoreau combed the beach of Fire Island for Margaret Fuller's effects, Emerson began his work on the biographical memorial volume, *Memoirs of Margaret Fuller Ossoli* (1852), that would become a bestseller, though today it is critically derided for its censorship of Fuller's life and work. In *Cape Cod* Thoreau produced a tribute of a very different sort, refusing to name his contemporary even once but shaping his narrative around Fuller nevertheless. The journey of *Cape Cod* invites many changes in perspective, and Thoreau explicitly points up the facility of making such dramatic shifts, destabilizing the narrator's own stances as soon as he takes them. Following some comments on the "shiftlessness" of mackerel fishing as a life's occupation, he writes, "Of course, *viewed from the shore*, our pursuits in the country seem not a whit less frivolous" (*CC* 144). Forcing the narrator's own 180-degree turn on the liminal edge of the shore, Thoreau emphasizes just how arbitrary—or at least physically ordained—all perspective is. In the last lines of the travelogue, after a (now very ironic) admission that the beaches of Cape Cod may never be fashionable, he concludes: "A storm in the fall or winter is the time to visit it; a light-house or a fisherman's hut the true hotel. A man may stand there and put all America behind him" (*CC* 215). The doubleness of this statement—putting something physically behind you, putting something mentally behind you—resonates with Thoreau's action throughout the text, first tracing then questioning the history of America's settlement, upending the hierarchy of sea and land, spirit and material.

In putting America behind him, Thoreau is also doing what Fuller did in the years following the publication of *Summer on the Lakes*, when the success of the travelogue inspired Horace Greeley to offer her the position of foreign correspondent for the *New York Tribune*, a post that would take her through Europe and to the center of the Italian revolutions and eventually end, on the eve of her return to America, off the coast of New York. Thoreau would again turn his back to the coast on his return to Concord, to undertake more landlocked writing. But in his exploration of both the metaphysical abyss and the historical influx from Europe, Thoreau composed a far more meaningful memorial to Fuller than did her closer ally Emerson, one that, knowingly or not, echoes the inscription on the monument at Mount Auburn Cemetery erected in her honor over the grave of her son:

> By birth a child of New England
> By adoption a citizen of Rome
> By genius belonging to the world

Notes

1. Megan Marshall, *Margaret Fuller: A New American Life* (New York: Houghton Mifflin, 2013), 379–90.
2. Walter Harding, *The Days of Henry Thoreau* (New York: Alfred A. Knopf, 1967), 278–79.
3. Harding, *Days of Henry Thoreau*, 273.
4. William Henry, *Coffin Ship: The Wreck of the Brig St. John* (Cork: Mercier Press, 2009), retrieved from http://books.google.com.
5. See Wai Chee Dimock, "Deep Time: American Literature and World History," *American Literary History* 13, no. 4 (Winter 2001): 755–75.
6. Paul Giles, "Transnational Thoreau: Time, Space, and Relativity," in *Thoreau at 200: Essays and Reassessments*, ed. Kirsten Case and K. P. Van Anglen (Cambridge: Cambridge University Press, 2016), 150.
7. Annette Kolodny, *In Search of First Contact: The Vikings of Vinland, the Peoples of the Dawnland, and the Anglo-American Anxiety of Discovery* (Durham, NC: Duke University Press, 2012), 151–212.
8. Kolodny, *In Search*, 147.
9. Kolodny, 12.

10. Richard J. Schneider, "Nature and the Origins of American Civilization in *Cape Cod*," in *Civilizing Thoreau: Human Ecology and the Emerging Social Sciences in the Major Works* (Rochester, NY: Camden House, 2016), 149.

11. Quoted in Marshall, *Margaret Fuller*, 213.

12. Margaret Fuller, *Summer on the Lakes, in 1843* (Boston: Little and Brown, 1844), 52–54.

13. Fuller, *Summer on the Lakes*, 54, 57.

14. Caleb Crain quoted in Michael Bronski, *A Queer History of the United States* (Boston: Beacon Press, 2011); Fuller, *Summer on the Lakes*, 54, 56.

15. As Walter Harding notes, Thoreau spoke to Desor in 1851 in Boston about some "strange jellyfish" he had found along the Massachusetts shoreline. Desor had made a special trip out to Cambridge the previous year to compare botanical notes with Thoreau. In this passage, Thoreau quotes from Desor's 1849 *Massachusetts Quarterly Review* article, "The Ocean and Its Meaning in Nature," but as Joseph Moldenhauer notes, minor errors in transcription suggest that Thoreau may have been citing from a manuscript draft of the essay. Walter Harding, *The Days of Henry Thoreau* (New York: Alfred Knopf, 1967), 294; *The Writings of Henry D. Thoreau: Cape Cod*, ed. Joseph J. Moldenhauer (Princeton: Princeton University Press, 1988), 384.

16. Robert Pinsky, introduction to *CC* xv, ix.

17. Margaret Fuller, "American Literature, Its Position in the Present Time and Prospects for the Future," in *Papers on Literature and Art* (New York: Wiley and Putnam, 1846), 122.

18. Fuller, *Summer on the Lakes*, 165.

3

BEYOND THE BORDERS OF TIME

THOREAU AND THE "ANTE-PILGRIM HISTORY" OF THE NEW WORLD

Michael C. Weisenburg

> Yet let us thank the purblind race
> Who still have thought it good
> With lasting stone to mark the place
> Where braver men have stood
>
> —Thoreau's *Journal*, 1837–47

In the latter half of his career, Henry David Thoreau became a historian. Although considerable scholarship exists on Thoreau's many personae—as poet, political thinker, activist, and proto-environmentalist—and while many have looked to Thoreau's relationship to time to better understand his role as philosopher, I propose to account for the historiographical investigations that comprise the foundation for many of Thoreau's more subtle arguments and run throughout his body of work. While there is substantial textual evidence to justify a reconsideration of Thoreau as historian, in this essay I will focus on how his engagement with the writings of French colonial explorers in his research for *Cape Cod* offers what Thoreau terms "the Ante-Pilgrim history of New England" (*CC* 179).

Thoreau did considerable historical research while working on *Cape Cod*, and much of that research finds its way into the text despite the narrative's close fidelity to the events of Thoreau's first excursion with Ellery Channing in 1849. Furthermore, Thoreau's historical reading prompted him to fundamentally change the way he thought about not only his work but also the world around him. So much so that he was inspired to revise such earlier efforts as *A Week on the Concord and Merrimack Rivers*, contextualize the problem of historical borders in such seminal works as *Walden,* and comment on how people and nations struggle against geographic and political borders in such writings as *A Yankee in Canada.* What we learn in considering these moments of historical border crossings is that, for Thoreau, the history of new world borders, their revisions and elisions, is just as important as his turn toward empirical science and his study of the natural world.

Often associated with a sense of place, Thoreau's historical asides offer a diachronic meditation that denies the purely sublime, or transcendental, experience of the present moment. Furthermore, by comparing competing colonial and regional histories, Thoreau is able to perform a self-conscious historiography that calls into question the teleological and nationalist histories of George Bancroft and the Anglocentric antiquarianism that insists on beginning with the Pilgrims, thus offering his readers an alternative, cosmopolitan history. While I will consider a variety of Thoreau's published works, periodical pieces, and journal entries to support my claims, of all of his texts, *Cape Cod* shows us that Thoreau was the most historically minded of the Transcendentalists. By reading *Cape Cod* in a discursive tradition of exploration, promotion literature, antiquarian histories, and pedestrian tours, we may better understand Thoreau's methods, by which he hoped to transcend the jingoism of his own historical moment not merely through reason and linguistic play but also through a detailed attunement to comparative and regional history. This essay will focus on those moments in Thoreau's oeuvre in which he uses geographic borders as a means of crossing temporal borders, thereby reconsidering not only the landscape but the history inscribed in the territory as well.

In chapter 5 of *Cape Cod,* Thoreau has a conversation with the Wellfleet Oysterman, who informs him that "'King George the Third . . . laid out a road four rods wide and straight the whole length of the cape,' but where it was now he could hardly tell" (*CC* 68). The exchange between the local and the traveler brings to the fore several problems of American history with which Thoreau struggles throughout *Cape Cod.* Questions of cultural origins, territorial control, sovereignty, memory, and storytelling are all jumbled up in this quaint, comic scene. As Thoreau muses on why time should seem so scrambled in the old man's recollections, he remarks, "There was a strange mingling of past and present in his conversation, for he had lived under King George, and might have remembered when Napoleon and the

moderns generally were born" (*CC* 71–72). In the spoken memories of the
Wellfleet Oysterman, Thoreau offers his readers a vignette of the limits of
historical narrative and the great difficulty in keeping the story straight and
recognizable. Just as our local antiquarian can no longer recall where the
British-American King's Road was, so too does the historian often have
trouble finding adequate sources to properly recover the full history of a
given place or time. Additionally, the Oysterman's confused and partial
history of the Cape is tied to his memories, which, like the jingoism that
pervaded American history of the early national and antebellum periods,
narrows the geographic scope and truncates the historic arc of his tale. The
great historians of the day, such as Jared Sparks and George Bancroft, so
deeply committed to the War for Independence and its systematic elision
of British America, were only so many Wellfleet Oystermen, scratching
their heads about where exactly it was that mad old King George lost his
American road.

I think this scene deserves more attention than it has previously enjoyed
because it is here that Thoreau reminds us that history is in the land as well
as in books. Ever the surveyor, he is constantly assessing the landscape of
the Cape and informing his readers of distances traveled and geographic
features that characterize the terrain. He opens the chapter on the Wellfleet
Oysterman with a comment about a "stone post in the sand,—for even
this sand comes under the jurisdiction of one town or another" (*CC* 62).
Here we find Thoreau's philosophies of time and place intersect. History
is much like the sand of Cape Cod, and just as Thoreau was a surveyor
of land, so was he also a surveyor of time. While he may not have had a
proper title or explicit jurisdiction, the past of the Americas was just as
much his as any other author's.

While thinking of Thoreau as a historian may seem a bit of a stretch to
twenty-first-century readers who are more accustomed to thinking of him
as poet, naturalist, and political iconoclast, his own friends and associates
would not find the claim so troubling. Thoreau's contemporaries were so
well aware of his historical interests that they often failed to give us a full
account of them. This fact of Thoreau's life was commonplace enough
that Emerson, in his eulogy on Thoreau, used it as merely one of many
asides to remind his audience of both Thoreau's capacious mind and his
rebellious temperament. Emerson's recounting of Thoreau's argument to
Harvard president and fellow historian Jared Sparks—"not only his want

of books was imperative, but he wanted a large number of books"—is a direct reference to Thoreau's historical awakening (*CW* 10:417). His request to access library holdings was similar to that of others of his intellectual circle. Emerson had argued for the same privileges in 1846 to aid in revising his "Representative Men" lectures, especially the lectures on Plato and Swedenborg, as well as material regarding Persian poetry that would influence specific elements of *Poems*.[1] What is different about Thoreau's research is that it increasingly became a pursuit to recover empirical history with an accumulative, cosmopolitan, and revisionist agenda. Whereas Emerson generally utilized his research as a means of discovering transhistorical ideals that helped affirm his own aesthetic arguments, Thoreau allowed the historical record to influence his arguments and guide his endeavors. Access to the major libraries of the Boston area afforded him the means to see the eastern coast of North America before it was New England. From the perspective of the past that Thoreau discovered in these overlooked historical works, he was better able to articulate how the borders of what became the United States were drawn and redrawn by the successive imperialist and nationalist narratives that laid claim to place.

To fully appreciate Thoreau's historiographical turn, we must establish how he situated *Cape Cod* within the dominant discursive modes of the history of his time before ultimately moving away from them. At the beginning of *The Archaeology of Knowledge*, Michel Foucault posits that the "epistemological mutation of history is not yet complete," and he raises several methodological problems, including "the building-up of coherent and homogenous corpora of documents . . . the establishment of a principle of choice . . . the definition of the level of analysis and of the relevant elements . . . [and] the specification of a method of analysis."[2] Foucault offers us a useful heuristic by which we may assess the cultural milieu of American historiography with which Thoreau was engaged. The dominant mode of historical writing in the early national and antebellum United States composed the archetype of its grand narrative primarily out of a British colonial and American Revolutionary archive. In privileging anglophone documents as their source texts, these scholars selectively obfuscated the earlier colonial history of French North America and set a precedent for writing a predominantly Anglo-American history. The Revolutionary generation, the first generation of U.S. historians, produced works that strove to create a national history that would justify the War of Independence and establish a sense of cultural belonging and logical inevitability. Although they were influenced by Enlightenment ideals of the universality of the human experience and the conjectural tradition of the Scottish School of Common Sense, their works ultimately turn toward a preoccupation with the nascent nation-state as constituting a fundamentally unique historical experience. The apparent political and intellectual novelty of the United States was a result of a narrative breach between Old World and New that created the conditions by which the next generation of Romantic historians were able to forge a national mythology.

This is no small point in American historiography. While the Revolutionary generation forced facts into a preconceived structure that assumed America's separation from Great Britain was inevitable, they did so under the aegis of the Enlightenment. For them, everything that transpired was logical, reasonable, and empirical. The Romantics took up this structure and cloaked it in mythology and hero worship. As Arthur H. Shaffer describes it, "The Romantic school was by contrast mystical and obscurantist. Its basic doctrine was a belief in the gradual development of a distinct and unique national spirit . . . It was an emotional approach to history, for it made no other rational attempt to explain the development of these national peculiarities."[3] It was this Romantic mode that drove most history in the period, regardless of the particular subgenre a given author was writing. Everything from academic history and national biography to pedestrian tours, local color and regional histories, and popular legends and folktales proliferated in this period, and all of them were dominated by a Romantic ideology of what would come to be known as "American exceptionalism." While Thoreau deploys some aspects of Romanticism, with affinities for blending the historical record within the genre of travel narrative, his empirical tendencies and his willingness to consider a more capacious and inclusive world afford his history a less nationalist, more cosmopolitan perspective. In a similar way that his scientific affinities lead to Thoreau's development into what Ellery Channing referred to as "the poet-naturalist," so too did his historical research present a manner in which he often wrote against the cultural grain, following where the evidence lead him.[4]

Thoreau's Transcendentalist peers were no less complicit in the production of nationalist mythology and hero worship. As Frank Shuffelton has pointed out, "[Emerson] shared with the great American romantic historians a belief in the hermeneutic possibilities of the representative man within the narrative of history."[5] Given the preponderance of the hero as a synecdoche for the people, it is little wonder that Ralph Waldo Emerson would claim, in his essay "History," that "all history becomes subjective; in other words, there is properly no History; only Biography" (*CW* 2:6). When we consider the importance of biography in the period, Emerson's remark seems rather run-of-the-mill. The first volume of Jeremy Belknap's *American Biography* was published in 1794 with a second volume published in 1798, Samuel Knapp's *American Biography* came out in 1833, Jared Sparks edited *The Library of American Biography* between 1834 and 1838, and Benson John Lossing published *Our Countrymen; or, Brief Memoirs of Eminent Americans* in 1855; these are only the highlights of middle-class academic histories, which in turn are only a small fraction of what Americans read. There were innumerable local and regional histories that focused on each state and county's exploits during the Revolution, countless newspaper and magazine articles that periodically reminded readers of the valor of the founding fathers, and a variety of penny press legends of Washington and his generals, such as those produced by George Lippard. We might even consider Cotton Mather's *Magnalia Christi Americana* and the works of Mason Locke Weems as establishing and refining the long tradition on which Emerson was commenting.

The great practitioner of this mode of history was, of course, George Bancroft, whose monumental *History of the United States from the Discovery of the American Continent* anachronistically reads the discovery of the New World within the borders of the United States. Indeed, its very title forecasts its fundamental assumption that the American continent was discovered so that the United States might come into being. Bancroft was interested in the colonial past of North America only insofar as it could be used as a backdrop for the Revolution and as a means of exploring the origins of national character. For Bancroft, America came "out of the soul of the people, and was an inevitable result of a living affection for freedom, which actuated harmonious efforts as certainly as the beating of the heart sends warmth and color and beauty to the system."[6] The rhetorical flourish with which Bancroft incorporates American history into the body politic of the Unites States is then religiously approbated by Bancroft's controlling theme of the creation of the United States as an act of divine providence. Such apocalyptic and millennialist themes were prevalent in colonial and early national New England, and these narratives were utilized to rationalize the inevitability of the American Revolution and the necessity of the United States to God's divine plan.[7] The United States thus becomes the greatest actor in the progress toward the perfection of history, as if the end of time were in search of its proper place.

Unlike Bancroft, whose assessment of history was bound by the borders of the United States, Thoreau uses a broader territory to recover the transformations of boundaries over time. His commitment to the historical record and his incorporation of a wide array of colonial histories in his works highlights an essential difference in his engagement with and writing of history, and the historicism of these works constitutes a fundamental aspect of Thoreau's turn away from Romanticism. Tacit in Romantic history is a desire to see the self reflected back from the past. It is a way of writing history that is essentially present tense and future-oriented.[8] In this respect, Emerson is the consummate Romantic philosopher when he argues, "There is no age or state of society or mode of action in history to which there is not somewhat corresponding in his life . . . He should see that he can live all history in his own person" (*CW* 2:5–6). For Emerson, history corresponds to the self. This self would be a hero for his people, and so, when he looks to the past, he is congenitally blind to the rich, multicultural, and cosmopolitan history it might offer. The reality of the past held little meaning for Emerson and other Romantic historians; the self-affirming narrative was what they were looking for. As Emerson argues elsewhere in his essay "History," "Who cares what the fact was, when we have made a constellation of it to hang in heaven an immortal sign?" (*CW* 2:6). Herein lies the fatal flaw of Romantic history, for when the facts of history are ignored, all we are left with is the myth, the fable, and when this fable is agreed on by those in power, it has the force to elide history, to subsume its facts and place them under erasure.

Thoreau became increasingly aware of the danger Romantic history posed to historical veracity and strove to recover the facts of North America's past, to give it a broader range of actors, a longer temporal arc, and a more affective social meaning—something that extends beyond borders, nations, and ideology. Laura Dassow Walls and Robert D. Richardson both point to Thoreau's trip to Canada in 1850 as a turning point in his thought, an "epiphany" that gave him a "whole new conception of the history of North America" that fundamentally influenced the development of *Cape Cod*.[9] However, Thoreau had long been interested in history, and his rekindled interest affects and pervades not just *Cape Cod* and *A Yankee in Canada* but also *Walden* and *The Maine Woods* as well as expansions and revisions he later made to *A Week on the Concord and Merrimack Rivers*. What the Canadian excursion did was make manifest for Thoreau an alternate possibility, a North America that might have been—that in fact still was. This realization was powerful enough to affect all his subsequent writings. While *Cape Cod* is perhaps Thoreau's greatest achievement in historiography, we see the development of his ideas concerning history forming in his journals of the period. For example, on January 21, 1852, he writes, "History used to be the history of successive kings—or their reigns the Williams—Henries—Johns Richards &c &c all of them great in somebody's estimations— But we have altered that considerably— Hereafter it is to be to a greater extent the history of peoples" (*PJ* 4:273). Here we see Thoreau's historical perspective coming into conflict with Emerson's notion of history as the record of the one mind common to all. In response to a mythology of hero worship, Thoreau began to write a history of how many peoples and their collective actions helped shape the development of a place over time.

One of the ways that Thoreau reminds his readers of the arbitrary nature of borders is by paying attention to the landscape and its specific history. In addition to the succession of different plant species and the migrations of animals, rivers often afford Thoreau an opportunity to meditate on the various histories of a place. For Thoreau, rivers, like the shifting sands of Cape Cod, are both constantly in flux and the sum total of their histories. If, as he quips at the end of "Where I Lived and What I Lived For," "time is but the stream I go a-fishing in," then those fish are so many facts of history that his fellow historical anglers are too impertinent to appreciate (*W* 98). The association of rivers with historical accretion across time in a place is found as early as the first edition of *A Week*. In her study of Thoreau's use of history in *A Week on the Concord and Merrimack Rivers*, Judith Broome Mesa-Pelly points out that "although Thoreau must, at times, rely on historical records, he is keenly aware of the way in which those documents create history," and "for Thoreau, history constantly rewrites itself by weaving together landscape, memory, and historical records."[10] As Thoreau worked up his trip with his brother, John, into material for his first book, he used the conceit of the river and its history as a means to comment on the social and political changes in the land over the past two centuries, thereby setting a rhetorical pattern of attaching as many historical and documentary references to a description of place as he could, a pattern that he would repeat and augment throughout his later writings.

Thoreau's attention to the pluralist, sedimentary history of place is found not only in his major works but in many of his essays and excursions as well. Just as he points out that the Concord River was once Muske-taquid, or Grass-ground River, so too does he recover the deep history of the St. Lawrence in *A Yankee in Canada*. Reporting that "in Champlain's day it was commonly called 'the Great River of Canada,'" Thoreau calls attention to the fact that "more than one nation has claimed it. In Ogilby's 'America of 1670,' in the map *Novi Belgii*, it is called 'De Grate River van Niew Nederlandt.' It bears different names in different parts of its course, as it flows through what were formerly the territories of different nations" (*Exc* 155). Just as rivers cross national borders in the present, they also cross the borders of time, and just as he is able to recover the Native American, French, Dutch, and English names of places across time, Thoreau is able to argue that "the Englishman's history of *New* England commences, only when it ceases to be, *New* France" (*CC* 183). These transformations are accomplished only by the elision of native place names.

If, as Richard Bridgman speculates, "because Thoreau did not live to see *Cape Cod* through the press, its last two chapters are particularly unkempt," then we who study early American literature and history are so much the poorer for it.[11] While I wish to emphasize the importance that history, topography, and surveying play throughout *Cape Cod*, it is the final chapter, "Provincetown," in which we see Thoreau striving toward a comparative historiography of the Americas. While I share Bridgman's concern that we do not have a clearly authoritative end of the work, I am not convinced that we should read the last two chapters as unkempt or unrealized. It is clear from his journal entries and his other published writings that Thoreau had historiographical ambitions for *Cape Cod* from its earliest inception. His journals from this period are filled with references to his researches on early exploration and promotional literature about the region.[12]

The importance of history and historical research to the overall structure of *Cape Cod* is difficult to overstate, but what I am most concerned with here is how Thoreau's use of the historical record calls into question the nationalist claims of his contemporaries. In the chapter "Provincetown," he explicitly takes Bancroft to task, criticizing him for not mentioning "Champlain at all among the authorities" of colonial history, even going so far as to cite Belknap as an authority who sanctions Champlain's importance to the history of New England (*CC* 179, 180). As he puts it: "It is remarkable that there is not in English any adequate or correct account of the French exploration of what is now the coast of New England, between 1604 and 1608, though it is conceded that they then made the first permanent European settlement on the continent of North America north of St. Augustine. If the lions had been the painters it would have been otherwise" (*CC* 179). Thoreau then continues to consider the (perhaps deliberate) historical elision of Champlain from the Anglo-American record. While Champlain is at the heart of Thoreau's criticism of Anglo-American history, he is by no means the sole historical example of deliberately excised explorers. Indeed, the list of Thoreau's references is quite long and includes the likes of Robert Beverley, William Bradford, William Brereton, Pierre François Xavier de Charlevoix, Christopher Columbus, Timothy Dwight, Richard Hakluyt, John Josselyn, Sieur de la Borde, and John Smith, to name just a few. Furthermore, the genres that Thoreau works to incorporate into his history range from antiquarian chorographies, cartography, and promotional tracts to topographical descriptions and natural histories. I've listed these authors and genres with the expressed desire to illustrate that Thoreau's "ante-Pilgrim history of New England" is not only an insistence on setting the historical record straight by pointing out that the French were engaged in North American colonialism before the English, although that is certainly one of Thoreau's major points, but that it is also a fundamental change in the manner by which Thoreau approached the writing of his text, demonstrating that civil history was of equal importance as natural history and emergent science to his philosophical and worldview.

In concert with or in supplement to Thoreau's concern with transcendental existence, the sublime, and being in the present is a counterbalance of competing histories, all of which influence and determine the present. While "Provincetown" is the most historically laden of its chapters, such moments of historical rumination punctuate the narrative of *Cape Cod*. Indeed, they are incorporated throughout Thoreau's body of work. Thoreau's attention to the empirical data of the environment around him not only influenced his ethics and his work as a naturalist but also imbued his narratives with a deep sense of history akin to what Wai Chee Dimock

has referred to as "deep time" and what Laura Dassow Walls has identified as "the emergent discourse of globalization" that is at the "heart of
modernity" and characterizes Transcendentalism as a problem.[13] Thoreau
responded to the problem of modernity and globalization by performing
such extensive historical research to account for the imposition of history
on the present. Thus, his writing is not only an ante-Pilgrim history but an
anti-Romantic history as well.

The irruption of the past into the present registers an ecology of time as
well as an ecology of region. Thoreau's historical asides are often associated
with a sense of place, which calls attention to the diachronic nature of the
landscape. Such moments allow Thoreau's work a temporal layering akin
to what we might term a cultural geology or sedimentary anthropology,
one that encourages his readers' present tense pause to reckon with the
past. Throughout *Cape Cod*, place is always encumbered with memory,
such as in the scene in "The Plains of Nauset," in which the landlord's brag
about his corn harvest from such seemingly barren land prompts Thoreau
to interject his narrative with references to Champlain's *Voyages* and *Mourt's
Relation*, as well as to speculate on the nature of past Native American
agriculture in the region (*CC* 29). Thoreau's historical meditations not only
expound on such moments of the past but also shift readers out of their
present experience, just as the sand dunes and the Cape itself are registered
to shift over time, drawing attention to the palimpsest that is Cape Cod,
both landmass and historical text. Kristen Case has argued more recently
that "Thoreau's insistence on the value of a deep knowledge of place" is
such that both his method and his epistemology are "precisely located . . .
and practice-based." Case goes on to argue that Thoreau's walking tours
can be understood as producing "dynamic topological reconfigurations."[14]
I would posit that not only did Thoreau practice such methodology in his
journals and Kalendars of natural history but that he also applied them to
his later travel writings.

Thoreau's situated methodology is tied not only to place but to time as
well, specifically to history. Thoreau shared this method of situated rela-
tionality with such minor and residual forms of historical writing as the
pedestrian tour and topographic histories, for example, those of Benson
John Lossing, whose popular *Pictorial Field-Book of the Revolution* was seri-
alized in *Harper's* from 1850 to 1852, representing "how middle-class Americans . . . read, wrote, and thought about their nation's past."[15] Thoreau's

reliance on the long historical traditions of the New World, especially French colonial history, and his hyperregional descriptions and topographies aid in surveying not just the landscape but also its past. Doing so allows him to account for the various historical phenomena that interrupt the present—be it the many Indian arrowheads he finds, the history of African American slaves in Concord, Massachusetts, or the precedent of French colonial activities in the geographic region that will come to be known as New England. Thoreau's deep historical research allows him to describe the historical landscape at length while remaining within the narrative of his walk along Cape Cod with Channing in 1849. By comparing the competing colonial and regional histories, Thoreau performs a self-conscious historiography that calls into question the teleological and nationalist histories of Bancroft and Lossing, who both insist on beginning with the Pilgrims and focusing on the Revolution, in order to offer his readers an alternative, cosmopolitan history. That Thoreau was so keenly aware of and invested in history is consistent with both his empiricism and his insistence on not taking the commonplace for granted.

With *Cape Cod*, Thoreau not only developed a deeper reliance on written history but also came to appreciate and foreground the fact that not all written histories are treated equally within any given historical moment, geographic region, or political context. In turning back to the historical record as he expanded and revised *Cape Cod*, Thoreau increasingly focused his attention on the global scope of the colonization of the New World. As early in the text as "The Plains of Nauset," he began to cite and compare how the Nauset Indians are represented in Champlain's *Voyages* with *Mourt's Relation*, bringing early French exploration to bear on the context of the English Pilgrims' presence in the New World as well as to situate both the French and the English in trade relations with the Indigenous people of the Cape, showing the three groups to be much closer neighbors in time and space than most of the nationalist histories that circulated in Thoreau's time would admit. At the very point that he began to perform a comparative history of the Cape, Thoreau also began to fold his subsequent trips to the Cape into the 1849 narrative, further emphasizing the diachronic nature of his text. At one point he comments, "There is a 'beach' on the west side of Eastham, which we crossed the next summer, half a mile wide, and stretching across the township, containing seventeen hundred acres, on which there is not now a particle of vegetable mould, through it formerly produced wheat" (*CC* 28). In continually returning to the writings of colonization, regional histories, and topographical descriptions, Thoreau produces what Mesa-Pelly refers to as his "unusual sense of parallel history," in which he is able to call attention to the competing aspects of French and English colonial dominance in North America and through which he may criticize his own historical moment of military expansion, which, Thoreau believes, is predicated on dubious arguments of originality, nationalism, and religious destiny.[16] By calling attention to both the constant flux of the present and the continual irruption of the past in the present, Thoreau's survey of the Cape Cod landscape and its past engenders his text, *Cape Cod*, with a political and ethical reconstitution that is revisionist in its methods.

Benjamin Vilhauer has drawn attention to Thoreau's interest in the discovery and colonization, especially with regard to Thoreau's priority of the French explorers, arguing, "In metaphorically equating history with the landscape, Thoreau parallels the shore with the present."[17] Yet given Thoreau's emphasis on the palimpsestic nature of Cape Cod, we might do better than merely read the equation of the past with landscape as metaphorical. For Thoreau, it was quite literal. The crisis of the shore is that, unlike Thoreau, few of his contemporaries were reading the landscape for the history that it contains. While many antebellum American historians relied on the historical record to justify the United States' imperial tendencies of the present and imagine a future American empire expanding its territorial bounds, Thoreau leveraged the history of the landscape to reorient his readers' perspectives with an eye toward historical borders as well as historical actors. Thoreau's extensive historical research on Cape Cod produces a narrative landscape through which he may collapse time and reveal the shoreline to be the full account of the history he has found there—that of Native peoples, French and English explorers, the Pilgrims, and New England fishermen and wreckers, traces of whom he comes across in his walking the Cape. In recovering the global and regional histories of Cape Cod, Thoreau is able to remove the nationalist topoi of his historical moment and recast the Cape as a cosmopolitan territory of diverse peoples. By surveying the Cape's history, he calls attention not only to the flux of the present but also the flux of the past, recalling its borders and, in doing so, reconstructing its titles and its deeds, if only in the narrative of his own *Cape Cod*.

I'd like to close with a final consideration of Thoreau's practice of surveying because I think it is integral to his practice of history and reminds us how deeply he thought about these matters in his daily life. In his work on Thoreau as surveyor, Patrick Chura argues that for Thoreau, surveying was a practical historical labor, stating, "Clearly, his natural inclination to study the environment and learn the histories of its fields, ponds, and woodlands helped Thoreau to locate old boundaries."[18] Thoreau understood his work to be not only the labor of making borders in the present but also of rediscovering the borders of the past. In December 1857, he was performing a considerable amount of surveying work. He recorded his thoughts on his labor in his Journal: "That is what I had been doing all my life—making or rather finding them—remaking what had been unmade bounds—where they were away."[19] It is Thoreau's ingrained commitment to rediscovering forgotten bounds and lost markers in the landscape that allows *Cape Cod*, a work that started out as an example of the popular genre of travel literature, to become a prescient critique of the American history of its day.

Notes

1. Emerson had claimed, and was awarded, the same privilege in 1846 by Edward Everett; see Emerson, *Letters of Ralph Waldo Emerson*, vol. 3, ed. Ralph L. Rusk (New York: Columbia University Press, 1939), 335–36. For Thoreau's initial request, see his letter of September 17, 1849, to Jared Sparks (*Corr* 2:35–36).

2. Michel Foucault, The *Archaeology of Knowledge*, trans. A. M. Sheridan Smith (New York: Pantheon Books, 1972), 10–11.

3. Arthur H. Shaffer, *The Politics of History: Writing the History of the American Revolution, 1783–1815* (Chicago: University of Chicago Press, 1975), 177.

4. William Ellery Channing, *Thoreau: The Poet-Naturalist, with Memorial Verses* (Boston, MA: Roberts Brothers, 1873).

5. Frank Shuffelton, "Emerson's Politics of Biography and History," in *Emersonian Circles: Essays in Honor of Joel Myerson*, ed. Wesley T. Mott and Robert Burkholder (Rochester, NY: University of Rochester Press, 1997), 56.

6. George Bancroft, *History of the United States from the Discovery of the American Continent*, vol. 7 (Boston, MA: Little, Brown, 1858), 301.

7. The rhetoric of apocalypse is a foundational subtext of British colonial and U.S. national identity that persists to this day. For an assessment of apocalyptic and millennialist themes in American history, see Ruth H. Bloch, *Visionary Republic: Millennial Themes in American Thought, 1756–1800* (New York: Cambridge University Press, 1985); Michael Lienesch, "The Role of Political Millennialism in Early American Nationalism," *The Western Political Quarterly* 36, no. 3 (September 1983): 445–65; and Matthew Avery Sutton, *American Apocalypse: A History of Modern Evangelicalism* (Cambridge, MA: Belknap Press of Harvard University Press, 2014).

8. See also Frederick Saunders and Thomas B. Thorpe, who wrote, "Other nations may glory in the past, but we are the people of the future," in *Voice to America* (New York: Edward Walker, 1850), 300.

9. Laura Dassow Walls, *Henry David Thoreau: A Life* (Chicago: University of Chicago Press, 2017), 300; Robert D. Richardson Jr. *Henry Thoreau: A Life of the Mind* (Berkeley: University of California Press, 1986), 216.

10. Judith Broome Mesa-Pelly, "Thoreau's 'Basket of a Delicate Texture': Weaving History in *A Week*," *The Concord Saunterer* 4 (1996): 179, 177.

11. Richard Bridgman, *Dark Thoreau* (Lincoln: University of Nebraska Press, 1982), 185.

12. For an exhaustive assessment of Thoreau's reading practices, see Robert Sattelmeyer, *Thoreau's Reading: A Study in Intellectual History with Bibliographical Catalogue* (Princeton, NJ: Princeton University Press, 1988).

13. Wai Chee Dimock, *Through Other Continents: American Literature across Deep Time* (Princeton, NJ: Princeton University Press, 2008), 3; Laura Dassow Walls, "Global Transcendentalism," in *The Oxford Handbook of Transcendentalism*, ed. Joel Myerson, Sandra Harbert Petrulionis, and Laura Dassow Walls (Oxford: Oxford University Press, 2010), 513.

14. Kristen Case, "Knowing as Neighboring: Approaching Thoreau's Kalendar," *J19* 2, no. 1 (Spring 2014): 122, 120.

15. Harold E. Mahan, *Benson J. Lossing and Historical Writing in the United States* (New York: Greenwood Press, 1996), 3.

16. Mesa-Pelly, "Thoreau's 'Basket,'" 182.

17. Benjamin Vilhauer, "The Theme of Time in Thoreau's *Cape Cod*: The Crisis of the Present Shore," *The Concord Saunterer* 16 (2008): 35.

18. Patrick Chura, *Thoreau the Land Surveyor* (Gainesville: University Press of Florida, 2010), 19.

19. Henry David Thoreau, *Journal*, "Journal, November 25, 1857–June 4, 1858," entry for December 31, 1857, http://thoreau.library.ucsb.edu/writings_journals_pdfs/J13f1-f3.pdf, 31.

4

MAKING THE INVISIBLE VISIBLE

THOREAU'S TEXTS AND/AS MAPPING PRACTICES

Julien Nègre

Henry David Thoreau's legacy is not only literary but cartographic, including numerous maps long neglected by critics—from the plans he drafted as a professional surveyor to the ancient charts he copied in the library at Harvard University.[1] In this essay, I attempt to clarify the role that these maps played in Thoreau's work as a writer by examining the recent processual turn in map theory. Following Lawrence Buell's suggestion that maps can be "more complexly productive than when seen merely as agents of cartographical imperialism," I show that Thoreau's map use was not a passive gesture of reception but an active engagement with maps.[2] I argue that Thoreau was drawn to maps as a unique clarification tool, one capable of revealing phenomena that would otherwise remain invisible. His "extravagant" and sauntering mind finds an unexpected ally in cartography, allowing him to conduct a controversial redistribution of spatiality and explore a new system of visibility.

I begin by examining the reasons why looking at Thoreau's maps in a "productive" way is a difficult but important task. I compare different approaches in map theory and show that the processual turn allows us to understand Thoreau's writings as a direct engagement with maps. To explore the implications of this paradigm shift, I then turn to some of the maps that Thoreau drew and to his texts. I relate Thoreau's interest in maps to his concern with issues of perception and visibility. In conclusion, I suggest that Thoreau's texts are not maps, of course, but can nonetheless be read as "mappings" in their effort to make the invisible visible.

Maps occupy a singular position in Thoreau's life and in his texts. As a volume such as *A Thoreau Gazetteer* makes clear, he was very familiar not only with the commercial and official maps of his own time but also with the history of cartography as a whole.[3] In his texts, but also in his papers and notebooks, references to specific maps abound (the final chapter of *Cape Cod* is a good example), as do tracings of ancient and modern maps that he made in libraries or during his travels—indeed, at the beginning of *The Maine Woods*, Thoreau explicitly describes how he produced a tracing of Moses Greenleaf's 1844 *Map of the State of Maine* that he found hanging on the wall in a tavern (*MW* 15).[4] Despite this familiarity and the presence of these cartographic documents in his papers, the role that maps and mapping played in Thoreau's work as a writer has rarely been truly investigated.[5] A comprehensive study such as Patrick Chura's *Thoreau the Land Surveyor* does provide insight into the complex experience of surveying, which is, however, only partially related to map use: the production of a survey is a complex process that involves collecting data and making measurements, of which the map is only the result.[6] Moreover, Chura's book examines passages in Thoreau's texts that refer to surveying practices, but it does not tackle the larger question of what role Thoreau's interactions with maps have played in the way he understood his work as a writer. The same is true of *A Thoreau Gazetteer*, whose purpose is strictly limited to "giv[ing] an idea of the places Thoreau describes in his own books"—a striking statement that seems to imply that these maps have a purely documentary and illustrative value and bear no relation to the texts themselves.[7]

While Thoreau is a writer often associated with maps (I am thinking here of the maps included in most modern-day editions of his texts or used on the covers of his volumes), it is also easy to neglect, at best, the maps he used by treating them as irrelevant or merely incidental (in much the same way that his interest in "science," facts, and data was long dismissed as insignificant until the groundbreaking work of Laura Dassow Walls) or, at worst, to define them as the direct antagonist of his writing—that against which his work as a writer is directed.[8] The latter view is supported by passages from his texts in which Thoreau explicitly stresses the importance of being "completely lost"—a statement that can easily be construed as a disinterest in, not to say a rejection of, maps (*W* 170). An oft-quoted passage from an 1858 journal entry emphasizes the toll that Thoreau's job as a surveyor had on his perception of the natural environment around

Concord, relating the drawing of plans to a form of "dry knowledge."[9] In this perspective, the map is associated with stasis, fixity, and barrenness, while writing is linked with fluidity, extravagance, and a certain richness of texture. This reading works well with *Walden*, in which the speaker can be described as moving away from the simplified and arid plan of the pond reproduced in "The Pond in Winter" to the exuberant fluidifications of "Spring."

This reading is also in tune with the larger critical context of the last thirty years. In the 1980s, following Foucault's warning that authoritative discourses are always gestures of domination and control, map theorists such as Brian Harley started to analyze maps in a critical light to show that they are inherently tools of power at the hands of those who commission them.[10] The legacy of "critical cartography" became the dominant paradigm in map theory in the 1990s and 2000s, with the publication of such popular books as *The Power of Maps* by Denis Wood (1992, followed by *Rethinking the Power of Maps* in 2010) and *How to Lie with Maps* by Mark Monmonier (1996).[11] In this perspective, the map is not only far less textured than the real world but is also seen as a highly suspicious tool of imperialism, territorial appropriation, and hegemony. This reading is particularly relevant in the context of Thoreau's own time: for example, on the maps of the American West published year after year in the 1840s and 1850s, the growing accuracy and the gradual disappearance of blank spaces can be read not so much as the *revelation* of what was hidden in those *terrae incognitae* as the deliberate *concealment* of entire populations (the presence of Native American tribes is not always figured on the map, thereby reinforcing the perception of an empty continent, available for pioneers to seize), violent episodes (massacres, forced migrations), and the economic systems of exploitation that made westward expansion possible (slavery).

To be sure, Thoreau himself was aware of both the limitations of maps and their ideological bias. Consider the following passage from his Journal, written on November 10, 1860: "How little there is on an ordinary map! How little, I mean, that concerns the walker and the lover of nature. Between those lines indicating roads is a plain blank space in the form of a square or triangle or polygon or segment of a circle, and there is naught to distinguish this from another area of similar size and form. Yet the one, may be covered, in fact, with a primitive oak wood, like that of Boxboro, waving and creaking in the wind, such as may make the reputation of a county, while the other is a stretching plain with scarcely a tree on it. The waving woods, the dells and glades and green banks and smiling fields, the huge boulders, etc., etc., are not on the map, nor to be inferred from the map" (*J* XIV:228–29). Thoreau spent the month of November 1860 deeply absorbed in his study of the question of the succession of forest trees. His journal entries for that month include literally hundreds of measurements of pine stumps and oak stumps, which he observed meticulously and on which he counted the annual rings. On the day when this entry was made, Thoreau visited a place called Inches Wood, located in Boxborough, less than eight miles west of Concord. Inches Wood was a primitive oak wood of beautiful ancient trees, and Thoreau was amazed to discover that such a place existed so close to Concord and that he had never heard of it. The passage draws a stark contrast between the map and the world but also, more obliquely, between the map and writing itself. The careful choice of adjectives focusing on what the map cannot depict (sounds, movements of air, what Thoreau calls in *The Maine Woods* "wind on our cheeks" [*MW* 71]) not only suggests that the map can offer a limited version of the real but also emphasizes what writing, and words, can accomplish.

At first sight, the passage reads as an indictment of maps and their limitations. Thoreau's rebuke makes sense when we look at maps from the perspective of what has been called the representational paradigm that dominated map theory until the 1990s. In that perspective, a map is envisioned first and foremost as a representation of the territory. That representation is produced by the cartographer, who makes a series of choices to convey to the map user a certain "truth." Drawing on Claude Shannon's work in information theory, this conception of maps was formalized into a "map communication model" in which the cartographer transmits to the user a certain amount of information through a channel, the map.[12] Thoreau seems to be working from this particular paradigm here: he thinks of himself as the end user of a process, and he criticizes both the choices made at the other end by the transmitter and the limitations of the channel itself.

As I will explain later, the map that Thoreau had in mind when he wrote this journal entry is probably Henry Walling's 1856 map of Middlesex County, on which Inches Wood indeed appears as a "plain blank space" (figure 1).[13] Walling's name is familiar to readers of Thoreau because he also

Figure 1. Henry Walling, *Map of Middlesex County, Massachusetts*, 1856, 146 cm by 147 cm, Library of Congress, Geography and Map Division, Washington, D.C.

published a map of Concord in 1852 which famously features the survey of Walden Pond performed by Thoreau himself.[14] The blank spaces on these maps (figure 2) make Thoreau's lament understandable: what is hidden in those empty areas? From the perspective of the representational paradigm, what Thoreau denounces is at the same time the technical limitations of maps, whose geometric shapes are utterly disconnected from the real world they are supposed to "represent," and the ideological orientation of the map, which shows human infrastructures (roads, mills) while neglecting the interests of another category of citizens, the "walkers and lovers of nature" (*J* XIV:228).

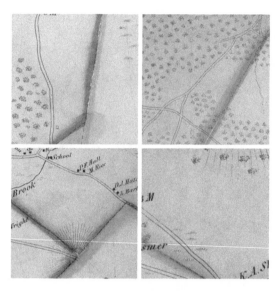

Figure 2. Details of blank spaces on Henry Walling's 1852 *Map of the Town of Concord*. Map reproduction courtesy of the Norman B. Leventhal Map & Education Center at the Boston Public Library, MA.

Looking at Thoreau's maps from this perspective, though, is limiting in at least two ways. First, if we demand that maps be representations of the world, they simply cannot escape the accusation of incompleteness: as the mapmaker needs to select specific categories of information to keep his map legible, the map is always incomplete and, for that reason, dissatisfying. Second, map use is primarily understood as, at best, a passive reception or, at worst, a confrontation with an ideologically biased object. In other words, the representational paradigm makes it impossible to envision a fruitful and more dynamic interaction between Thoreau and his maps.

More recent theoretical developments offer a different perspective on the work that maps do. Instead of a unidirectional model of map communication in which the map is crafted by the mapmaker and transmitted to the user, other critics have the map users themselves play an important role in defining what a map is and does. Alan MacEachren's 1995 "cartography cube," for example, took into account the dimensions of interactivity and customization to evaluate the status of a given map.[15] A new paradigm, usually referred to as the "processual turn" in map theory, eventually emerged in the late 2000s.[16] In this processual perspective, maps are not envisioned as ontologically stable objects solely shaped by the mapmaker but rather as being "in a constant state of becoming . . . they are 'mobile subjects' whose meaning emerges through socio-spatial practices of use that mutate with context and is contested and intertextual."[17] The point here is not to question the hegemonic dimension of maps foregrounded by critical cartography, but to emphasize the importance of reception. A map is shaped and defined by the multiple practices of its user: it might be folded, rolled, traced, annotated, cut into pieces, recycled, etc., each of these gestures altering its nature and its agency.

From that viewpoint, a map and its tracing, for example, are not the same map. When Thoreau copied Greenleaf's map by hand, he produced a document whose nature and meaning were, in effect, different from the original. Instead of focusing on the ontological essence of maps, the processual approach is more interested in the ontogenesis of maps—how a map is "(re)made *every time* mapping practices are applied to the pattern of ink." One consequence of this reading is that "maps do not emerge in the same way for all individuals."[18] In other words, a "map" (its meaning and significance) exists only in the specific context in which it is used, and depending on how it is read by the user. One of Thoreau's surveys, for example, can be read as containing two maps in one. On November 24, 1851, as Ray Angelo explained in a 1979 article, Thoreau was surveying a lot in Concord when he discovered a very rare specimen of climbing fern.[19] The plant was so rare that Thoreau only revealed its location to a small number of friends, with the result that a few decades after his death its location was lost. In the 1970s, though, Angelo noticed that Thoreau had noted its location on the plan he was drawing that day.[20] And, sure enough, when Angelo visited that spot, he saw that the climbing fern was still there, growing in secret. On his survey, Thoreau noted the presence of a nonhuman feature, unrelated to the "official" function of his plan. While his employer probably only saw a survey of his property and potentially overlooked the presence of the fern, Thoreau would read the map in a much different way. The map is not the same, depending on who is holding it.

This approach profoundly changes the question of the map's incompleteness, which tends to be foregrounded by representational and postimperialist perspectives. In the processual perspective, the import is not what the map shows or doesn't show but what the user sees or doesn't see. This

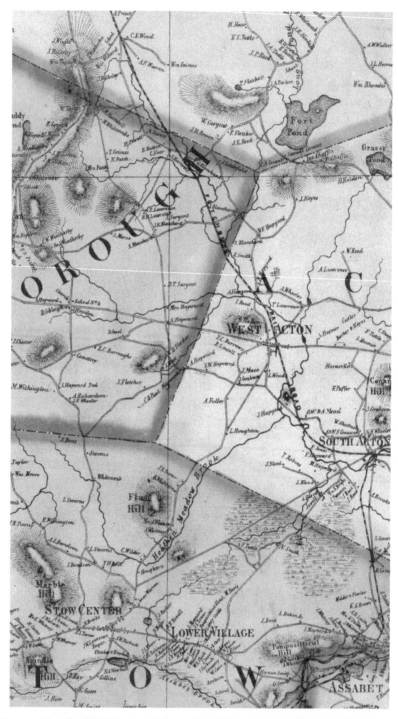

Figure 3. Detail of Walling's 1856 map of Middlesex County (figure 1). This area was traced by Thoreau (see figure 4). Library of Congress, Geography and Map Division, Washington, D.C.

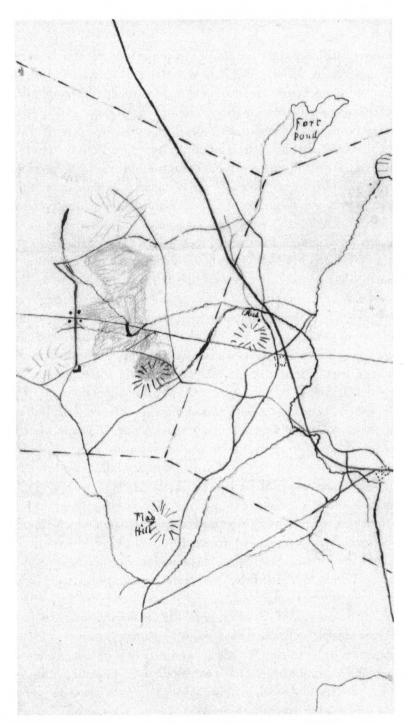

Figure 4. Thoreau's tracing of Walling's map (figure 3). The shaded area represents Inches Wood. The Morgan Library & Museum, New York, MA 1302.38. Purchased by Pierpont Morgan, with the Wakeman Collection, 1909.

allows for a radically different reading of Thoreau's journal entry about the
absence of Inches Wood on the map. What is being voiced here is perhaps
not so much a definitive repudiation of maps as irredeemably incomplete
but the starting point of an alternative reading of the map.

This is corroborated by the existence of a document recently brought to
light among Thoreau's papers: a local map drawn by Thoreau himself on
which he has carefully inscribed the contours of the never-before-mapped
Inches Wood (figure 4).[21] This map can be found on a loose sheet of tracing paper kept with volume 32 of Thoreau's journals at the Morgan Library
in New York City. This particular notebook contains Thoreau's journal
between July 23 and November 22, 1860, which corresponds to the time
frame of the entry in which Thoreau noted the absence of Inches Wood on
his map. The map may have been traced by Thoreau on the occasion of his
second visit to the wood on November 16, a few days after his first excursion there. The dimensions of this tracing exactly fit those of Walling's
1856 map of Middlesex County. The details are also perfectly identical on
both maps, such as the location of houses or the placement of toponyms.
Walling's was the most detailed map of this area available in 1860, and
these details simply do not appear on other contemporary maps of the
same region. This suggests with almost absolute certainty that Walling's
map was the source of the tracing, as well as the map Thoreau refers to in
his journal. In other words, the November 10 journal entry voices Thoreau's surprise—and possibly his disappointment—but it does not signal
that he casts the map aside. On the contrary, it is the starting point of an
even more complex and active engagement with that same map.

These elements offer a way to bypass the theoretical dead end that appears
when we demand that maps be representations of the world—which they
are not and which makes it impossible to imagine any interaction between
them and Thoreau's texts. In the processual perspective, an entirely new
map emerges from Thoreau's tracing and his additions to Walling's original
work. By following the logic of the processual perspective to its end, it also
becomes possible to consider that Thoreau's writing is in itself a form of
engagement with the map. Writing about a place by using a map as a reference point is a form of interaction comparable with annotating it, correct-
ing it, or tracing it. As such, writing "takes part" in the map's ontogenesis
(the emergence of its meaning for its user, in a specific situation). Thoreau's
tracing, for example, shows that, in the interstices of human infrastructure,

Walling's map does reveal the blank spots where the human presence is the least evident and in which such places as Inches Wood exist.

Just as the tracing offers an alternative reading of the map, Thoreau's texts also foreground what tends to be overlooked within a given space, which is the case in this passage from "Walking": "I can easily walk ten, fifteen, twenty, any number of miles, commencing at my own door, without going by any house, without crossing a road except where the fox and the mink do. First along by the river, and then the brook, and then the meadow and the wood-side. There are square miles in my vicinity which have no inhabitant. From many a hill I can see civilization and the abodes of man afar. The farmers and their works are scarcely more obvious than woodchucks and their burrows . . . In one half hour I can walk off to some portion of the earth's surface where a man does not stand from one year's end to another" (*Exc* 191–92). Thoreau is referring here to the literal experience of walking and to his own knowledge of the fields and woods around the village. But the passage can also be read as an exercise in map reading, in which Thoreau detects and reveals the areas where human presence is imperceptible. The map, read as a negative, becomes a positive map of what it supposedly does not represent. Woodchucks and their burrows, invisible on the maps, become visible and central in Thoreau's text. They are more "obvious" than the works of men, which recede into the background. A cartographic reorganization is at work in the text, as the end of the essay explicitly suggests: "The walker in the familiar fields which stretch around my native town, sometimes finds himself in another land than is described in their owners' deeds, as it were in some far away field on the confines of the actual Concord . . . These farms which I have myself surveyed, these bounds which I have set up appear dimly still as through a mist; but they have no chemistry to fix them; they fade from the surface of the glass" (*Exc* 217–18). Within the text, the physical markings used to inscribe the framework of human activity and land-ownership fade away, revealing instead the hidden map of what Thoreau calls in *The Dispersion of Seeds* "the neglected spots" on the territory of Concord (*Faith* 45).

A text such as "Wild Apples" illustrates Thoreau's interest in putting those neglected spots "on the map" by devoting entire sections of his essay to places and specimens that usually remain unseen. The text moves from the straight rows of "civilized apple-trees" to the "devious" (literally, out of the way) specimens of wild apple trees that have escaped from orchards and sprung up in unsuspected places, in the middle of the woods or even on a cliff: "Going up the side of a cliff about the first of November, I saw a vigorous apple-tree . . . The owner knows nothing of it. The day was not observed when it first blossomed, nor when it first bore fruit, unless by the chickadee" (*Exc* 269–70). Thoreau insists that the tree was there but remained invisible. Only the chickadee witnessed its growth. The text, on the contrary, makes this undocumented tree visible on the map of our surroundings. To borrow a phrase used by Joan Burbick, Thoreau's text becomes a "technology of seeing."[22]

The first category of phenomena which this technology makes visible is environmental and nonhuman in nature: it consists of plants and animals, but also entire ecosystems. Such is the case with the wetlands of Concord and, more specifically, the bogs around the village that Thoreau loved to visit. The swamps, as he called them, were special and "sacred" places for him, as he makes clear in "Walking" when he exclaims, "Bring your sills up to the very edge of the swamp!" (*Exc* 205). Thoreau is more specific in his Journal and in several passages of *Wild Fruits* when he describes in detail his visits to two swamps in particular: Gowing's Swamp and Beck Stow's Swamp, located close to each other just east of the village.[23] Thoreau went as far as to draw two maps of Gowing's Swamp, which are reproduced in his Journal (figures 5 and 6). One of them outlines the general layout of the swamp, while the other is a map of the distribution of plant species.[24] The sketches allow him to make visible the ecological structure of an ecosystem that remains invisible to others because it is financially unprofitable and aesthetically unpleasant. Thoreau's texts and his hand-drawn maps perform the same work here. They share a common interest in clarifying what is hidden in those neglected areas of the village's territory. Thoreau's observations and his sketches of the swamp are now well known to local environmentalists, who have been using Thoreau's notes as the basis for their studies of this wetland's complex and fragile ecosystem.[25]

The environmental unseen is not the only thing that Thoreau's texts make visible. The human members of the community whose presence is inconspicuous and whose voices are rarely heard are also put on the map. The vocabulary of territorialization, which tends to fade away and recede in the distance in "Walking," reemerges in "Wild Apples," for example, suggesting that the essay delineates a territory—even though Thoreau is here describing "extra-vagant" trees that have leaped the fence of surveyed

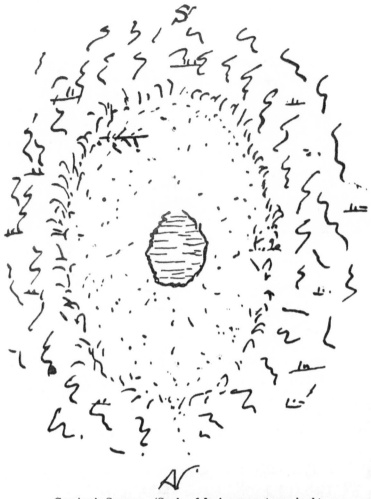

Gowing's Swamp. (Scale of forty paces to an inch)

Figure 5. Thoreau's sketch of Gowing's Swamp, February 3, 1860 (*J* XIII:125).

farms, just like the cow in *Walden*. At the beginning of the essay Thoreau writes, "My theme being the Wild Apple, I will merely glance at some of the seasons in the annual growth of the cultivated apple, and pass on to my own special province" (*Exc* 264). The phrase "my own special province" seems innocuous at first sight. It is a dead metaphor: the province here is understood as a field of study, an area of specialization. But I would

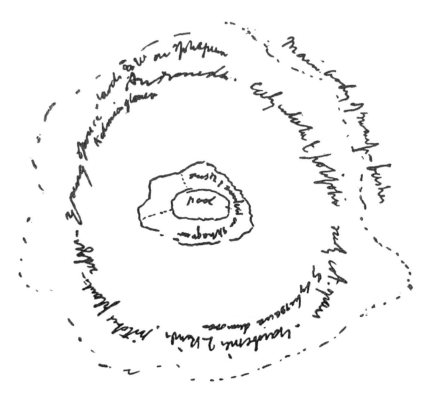

Figure 6. Thoreau's sketch of plant distribution in Gowing's Swamp, August 23, 1854 (*J* VI:467).

argue that Thoreau's text remotivates the signifier by subtly drawing attention to its original meaning. In effect, Thoreau marks the contours of an actual province, a domain in space which is coterminous with the "square miles" evoked in "Walking," on which the presence of humans becomes imperceptible. On the next page, Thoreau adds: "As you are going by the orchards and gardens, especially in the evenings, you pass through a little region possessed by the fragrance of ripe apples, and thus enjoy them without price, and without robbing anybody" (*Exc* 265). Here again, the term *region* suggests that Thoreau is tracing out a series of interstitial spaces. The term *possessed* reimports into the text the language of land appropriation, but it is applied here to a sweet, intangible smell that disintegrates the structures of ownership.

Read in this light, "Wild Apples" is about planting a flag and marking off an entire area, or at least a dimension in space. Its owners are clearly identified in the text. They are the "lovers of nature" evoked in the Journal, those who can appreciate the taste of the wild apples: "They belong to children as wild as themselves,—to certain active boys that I know,—to the wild-eyed woman of the fields, to whom nothing comes amiss, who gleans after all the world,—and, moreover, to us walkers. We have met with them and they are ours" (*Exc* 277). It is noteworthy that Thoreau says "we" instead of "I." This new community includes all those who operate, more or less willingly, outside the constraints of labor and profitability and are thus free to roam the woods: children, saunterers, and the strange figure of the eccentric woman. The list matches the list of "good" visitors evoked in *Walden*, when Thoreau says that only "girls and boys and young women" seemed glad to be in the woods—as opposed to the "farmers" and "men of business" (*W* 153). The point here is precisely not to be occupied by "busi-ness," hence the presence in this group of "young" women, a phrase which, as Laura Dassow Walls argues, probably refers to young unmarried women who are not yet preoccupied with the demands of domesticity.[26] Commenting on the time he spends in Beck Stow's Swamp, Thoreau notes in *Wild Fruits*: "If anybody else—any farmer, at least—should spend an hour thus wading about here in this secluded swamp, bare-legged, intent on the sphagnum, filling his pocket only, with no rake in his hand and no bag or bushel on the bank, he would be pronounced insane and have a guardian put over him" (*WF* 168). The tone is humorous, but Thoreau is also emphasizing how polemical his unconventional spatial practices are. The image of the guardian suggests that he could be silenced and his liberty of movement restricted. In other words, those who can "see" the wild apples, and thus also the "neglected spots" on the map of Concord, are also those who tend to remain unseen in the community and whose voices cannot be heard.

The French philosopher Jacques Rancière has argued that the way a person occupies time and space (what he calls "the sensible") defines his or her place in the community and "what is visible or not in a common space."[27] Beyond the spatial reordering that Thoreau's alternative reading of the map produces, at stake is also making visible those who occupy and live in those invisible, neglected spots: children, women, persons with disabilities, and persons of color. In the chapter "Former Inhabitants" of *Walden*,

Thoreau evokes the ghostly presence in the woods around Walden Pond of a series of isolated individuals, most of them former slaves or descendants of former slaves, who spent their lives on the margins of the community. Not much remains, Thoreau explains, of their dwellings, except, here and there, a "dent in the earth" and, characteristically, the plants that their children have sown and that now grow in the middle of the woods. "Still grows the vivacious lilac a generation after the door and lintel and the sill are gone," Thoreau notes, adding, "I mark its still tender, civil, cheerful, lilac colors" (*W* 263–64). The verb "I mark" means here "I notice," but it also refers to the performative gesture of inscription that alters the surface of the map: with this very sentence, Thoreau inscribes this neglected spot on the territory of the village, just as he had inscribed the presence of the climbing fern on his survey. The creation of what Elise Lemire calls "a landscape of memory" that counters "white memory practices" is achieved here by putting specific plant specimens on the map—thereby bridging the human and the environmental unseen.[28] Thoreau's adjectives refer both to emotions (tender, cheerful) and to a certain of form of collective gathering: "civil" refers both to the existence of a community and to the efforts made to maintain it (to act in a civil manner). Just as in "Wild Apples," the text gestures toward the delineation of an (alternative) community.

In her essay "Unspeakable Things Unspoken," Toni Morrison comments on the invisible presence (or visible absence) of nonwhite figures in nineteenth-century American literature. She writes: "We can agree, I think, that invisible things are not necessarily 'not-there'; that a void may be empty but not be a vacuum. In addition, certain absences are so stressed, so ornate, so planned, they call attention to themselves; arrest us with intentionality and purpose, like neighborhoods that are defined by the population held away from them."[29] The exercise in vision that Morrison encourages here is comparable with Thoreau's alternative reading of the map: an absence, or a plain blank space on the map, is not necessarily the sign that there is nothing there. On the contrary, it can be read as the telltale "mark" of a hidden presence.

Thoreau's descriptions of Gowing's Swamp effectively altered the local map by turning the bog into a place worthy of our attention and protection. The swamps that Thoreau cherished are now literally "on the map." They appeared there as early as 1906 when Herbert Gleason included them on the map he prepared for the Houghton Mifflin edition of Thoreau's writings. They are also shown on the maps that Brad Dean included at the end of *Faith in a Seed* and *Wild Fruits*.[30] In the same way, the chapter "Former Inhabitants" alters our perception of the territory of Concord and its complex racial history. As Elise Lemire explains in *Black Walden*, the chapter is what originally prompted her to examine "slavery and its aftermath in Concord" and to produce the map included in her book, on which the location of the houses of the former inhabitants finally appear.[31] Today, a boulder with an inscription marks the approximate site of Brister Freeman's house, and two of the "benches by the road" of the Toni Morrison Society have been placed in or near Concord to commemorate Caesar Robbins, a former slave and Revolutionary War veteran, and Brister Freeman himself. The maps of Concord that we are familiar with today have been altered by Thoreau's texts.

The relationship between Thoreau's texts and his maps works both ways. Maps are an irreplaceable starting point. They allow Thoreau to understand the general configuration of a given place, as in the first pages of *Cape Cod*, for example, when he explains that he first planned his journey and his trajectories by carefully examining his map (*CC* 4).[32] But the map is also altered, in return, by how Thoreau uses it. Not only do his annotations and inscriptions change what it figures, but the texts themselves also complement and complicate the maps—his own and those we use today.

Thoreau's texts, of course, are not maps. A map, in the strictest sense, is always an image. Thoreau's texts also differ from maps in that they do not perform exactly the same work. As John Krygier and Denis Wood argue, the map asserts the validity of two existential propositions: first, *this is* (such a thing does exist); second, *there is* (it exists in specific locations in the world). Combined, these two existential propositions produce the cartographic proposition itself, which is *this is there* (or *there is this*).[33] This is what the map proclaims to its reader, just as medieval maps proclaimed "here be dragons." The reason why Thoreau's texts are not maps is that they almost never assert such a proposition. As Lawrence Buell noted in *The Environmental Imagination*, the text of *Walden* remains very vague regarding the exact location of the different places it mentions: "For the most part we cannot tell where anything is located in relation to anything else."[34] The chapter "Former Inhabitants" is crucial because it proclaims both that "this was" (the people he mentions by name existed on the margins of the community) and that "there is" (the physical traces of their presence can still be detected in our world). But the text of *Walden* never proclaims "this is there"; it does not provide the coordinates of specific locations.

Thoreau's hand-drawn maps and his texts, though, share a common interest in identifying, clarifying, and naming "what is there." In his more recent reflections on politics in the new climate regime, Bruno Latour emphasizes the importance of description in the age of the Anthropocene. Using the example of the *cahiers de doléances* (the lists of grievances collected in "ledgers of complaints") written by the people at the onset of the French Revolution between January and May 1789, Latour describes as a gesture of "inscription" or "*geo-graphy*" the fact that "in a situation of financial disaster and climatic tension, all the villages in France, all the cities, all the corporations, not to mention the three estates, managed to describe fairly precisely their living environments."[35] To Latour, the episode is a model because, in our age of climate change and political disorientation, "everything has to be *mapped out* anew."[36] Describing our "environment," in the strictest sense of "what is around us," is, in Latour's view, a mapping gesture that amounts to clarifying the multiple connections and relations that constitute our world. Even though they do not provide locations, Thoreau's texts work as "mappings" in the sense that they strive to make visible what is otherwise invisible—thereby enriching the work of description that, according to Latour, is so crucial in our time. The map is one of the "realometers" that allow him to proclaim, as he does in *Walden*, "this is, and no mistake"—an existential proposition that matters more to him than the cartographic proposition itself, *this is there* (*W* 97). From that perspective, Thoreau's texts are not "ordinary" maps, but they effectively work as "extra-ordinary" mappings.

Notes

1. See my article on Thoreau's tracings and their significance in his writings: Julien Nègre, "From Tracing to Writing: The Maps that Thoreau Copied," *Nineteenth-Century Prose* 44, no. 2 (Fall 2017): 213–34.

2. Lawrence Buell, *The Environmental Imagination: Thoreau, Nature Writing, and the Formation of American Culture* (Cambridge, MA: Harvard University Press, 1995), 270.

3. Robert F. Stowell, *A Thoreau Gazetteer*, ed. William L. Howarth (Princeton, NJ: Princeton University Press, 1970). The *Gazetteer* was officially "approved by the

Editorial Board as a supplement to *The Complete Works of Henry David Thoreau*" project, founded in 1966 (i). The volume appeared even before publication of the Princeton Edition of *Walden* (1971).

4. Moses Greenleaf, *Map of the State of Maine with the Province of New Brunswick*, 3rd ed., 131 cm by 104 cm, scale 1:570,240 (Philadelphia: engraved by J. H. Young and F. Dankworth, 1844), http://www.davidrumsey.com/luna/servlet/s/7c6wjn.

5. For a pioneering study of Thoreau's interaction with ancient maps, see John W. Hessler, "From Ortelius to Champlain: The Lost Maps of Henry David Thoreau," *The Concord Saunterer*, n.s., 18 (2010): 1–26.

6. Patrick Chura, *Thoreau the Land Surveyor* (Gainesville: University Press of Florida, 2010).

7. Stowell, *Thoreau Gazetteer*, xi.

8. The dust jacket of *A Thoreau Gazetteer* is a good example of the implicit association between Thoreau and cartography: it features a composite image on which Thoreau's face (based on Samuel Worcester Rowse's 1854 portrait) is merged with the map of the Concord area created by Herbert Gleason for the 1906 edition of Thoreau's works. The image suggests that Thoreau's face emerges from the map (he is visible to us today because we read him against this specific background), but also that the map emerges from his face: Concord is visible to us because we read this area through the prism of Thoreau's texts. The image has been used since 1981 on the dust jackets of the volumes of the *Journal* published by Princeton University Press.

9. "I fear this particular dry knowledge may affect my imagination and fancy, that it will not be easy to see so much wildness and native vigor there as formerly" (*J* X:233, January 1, 1858).

10. J. Brian Harley, "Deconstructing the Map," *Cartographica* 26, no. 2 (Spring 1989): 1–20.

11. Denis Wood, *The Power of Maps* (New York: Guilford Press, 1992); Denis Wood, with John Fels and John Krygier, *Rethinking the Power of Maps* (New York: Guilford Press, 2010); Mark Monmonier, *How to Lie with Maps* (Chicago: University of Chicago Press, 1996).

12. Rob Kitchin, Chris Perkins, and Martin Dodge, "Thinking about Maps," in *Rethinking Maps: New Frontiers in Cartographic Theory*, ed. Martin Dodge, Rob Kitchin, and Chris Perkins (New York: Routledge, 2009), 6.

13. Henry Francis Walling, *Map of Middlesex County, Massachusetts*, scale 1:50 000, approximately 146 by 147 cm (Boston: Smith & Bumstead, 1856), Library of Congress, Washington, D.C., http://hdl.loc.gov/loc.gmd/g3763m.la000316.

14. Henry Francis Walling, *Map of the town of Concord*, scale 1:18,400, approximately 60 by 78 cm (Boston, 1852), Norman B. Leventhal Map & Education Center, Boston, MA, https://collections.leventhalmap.org/search/commonwealth:1257bc79t.

15. Alan M. MacEachren, *How Maps Work: Representation, Visualization, and Design* (New York: Guildford, 1995), 358.

16. Kitchin, Perkins, and Dodge, "Thinking about Maps," 20–23. The processual perspective was explored notably by Rob Kitchin and Martin Dodge in "Rethinking Maps," *Progress in Human Geography* 31, no. 3 (2007): 331–44. See also Vincent J. Del Casino and Stephen P. Hanna, "Beyond the 'Binaries': A Methodological Intervention for Interrogating Maps as Representational Practices," *ACME: An International E-Journal for Critical Geographies* 4, no. 1 (2005): 34–56.

17. Kitchin, Perkins, and Dodge, "Thinking about Maps," 20.

18. Kitchin, Perkins, and Doge, 21.

19. Ray Angelo, "Thoreau's Climbing Fern Rediscovered," *Thoreau Society Bulletin* 149 (Fall 1979).

20. The plan is available online on the Concord Free Public Library website: https://concordlibrary.org/special-collections/thoreau-surveys/89. The Latin name of the plant (*Lygodium*) appears in the upper part of the image. The plant still exists today and is well known to local botanists.

21. Morgan Library, New York, accession number MA 1302.38. The map was noticed by Dennis Noson, a specialist of Thoreau's maps and surveys and the author of a transcript of his Field Notes. I warmly thank Dennis for bringing this document to my attention.

22. Joan Burbick, *Thoreau's Alternative History: Changing Perspectives on Nature, Culture, and Language* (Philadelphia: University of Pennsylvania Press, 1987), 24.

23. On the importance of these specific swamps for Thoreau, see Don Scheese, "Thoreau's *Journal*: The Creation of a Sacred Place," in *Mapping American Culture*, ed. Wayne Franklin and Michael C. Steiner (Iowa City: University of Iowa Press, 1992), 142–46. See also William Howarth, "Reading the Wetlands," in *Textures of Place: Exploring Humanist Geographies*, ed. Paul C. Adams, Steven Hoelscher, and Karen E. Till (Minneapolis: University of Minnesota Press, 2001), 71.

24. Figure 5, *J* XIII:125, February 3, 1860; Figure 6, *J* VI:467, August 23, 1854. Figure 6 is also reproduced in *PJ* 8:291.

25. In 2010, a botanical inventory prepared by Cherrie Corey in the continuity of Thoreau's work played a decisive role when a development project close to the swamp threatened to disrupt its ecosystem. The full report is available at https://drive.google.com/file/d/0BwDoS2X2FmxaNllzMW5wSkppbHc/view?usp=sharing.

26. Laura Dassow Walls, "*Walden* as Feminist Manifesto," *Interdisciplinary Studies in Literature and the Environment* 1, no. 1 (Spring 1993): 137–44.

27. Jacques Rancière, *The Politics of Aesthetics*, trans. Gabriel Rockhill (New York: Continuum, 2004), 12–13.

28. Elise Lemire, "Repeopling the Woods," in *Thoreau at 200: Essays and Reassessments*, ed. Kristen Case and K. P. Van Anglen (Cambridge: Cambridge University Press, 2016), 72.

29. Toni Morrison, "Unspeakable Things Unspoken: The Afro-American Presence in American Literature" (Tanner Lectures on Human Values, University of Michigan, October 7, 1988), https://tannerlectures.utah.edu/_documents/a-to-z/m/morrison90.pdf, 136.

30. The map in *Wild Fruits* is not accurate: Beck Stow's Swamp is placed just south of Lexington Road, along the Mill Brook, whereas in reality it is located farther to the north, where the New Bedford Road meets the Old Bedford Road. The same error appears on Map Nineteen in Stowell, *Thoreau Gazetteer*, 37.

31. Elise Lemire, *Black Walden: Slavery and Its Aftermath in Concord, Massachusetts* (Philadelphia: University of Pennsylvania Press, 2009), 6.

32. In my article on Thoreau's tracings, I identify Simeon Borden's 1844 *Topographical Map of Massachusetts* as Thoreau's source in this passage. See Nègre, "From Tracing to Writing," 223–24.

33. John Krygier and Denis Wood, "Ce N'est Pas le Monde (This Is Not the World)," in *Rethinking Maps: New Frontiers in Cartographic Theory*, ed. Martin Dodge, Rob Kitchin, and Chris Perkins (New York: Routledge, 2009), 198–99.
34. Buell, *Environmental Imagination*, 135.
35. Bruno Latour, *Down to Earth: Politics in the New Climate Regime*, trans. Catherine Porter (Medford, MA: Polity, 2018), 97.
36. Latour, *Down to Earth*, 33; emphasis added.

5

RHETORIC OF EMPIRE AND POETIC BORDERLANDS IN THOREAU'S "WALKING"

François Specq

Thoreau's "Walking" has long been hailed as a milestone in the development of environmentalism, providing the environmental movement with one of its rallying cries, "In Wildness is the preservation of the world." A closer look at the essay, however, has led a number of scholars to raise the seemingly contradictory issue of Thoreau's embrace of the rhetoric of Manifest Destiny, as he celebrates westering as America's—and his own—supreme realization.[1] Both approaches, I will claim, have actually been reductive, failing to give a proper account of the various strands of what is arguably Thoreau's most complex essay. Through a reading that will concentrate on Thoreau's rhetoric, teasing out the main implications of the contrast he draws between westward expansion and a Concord swamp, this essay demonstrates how Thoreau employs the dominant rhetoric the better to subvert ideological assumptions and promote his own dissenting views.[2] In effect, Thoreau cast the spell so as to break it: the strategy of "Walking" means to overturn widely accepted notions and dismantle the historical discourse of westward movement. Far from adhering to the rhetoric of Manifest Destiny, or even to any "new nationalism," as Andrew Menard has argued, "Walking" unflinchingly gave pride of place to Thoreau's deeply challenging poetics of inhabitation.[3]

Dismantling the Westering Myth

After his opening celebration of walking as going "to the holy land" (*Exc* 185), Thoreau devotes several pages to extolling the West and westward movement in a way that seems to embrace Americans' exalted view of their place in history—a view that ultimately amounts to the claim that the nation's mission is divine, in accord with the ideology known as "American exceptionalism." But, I will argue, that is the better to highlight his dissent, which Thoreau voices through his subsequent focus on the Concord swamps:

> Hope and the future for me are not in lawns and cultivated fields, not in towns and cities, but in the impervious and quaking swamps. (*Exc* 204)

> Yes; though you may think me perverse, if it were proposed to me to dwell in the neighborhood of the most beautiful garden that ever human art contrived, or else of a dismal swamp, I should certainly decide for the swamp.— How vain then have been all your labors, citizens, for me! (*Exc* 205)

> When I would recreate myself, I seek the darkest wood, the thickest and most interminable, and, to the citizen, most dismal swamp. I enter a swamp as a sacred place—a *sanctum sanctorum*. (*Exc* 205)

The pivotal moment is a complete semantic reorientation or refocusing: "The West of which I speak is but another name for the Wild; and what I have been preparing to say is, that in Wildness is the preservation of the world" (*Exc* 202). From this point on, the West/wild is relocated to the outskirts of Concord, Massachusetts, thus radically taking the exact opposite position to transcontinental mobility. This is in line with Thoreau's well-known taste for paradox. Rhetorically speaking, as a consequence of his folding the West back on the wild, Thoreau rechannels (or, literally, re*orients*!) the rhetorical energy accumulated through his celebration of westward expansion into his praise of "the Wild."

Such a radical redefinition moves the focus of the essay from space to place, from the distant (transcontinental spatiality) to the local, from progress to "burying" or "burrowing." Instead of a vectorized relation to the land, Thoreau's (unconventional) emphasis on local mobility back East foregrounds a form of mobility akin to what French theorist Guy Debord called *dérive,* or drifting.[4] It reinstates a contrast between outward and inward mobilities, to the clear benefit of the latter. Thoreau meant to counter the excess of *sense*—meaning and direction—inherent in westward expansion and the standard historical narrative. His essay's structure

revolves around a contrast between westward progress as unidimensional/
unidirectional advance and a process of *repeated* departure. He refers to
unidimensional advance as "locomotiveness," which suggests constant
progress (from one locality to another), restlessness, and mechanical
motion: "Who but the Evil One has cried Who! to mankind?— Indeed,
the life of cattle, like that of many men, is but a sort of locomotiveness,
they move a side at a time, and Man by his machinery is meeting the horse
and ox half way" (*Exc* 211).

By contrast, Thoreau's series of departures and homecomings are repet-
itive—or iterative (from Latin *iter*, way)—but not mechanical. What
matters is less that Thoreau returns home every night than that he departs
every day.

Another crucial change is a refocusing on a dystopian place. The swamp,
as supreme embodiment of "a Wildness whose glance no civilization can
endure" (*Exc* 202), is a place that, within American history, economy, and
society, is fundamentally heterogeneous, leading away from America as
world of progress and commerce, and away from a movement of appropriation (as embodied by imperial frontier narratives), toward what Lawrence
Buell has called an "aesthetics of relinquishment"—one that privileges
retreat, simplicity, and a bracketing of the self as conducive to an inner
awakening: "I derive more of my subsistence from the swamps which sur-
round my native town than from the cultivated gardens in the village" (*Exc*
204).[5] Against a celebration of "the West" as a framework in which spatial
and historical narratives are interlocking and commensurate, the swamp
passage, radically dissociating place from the standard historical narrative,
features the incommensurable, the heterogeneous, the dystopian. Whereas
westward expansion pointed to a utopian promise, an ideal remotely and
abstractly situated, the swamp, from a standard point of view, represents
an inverted utopia or dystopia.

I suggest that it is also "dyschronic," in the sense that it is related not to
the teleological linearity of westward expansion but to the transhistorical
neighborliness of "deep time." Forsaking the eagle-eye view of history, the
focus on the swamp establishes a view from within the midst of things,
one that heeds the complexity of history as well as the gravitational pull
of culture. While the West is "planar" (flat, two-dimensional), the swamp
is "planetary" (deep, three- or multidimensional).[6] Thoreau emphasizes
the unsurveyable nature of the swamp ("survey" is a word he uses several

times), as opposed to the survey of history and of the land that is central to the essay's earlier section. When the land is surveyed, it is at the expense of the real itself, as Thoreau—a professional surveyor himself—powerfully suggests through his striking apologue of the "Prince of Darkness" (*Exc* 191). Thoreau here embodies the Transcendentalists' understanding of the intellectual's or "scholar's" mission as that of awakening thinking in others, so as to free what Emerson called their "imprisoned spirits, imprisoned thoughts."[7] The swamp itself is an "imprisoned thought" or, in more contemporary terms, a return of the historically repressed, even as it conveys the pent-up truth that there are gaps in continental expansion.

Finally, the focus shifts from the physical to the metaphysical: the structure of Thoreau's essay leads from geographic West to metaphysical West, but this metaphysical West is in no way beyond (*meta*) but *within* the locus of ordinary experience—which, after all, is never so ordinary, as Thoreau makes clear, but an ever-renewed source of beauty: "When we reflected that this was not a solitary phenomenon, never to happen again, but that it would happen forever and ever an infinite number of evenings, and cheer and reassure the latest child that walked there, it was more glorious still" (*Exc* 221).

Poetics of (Im)mobility

What Thoreau effects, in terms of rhetoric, is a "denarrativization" of space: the national narrative of space gives way to a poetics of place that is both personal and intercultural. As Thoreau breaks the hold of the westering myth, space is no longer absorbed and dissolved in a grand narrative or teleological script (*translatio imperii*, Manifest Destiny), as the essay resists finality and the restless trajectories of national expansion. Instead, space unfolds through poetics: plot displaces plot—the heterogeneous, heterotopic plot of land ("fertile spot" and "plot"), with its attendant poetics of place, displaces the plot of the spatiohistorical narrative (*Exc* 204). Thoreau's purpose is not really to produce the reverse of mobility, that is, immobility, but a countermobility, or alternative form of mobility—a mobility of connection versus a mobility of appropriation. The shift is from quantitative to qualitative. What most deeply defines the mobility of connection is not so much slowness as quality of movement: Thoreau's essay emphasizes movement "to and fro" (*Exc* 191), or the nonlinear, forever tentative mobility inherent in living what he famously called a "border life." As he writes, "For my part, I feel, that with regard to Nature, I live a sort of border life, on the confines of a world, into which I make occasional and transient forays only, and my patriotism and allegiance to the state into whose territories I seem to retreat are those of a moss-trooper" (*Exc* 217).

Thoreau's emphasis on a "border life" was deliberately meant to counter the overall focus on the historical and geographic complex of the "frontier," the limit of the settled regions of the United States as they gradually moved west. Thoreau distances himself from any dragooning into the cohorts of westward migrants to become instead "a moss-trooper"—deliberately suggesting that he is not a bandit but an outlaw to some extent, a "member of an undisciplined group."[8] His resistance to the primacy of the historical narrative trains the mind and the eye of the reader to different modes of reading space or relating to it. His passion for the swamp, enhanced by this refocusing and magnifying, is bent on recovering mysteries. As opposed to the standard narrative of progress that brings everything into the bland light of conquest and does away with chiaroscuro (see the adjective "dusky" in "dusky knowledge" [*Exc* 214])—in which a mobility of appropriation erases, or conceals, the indomitable enigma of the world—Thoreau promotes a mobility of connection, with a "psychogeographic" emphasis on recapturing one's physical and emotional ties to one's environment.[9] In the swamp, the walker is—literally and metaphorically—in the thick of things, not in the thin of vectorized space: "When I would recreate myself, I seek the darkest wood, the thickest and most interminable, and, to the citizen, most dismal swamp. I enter a swamp as a sacred place—a *sanctum sanctorum*" (*Exc* 205).

Thoreau defamiliarizes the standard historical narrative by framing it in his essay—thus containing it and putting it into perspective—and by recovering a cosmopolitan cultural archive, as against the planarity of the westering myth. Thoreau's swamp beautifully encapsulates the creative tension of the vernacular and the cosmopolitan. Whereas "the world with which we are commonly acquainted leaves no trace, and it will have no anniversary" (*Exc* 218)—for with no temporal depth, no anniversary is possible—attentiveness and independence of mind preserve or recover the world of culture, as the rich intertextual and intercultural layering of Thoreau's essay testifies. The swamp is clearly associated with a plurilingual vision, in which the lingua franca of conquest is replaced by the *gramatica parda* (or "wild and dusky knowledge" [*Exc* 214]) of inhabitation, as Thoreau is eager not to replicate the semantic hegemonies of imperial rhetoric: the variegated color of the leopard's skin means an acceptance of the diverse, the obscure, the confused, the diffuse, the uncertain, as opposed to the overbearing clarity of the nationalist narrative. Whereas standard discourse claims that "it is too late to be studying Hebrew" (*Exc* 201), Thoreau demonstrates an intense awareness of sedimented culture: he propounds a literature that is the custodian of all eras and cultures, one that rejects a *translatio studii* which is the cultural counterpart of the *translatio imperii*, celebrating instead a nurturing dialogue between "coming ages" and ages past: "A township where one primitive forest waves above, while another primitive forest rots below—such a town is fitted to raise not only corn and potatoes, but poets and philosophers for the coming ages. In such a soil grew Homer and Confucius and the rest, and out of such a wilderness comes the reformer eating locusts and wild honey" (*Exc* 206).

"We have advanced by leaps to the Pacific, and left many a lesser Oregon and California unexplored behind us," Thoreau rhapsodized in the conclusion to "Ktaadn" (*MW* 82). The swamp can be analyzed as an embodiment and a return of the (historical and cultural) repressed. Thoreau was undoubtedly eager to explode the force of containment and the dominion of the standard, monopolistic narrative of American progress. As against the unidirectional, the linear, the planar, he foregrounds a model that is a palimpsest, a layered archive, a cultural compost or "mould" (*Exc* 214), made of multiple "trace[s]" that are democratically compounded together; note that mosses and lichens are not only the most primitive members of the plant kingdom but also the most ordinary of plants, humble and overlooked. Thoreau clearly favors sedimentation over dissemination—that is, westward expansion only disseminates culture, rather than "improving" it—producing depth and complexity. The swamp fuses the dystopic with the utopic.[10]

Whereas Thoreau's activity as a "walker," systematically heading west, seems to fit into a personal and national narrative scheme, the following section reframes the perspective on the swamp as unassimilable, untamable "plot" (*Exc* 204). The swamp is personal, totally irreducible to the progressive scheme of the nation, taking instead the exact opposite position or direction, one distrustful of grand narratives: it puts into relief a lacuna, a gap within the national narrative. The untamable is no other than "the wild," a notion that, in Thoreau's mind, is directly linked to will and points to his essay's political substratum.[11]

The Wild and the Politics of Will

Indeed, it is often overlooked that the Compromise of 1850 and the Thomas Sims case in April 1851 were "the crucible in which . . . 'Walking' was originally written and delivered."[12] A crucial component of the literal and figurative reorientation of Thoreau's essay resides in his folding back not only the West on the wild but also the wild on the will. "Walking" thus obliquely confronts the reader with politics, which is primarily seen as a matter of will—or absence thereof—even as Thoreau had seemed to leave the topic aside in the opening paragraph of the essay's original lecture version: "I feel that I owe my audience an apology for speaking to them tonight on any other subject than the Fugitive Slave Law, on which every man is bound to express a distinct opinion, but I had prepared myself to speak a word now for Nature—for absolute freedom & wildness."[13] The truncated sentence still reverberates in the published essay, at the heart of which lies the (fanciful) theory of the derivation of *wild* from *willed*, which is made explicit in a passage from the Journal: "Trench says a wild man—is a *willed* man. Well then a man of will who does what he wills—or wishes—a man of hope and of the future tense—for not only the obstinate is willed but far more the constant & persevering— The obstinate man properly speaking is one who will not. The perseverance of the saints is positive willedness—not a mere passive willingness— The fates are wild for they *will*—& the Almighty is wild above all" (*PJ* 5:457–58). This passage refers to English archbishop and author Richard Chenevix Trench, who thus speculated in *On the Study of Words* that "'wild' is the participle past of 'to will'; a 'wild' horse is a 'willed' or self-willed horse, one that has been never tamed or taught to submit its will to the will of another; and so with a man."[14] Wild nature, then, is nature removed from human will. In facing it, one abandons a desire for both direction and meaning, instead immersing oneself in the beautiful order of the Κόσμος, or cosmos (*Exc* 217).

The wild is that which has its own will and thus is beyond our control. This is what the wild swamp stands for, as it evades the grip of the grand national narrative of territorial expansion and domination. Hence also

Thoreau's idea that God is supreme, radical, wildness, a notion that, in the context of "Walking," echoes the famous biblical phrase "to walk with God": this is a metaphor for yielding to God's will, for abdicating one's petty sovereignty, and not, as one might think, for parading like a god.[15] "Walking" is a political essay insofar as it celebrates the will, as against the compliance of the "herds" of migrants, mindlessly fleeing the scene of the national tragedy of slavery and such legal instruments as the Fugitive Slave Law. That law was very much on Thoreau's mind as he was preparing his lecture in the aftermath of the Thomas Sims case, as testified by his allusion to it (*Exc* 221). "Wild," thus reshaped as an expression of the full power of the will (and "not a mere passive willingness"), is the opposite of "instinct," which Thoreau associates with the "instinct in birds and quadrupeds" (*Exc* 197), thus denouncing the tameness of those who migrate westward. In this way, he vigorously keeps his distance from a pre-Turnerian vision of the American West as both the fundamental source of American democracy and the formative zone of national cultural identity, deconstructing the prevailing narrative of a westward progress of liberty. Through his eyes, we come to see the American people as literally fleeing away across the Great Plains from the scene where liberty is threatened: westward expansion is an act of moral and political desertion.

"Walking" thus enacts a repoliticizing of what had become so straight-forward as to appear depoliticized. Walking, understood now not as transcontinental progress but as peripatetic ambulation, emerges as a form of resistance that questions social and ideological formations, countering a movement that had become a national mystique; at the very moment when the eyes of the nation were focused on the West, turning one's own eyes toward the East intrinsically bespeaks dissent. In this respect, the very construction of the essay, which exacerbates the contrast between West and East, only further emphasizes Thoreau's dissent.[16] When, in his opening paragraph, Thoreau announces that he "wish[es] to speak a word . . . for absolute Freedom," he is not actually evading politics but questioning a simplistic understanding of "merely civil" liberty (*Exc* 185)—that is, more abstract, less substantial—to claim instead the truth of his equation, Free-dom = Wildness. "In short, all good things are wild and free," he declares, defending "the uncivilized free and wild thinking" (*Exc* 210, 207). What he rejects in "Walking," then, is "politics" in a narrow sense, which he dis-misses as "the cigar smoke of a man" (*Exc* 192), rather than the political as communal project and moral imperative; in Thoreau's way of thinking, "a Freedom . . . merely civil" is to "absolute Freedom" what willingness is to will—a matter of convenience, rather than of principle. Hence he reiterates his higher law philosophy: "The man who takes the liberty to live is superior to all the laws both of heaven and earth, by virtue of his relation to the Law-maker"—a classic formulation of the equivalence of self-reliance and God-reliance (*Exc* 216). Whereas "American Liberty . . . is to some extent a fiction of the present," in which "the majority" tend to be "submissive members of society" (*Exc* 209, 211), Thoreau perceives higher law as the cornerstone of any healthy political life, one that would first and foremost guarantee complete liberty for all.

Experience and the Unsettling of Knowledge

Thoreau's displacement of *the West* counters the way this term normalizes, and makes normative, movement and mobility, enabling the reappropriation of space on a different basis, to dissociate us from the idea of the West as a national space. In the rhetorical economy of "Walking," this move is realized through the dialogic potential of poetics and everyday personal practice, not unidimensional or monologic historical discourse. The swamp, as a concrete and symbolic embodiment of this reorientation, corresponds to Henri Lefebvre's notion of "differential space," that is, space that resists the homogenizing forces of contemporary life.[17]

"Walking" clearly establishes two very different orders of reality. What Thoreau celebrates, in his alternative geography, is not the expanding (space of the) nation but the expanding power of place poetically considered— that is, space as phenomenologically perceived, conceived, and lived, as Lefebvre suggested.[18] The union of knowledge and experience defines the truth of both, as Thoreau makes clear in *A Week on the Concord and Merrimack Rivers* through his famous definition of the "frontier" as situated "where man fronts [or engages with all one's will] a fact": "The frontiers are not east or west, north or south, but wherever a man *fronts* a fact, though that fact be his neighbor, there is an unsettled wilderness between him and Canada, between him and the setting sun, or, further still, between him and *it*. Let him build himself a log-house with the bark on where he is, *fronting* IT and wage there an Old French war for seven or seventy years, with Indians and Rangers, or whatever else may come between him and the reality, and save his scalp if he can (*Wk* 304)." Thoreau was thus already in his first book countering the primacy of the "frontier." When he proclaims, in "Walking," that "life consists with Wildness" (*Exc* 203), he is voicing his confidence that our poetic sense enlarges the scope of experience, not simply out in the West but altogether outside and even against the realm of physical expansion. It is a matter of reconnecting oneself to the immediate world of daily experience: "I would say to the Society for the Diffusion of Useful Knowledge, sometimes—Go to grass. You have eaten hay long enough" (*Exc* 215). Whereas westward progress operates as an expansion, or dissemination, of the actual or known world, the poetic sense opens the realm of the possible and the never-so-familiar: "There is in fact a sort of harmony discoverable between the capabilities of the landscape within a circle of ten miles radius, or the limits of an afternoon walk, and the three-score-years and ten of human life. It will never become quite familiar to you" (*Exc* 190–91). For Thoreau, the writer's task is to treasure and preserve the (forever) unknown: truth is an ongoing question rather than an answer. The link he traces between the wild and the unsettling of knowledge leads away from Bacon's "Knowledge is power" (quoted in *Exc* 214)[19] to a stance à la Montaigne: "Methinks there is equal need of a Society for the Diffusion of Useful Ignorance, what we will call Beautiful Knowledge, a knowledge useful in a higher sense; for what is most of our boasted so-called knowledge but a conceit that we know something which robs us of the advantage of our actual ignorance? What we call knowledge is often our positive ignorance, ignorance our negative knowledge . . . A man's ignorance sometimes is not only useful, but beautiful, while his knowledge, so called, is oftentimes worse than useless beside being ugly" (*Exc* 214–15).[20] Here again, Thoreau does not merely establish equally potent polarities, even though he claims there is an "equal need," because that equality is immediately displaced by the imbalance implied in "higher sense."

Thoreau even goes on to appear as a latter-day Socrates when he emphasizes the necessity of self-knowledge: "Which is the best man to deal with, he who knows nothing about a subject, and what is extremely rare knows that he knows nothing,—or he who really knows something about it, but thinks that he knows all?" (*Exc* 215). And when he defines genius as that which "shatters the temple of knowledge" (*Exc* 208), he alludes, even more pointedly, to Christ before the Doctors of the Faith, echoed in Emerson's desire to "unsettle all things."[21]

In this respect, "Walking" features a crucial paradigm shift: as we move through the essay, it becomes absolutely clear that the fundamental task of mankind is not "to improve the land" but to improve everyday life.[22] More specifically, Thoreau's concern is to improve *time*, as he makes clear in some of his more memorable phrases toward the end of the essay, when he preaches "a newer testament—the Gospel according to this moment," and affirms his belief that "we cannot afford not to live in the present" (*Exc* 220)—whereas, let us remember, earlier in the essay the West was equated with the future, echoing such propagandists as John O'Sullivan. Taken as a whole, in the full extent of its rhetorical construction, "Walking" creates a tension between celebration of the West, thus the movement of history and power of narrative, and celebration of place, thus an all-encompassing timelessness and the power of poetry. What is played out through this contrast is an overtaking of (spurious) historical truth by (incontrovertible) poetic truth.

The Method of "Walking"

In the concluding section, Thoreau circles back to the question of "the art of walking": here, as though to emphasize the obvious reorientation played out by his essay, he echoes and substantiates his opening proclamation that "in my walks, I would fain return to my senses" (*Exc* 190, 221). The very use of "return," instead of "progress," underscores his volte-face, and his signature pun on "sense" points to the derisive nature of the essay's earlier part, in which he was almost literally—but playfully—"out of his senses," a frenzied *vates* of expansion. Structurally, "Walking" retraces its steps, like the author's parabolic homecoming on his afternoon walks.

Yet while Thoreau circles back to his opening theme, that of walking to the "holy land," of course this has been considerably modified by the intervening developments. The most crucial difference is that the speaker's sense of mobility has now been freed, and even purged, of any kind of heroic presumption—to the point of appearing to some readers to be tinged with melancholy.[23] The counterpart of this "absolute freedom" is an openness to the newness of the familiar, for the individual is neither bound to the standard historical discourse nor to inherited culture sensu stricto. The energy liberated by this about-face is captured and rechanneled into the essay's final pages, in which imagination, or wildness, is spectacularly substituted for the actual, or tameness: "As the wild duck is more swift and beautiful than the tame, so is the wild—the mallard—thought, which, 'mid falling dews wings its way above the fens" (*Exc* 207). At stake here is a recovery of the "fancy and imagination" that characterized Greek mythology, poetic truth as opposed to historical truth (*Exc* 209).

Thus the imagination propounded by Thoreau is resolutely distinct from the one that produces the chimera of westward expansion. True imagination has to do with obscure forces, with emotions and deep feelings. Eager to stimulate his readers' imagination, he appeals to such visionaries as Chaucer, Moses, Homer, Christ, Dante, and Bunyan, who all come from the "deep time" of transhistorical culture, as imagined witnesses to our experience of the world, as opposed to the superficiality of standard historical time or of false mythology. While reason preposterously seeks to establish the seemingly necessary and universal westering movement, imagination helps us to regain or retain contact with the possible, to reinvent the ordinary. It turns out that the imagination of the West is actually a check on true imagining: it is imagination standardized, predefined.

Walking—and "Walking"—is thus a *method*, not in the derivative sense of a systematic, rational procedure but in the literal sense of following or accompanying something on its way, a process that unites knowledge and life, and thus destabilizes knowledge, producing what Thoreau calls *Gramatica parda*, or a "wild . . . knowledge" intrinsically imbued with life, since "life consists with wildness" (*Exc* 214, 203). Walking is revealed as Socratic method and the essay as dispensing Socratic irony. When Thoreau writes that "the highest that we can attain to is not Knowledge, but Sympathy with Intelligence" (*Exc* 215), he offers not postmodern diffidence but life-affirming questioning in the tradition of Socrates and Montaigne.

Just as Montaigne conceived of his *Essays* as a means to reclaim the world of ordinary experience, so does Thoreau open up a passage, not toward the West of the pioneers or the gold-seeking forty-niners but toward new areas of experience. It is no coincidence that the essay concludes on a trance-like evocation of Spaulding's Farm (*Exc* 218–19), which stands for the farms deserted by westering migrants. Because its former owners have left, it is now overgrown and ghost-like—the inverted mirror image of Manifest Destiny, a point highlighted by the almost exclusive use of sentences in the negative form, as though to counter the all-assertive rhetoric of the *translatio imperii*. And, like Montaigne, Thoreau extols and tries to preserve a form of methodological ignorance, in agreement with his acknowledgment that "we have a wild savage in us" (*Exc* 213). This brings to mind Maurice Merleau-Ponty's characterization of Montaigne as putting not "self-satisfied understanding but a consciousness astonished at itself at the core of human existence."[24] Thoreau, for his part, puts not self-satisfied historical progress but an ever-expanding consciousness at the core of human existence: the drifting or rambling inherent in walking mirrors the drifting of a mind, or resistance to dogmatism. Walking, in Thoreau's essay, is a decidedly *skeptical* gesture, not a triumphant one.

Conclusion

As he dislocates, and relocates, the West, Thoreau clearly exposes the hubris of the nation and counters its Americanocentrism, its celebration of its dominant, exceptionalist worldview. In so doing, he also breaks out of the grip of the narrative of "the West" as unique trajectory, one repressing spatial and historical heterogeneities within the nation—as he had also done in "Ktaadn"—and he resists the presupposition that the United States is socially and politically a homogeneous whole.

Such a stance is inseparable from an alternative sense of mobility. Thoreau may seem to be immobile, not because he does not move but because he refuses to synchronize with commonly accepted social and historical rhythms. He evinces a form of hidden or secret mobility, one that he encapsulates in his notion of a "border life." What Thoreau does in "Walking" is to recover alternative mobilities, opposed to the simplistic mobility associated with the mythology of westward expansion. He complexifies, "delinearizes," mobility; he also suggests that mobilities cannot exist or be beneficial without relative immobilities, or moorings. It is because he returns home every night that Thoreau can benefit from the mobility offered by his afternoon walk.

Thoreau's "Walking" is meant to check, if not to pull down, human presumption—the presumption inherent not only in the way conquest is legitimized but also in historical knowledge tinged with propaganda. Because he reacts against any excessive intelligibility of human history, his stance is thus resolutely skeptical. The movement of his essay is first to open us to the possibility of the strange and the remote, then to take us back to the familiar, so we see the extraordinary within the ordinary.

This skeptical movement is not meant to dwell in deep-seated doubt but to enable us to perceive the world anew. Like Montaigne, Thoreau was intent on pulling down the wall of certainty and on removing the veils of delusion so as to open up the horizon of the possible.

Notes

1. Richard J. Schneider, "'Climate Does Thus React on Man': Wildness and Geographic Determinism in Thoreau's 'Walking,'" in *Thoreau's Sense of Place: Essays in American Environmental Writing*, ed. Richard J. Schneider (Iowa City: University of Iowa Press, 2000), 44–60, 46. Kris Fresonke considers that Thoreau's "enthusiasms are briskly patriotic" and that he "sometimes struggled with and against manifest destiny without acknowledging his rhetorical complicity in it," in *West of Emerson: The Design of Manifest Destiny* (Berkeley: University of California Press, 2003), 131, 133. Although he is aware of the complexity of Thoreau's stance, David M. Robinson argues that "his implicit endorsement of the ideology of 'manifest destiny' here indicates the limits of his critical awareness of the oppressive and destructive nature of America's western imperialism"; see *Natural Life: Thoreau's Worldly Transcendentalism* (Ithaca, NY: Cornell University Press, 2004), 155. In another essay, Robinson describes what he perceives to be a tension "between the desire to preserve the wild and the desire to make use of it"; see "Thoreau's 'Walking' and the Ecological Imperative," *Approaches to Teaching Thoreau's* Walden *and Other Works*, ed. Richard J. Schneider (New York: The Modern Language Association of America, 1996), 171. Danielle Follett argues that Thoreau was along the lines of what would now be called "sustainable development." While Follett is right to emphasize Thoreau's pervasive desire to link wildness and civilization, nature contributing to a "healthy civilization" ("'Give Me a Culture That Imports Much Muck from the Meadows': Thoreau, le 'Sauvage' et la 'Culture,'" in *Littérature et politique en Nouvelle-Angleterre*, ed. Thomas Constantinesco and Antoine Traisnel [Paris: Editions Rue d'Ulm, 2011], 97), I think her approach tends to tone down Thoreau's more radical aspects.

2. My analysis of "Walking" will thus extend along somewhat different lines Laura Dassow Walls's apt remark that "Thoreau reclaims the rhetoric of Manifest Destiny to his own use" (*Seeing New Worlds: Henry David Thoreau and Nineteenth-Century Natural Science* [Madison: University of Wisconsin Press, 1995], 236). My reading is also congruent with Stephanie LeMenager's general framework in *Manifest and Other Destinies: Territorial Fictions of the Nineteenth-Century United States* (Lincoln: University of Nebraska Press, 2004), in which she considers the various ways U.S. writers of the nineteenth century (such as Cooper, Irving, Melville, or Twain) "began to articulate a postwestern and postcontinental cultural criticism" (16).

3. Andrew Menard, "Nationalism and the Nature of Thoreau's 'Walking,'" *New England Quarterly* 85, no. 3 (December 2012): 610.

4. Guy Debord, "Théorie de la Dérive," trans. Ken Knabb, *Les Lèvres Nues* 9 (November 1956), http://www.cddc.vt.edu/sionline/si/theory.html.

5. Lawrence Buell, *The Environmental Imagination: Thoreau, Nature Writing, and the Formation of American Culture* (Cambridge, MA: Harvard University Press, 1995), 143–79.

6. My thinking is here indebted to notions developed by Wai Chee Dimock, *Through Other Continents: American Literature across Deep Time* (Princeton, NJ: Princeton University Press 2006). Dimock coins the term deep time so as to specifically "denationalize" American literature, instead placing it in "a set of longitudinal frames, at once projective and recessional, with input going both ways, and binding continents and millennia into many loops of relations, a densely interactive fabric" (4). Dimock herself traces her focus on temporal and spatial scale enlargement back to Gayatri Chakravorty Spivak's notion of "planetarity," in *Death of a Discipline* (New York: Columbia University Press 2003), 71–102.

7. "I have quite other slaves to free than those negroes, to wit, imprisoned spirits, imprisoned thoughts," *The Journals and Miscellaneous Notebooks of Ralph Waldo Emerson*, vol. 13, ed. Ralph H. Orth and Alfred R. Ferguson (Cambridge, MA: Belknap Press of Harvard University Press, 1977), 80.

8. "Moss-trooper," strictly speaking, refers to "a member of any of the marauding gangs which, in the mid-seventeenth century, carried out raids across the 'mosses' of the Scottish Border; a Border pillager or freebooter" (*Oxford English Dictionary*, s.v. "moss-trooper"), a meaning consonant with Thoreau's insistence on living a "border life." However, Thoreau also literalizes or regrounds the expression, evoking his fondness for mosses, as if to criticize "mass-troopers" or regimented individuals. He certainly likes to suggest he is a latter-day outlaw or undisciplined individual.

9. See Guy Debord, "Introduction to a Critique of Urban Geography," for the notion of "psychogeography" and his remark that "the sudden change of ambiance in a street within the space of a few meters; the evident division of a city into zones of distinct psychic atmospheres; the path of least resistance which is automatically followed in aimless strolls (and which has no relation to the physical contour of the ground); the appealing or repelling character of certain places—all this seems to be neglected" (trans. Ken Knabb, *Les Lèvres Nues* 6 [September 1955], http://www.cddc.vt.edu /sionline/presitu/geography.html). Although Debord considers urban environments, his approach may be extended to any form of inhabiting the world.

10. In this regard, Andrew Menard's emphasis on what he regards as Thoreau's foregrounding of a "new nationalism" seems to me to be misleading. For Thoreau, beauty was an existential and spiritual principle, not "a means to nationhood" or the foundation of a Herderian "natural community" (Menard, "Nationalism," 610, 618).

11. Julien Nègre also regards "Walking" as "a decidedly political text," in the broad sense that walking "determines the place of the speaker/walker within the community." While my argument is fundamentally congruent with Nègre's reading, I am here considering the idea of the "political" in the more specialized sense. See Nègre, "Perambulating the Village: Henry David Thoreau and the Politics of 'Walking,'" in *Walking and the Aesthetics of Modernity*, ed. Klaus Benesch and François Specq (New York: Palgrave, 2016), 229–40.

12. Laura Dassow Walls, *Henry David Thoreau: A Life* (Chicago: University of Chicago Press, 2017), 318.

13. Lecture draft, 1851, MS Am278.5, folder 21B, Houghton Library, Harvard University, Cambridge, MA; facsimile in *The Essays of Henry D. Thoreau*, ed. Lewis Hyde (New York: North Point Press, 2002), 148.

14. Richard Chenevix Trench, *On the Study of Words* (New York: Redfield, 1852), 203.

15. Gen. 5:21–24 (Enoch) and 6:9 (Noah).

16. I am here drawing on and extending Michel de Certeau's analysis of urban walking. See his "Walking in the City," in *The Practice of Everyday Life*, trans. Steven Rendall (Berkeley: University of California Press, 1988), 91–110.

17. Although Lefebvre's analysis is meant to apply to urban space, its main thrust is relevant to an understanding of the dynamics of Thoreau's "Walking." See Henri Lefebvre, *The Production of Space*, trans. D. Nicholson-Smith (Oxford: Blackwell 1991), esp. chap. 1, "Plan of the Present Work," and chap. 6, "From the Contradictions of Space to Differential Space."

18. Lefebvre, *Production of Space*, 33, 38–39.

19. Whether Francis Bacon did pen this aphorism, which is commonly attributed to him, is beyond the scope of this essay. But the notion seems to be warranted by the formidable plan he canvassed to ensure human domination of nature through experimental science, from *The Advancement of Learning* to the *Novum Organum*.

20. Montaigne specifically brings forward the notion of "doctoral ignorance" in chapter 54 of the *Essays*: "A man may say with some colours of truth that there is an Abecedarian ignorance that precedes knowledge, and a doctoral ignorance that comes after it; an ignorance that knowledge creates and begets, at the same time that it despatches and destroys the first"; see Montaigne, *Essays*, trans. Charles Cotton (London: Reeves and Turner 1877), 1:414). One may also note that Thoreau's musings about names in the pages immediately preceding his discussion of knowledge (*Exc* 212–13) seem to echo chapter 46 of Montaigne's *Essays*, "Of Names."

21. Ralph Waldo Emerson, "Circles," in *Essays and Lectures*, ed. Joel Porte (New York: Library of America, 1983), 412.

22. "Now a days, almost all man's improvements, so called, as the building of houses, and the cutting down of the forest, and of all large trees, simply deform the landscape, and make it more and more tame and cheap" (*Exc* 191).

23. In William Rossi's view, "the fact of decay and death pervades the remainder of the essay, as the speaker walks the fine line between hope and melancholy." See "'The Limits of an Afternoon Walk': Coleridgean Polarity in Thoreau's 'Walking,'" *ESQ* 33, no. 2 (1987): 104.

24. Maurice Merleau-Ponty, "Reading Montaigne," in *Signs*, trans. R. McCleary (Evanston, IL: Northwestern University Press, 1964), 203.

PART II
CROSSING BOUNDARIES

WALDEN;

OR,

LIFE IN THE WOODS.

By HENRY D. THOREAU,

AUTHOR OF "A WEEK ON THE CONCORD AND MERRIMACK RIVERS."

I do not propose to write an ode to dejection, but to brag as lustily as chanticleer in the morning, standing on his roost, if only to wake my neighbors up. — Page 92.

BOSTON:

TICKNOR AND FIELDS.

M DCCC LIV.

Figure 7. Henry David Thoreau, *Walden* (Boston: Ticknor and Fields, 1854), title page of first edition, first printing.

6

OPENING *WALDEN*

Henrik Otterberg

Walden's title page, in its now-classic, original 1854 guise, offers at once a graphic and a linguistic portal, ushering the prospective reader toward a narrative of a new, transformed existence. Playing boldly with light and shade, its central engraving of a house in a wood-girdled glade announces the comprehensive nature of *Walden*'s invitation. A sunbathed window overlooks a benign pastoral clearing, while a half-obscured woodshed to the side of the house hints at a georgic site of revolving seasonal work. Behind these Virgilian topoi of leisure and diligence, a cluster of towering, dark, cypress-like pines remains to suggest the heroic dimensions to the proffered project. The cleared site, its viewer is made to understand, is also one of necessary bravery. The dweller here will be a Tityrus, Hesiod, and Æneas folded into one.

No person or animal is visible on the title page engraving, only an increasingly tenebrous path to the front door of its small house, cloaked in shadow. The lure of transition, then, seems to accommodate both clarity and obscurity, opportunity and risk—even as the qualifying subtitle, "*or, Life in the Woods*," adds dense fibers to the signal of crystal waters. To reinforce the promise of his narrative, Thoreau appends an introductory motto below the house engraving, where the depicted path has morphed into a virtual river of light: "I do not propose to write an ode to dejection, but to brag as lustily as chanticleer in the morning, standing on his roost, if only to wake my neighbors up." Thoreau's claim, however, is referenced as a forward-looking citation deep in his ensuing narrative—while once there, the reader is abruptly reverted back to the title page, with an "As I have said" prefixing what was purportedly the proper locus of his introductory quote.[1]

The spatiotemporal effect of this juxtaposition is somewhat spectral—Where does Thoreau's motto actually belong?—yet entirely appropriate to the title page illustration, conjuring up as it simultaneously does both presence and absence, something both fulfilled and yet to come. Indeed, the bulk of the ensuing pages of *Walden* assume the character of glassine, of more or less transparent envelopes containing distinct impressions, sights, sounds, and other observations garnered over several years, skillfully dressed into a seasonal *Sammelband* evoking a redemptive yearly cycle. Saliently, amid all the deft narrative weaving, Thoreau is never shy about his incessant creative process of sorting, adding, and reordering, tellingly beginning his narrative with the phrase, "When I wrote the following pages." *Walden* is thus a self-admitted, ambitious palimpsest and fruitfully approached as such.

Thoreau's Mystic

Walden's title page portal, with its introductory engraving and motto, ultimately relates to Thoreau's self-designation not only as a transcendentalist and a naturalist but also, and pointedly, as a *mystic*. My contention is that this largely overlooked aspect of Thoreau's self-fashioning holds a key to his aesthetic impulses of overlaying and interweaving his texts and their references with significance. "Mystic" once connoted a skilled exegete, able to discern several levels of spatial, social, ecclesiastical, and temporal meaning in scripture. Conversely, it also designated those devoted to such multilayered sensitivity in their own work. Paying special attention to the image of chanticleer, with a view to unpacking its connotations and reverberations for Thoreau both private and public, will yield dividends in this respect. Thoreau's ethics of writing, setting much store as he did on the responsibility of the reader to make sense and significance of his words, beyond their horizons of authorial significance, are also set in motion by his title page. Insofar as his readers choose to enter *Walden* proper then, it behooves them to secure the necessary leisure, resolve, and courage to approach their own independence and freedom through its profusion of assertions, subtle hints, and occasional maieutics.

We know that Thoreau revisited his landscapes and their associated phenomena again and again, to understand them and, by extension, himself the better, accreting an ever-firmer backbone to his environmentally focused writings. He also delved into a welter of topical literature to strengthen his ken and kept at his journalizing and charting. And so his nature-oriented writings gained a wide radial texture as well as depth of resonance. A flower would be inspected on its own terms—its structure, appearance, and aroma; its formation, unfolding, and bloom; its retreat and eventual decay. But also its botanical neighborhood, its hidden roots underground (clasping hands with those of others against the inclement seasons, as he once put it [*PJ* 4:385]), as well its hang-around insects, birds, and animals: considering its full *and-scape*, as it were. In effect, Thoreau asked, What music does the flower play? And so proceeded to carefully inspect the instrument, the player, her section, and finally the full ensemble, each stage, so defined, playing a role in widening rings to form an orchestra—strings very much attached.

Something similar, I believe, can be said of Thoreau's aesthetic and interpretive outlook in general. He designated himself a mystic, after all, and this in a contemporary sense often lost to us today. When calling up Thoreau's famous self-description in his 1853 Journal, occasioned by an offer of membership from the Association for the Advancement of Science, we tend to ignore what Thoreau states as his first vocation and hurry instead to focus on the two more familiar and recognizable ones. Here is what Thoreau writes: "The fact is I am a mystic—a transcendentalist—& a natural philosopher to boot" (*PJ* 5:469). It is tempting to think Thoreau's spark may have been the May 20, 1838, meeting of the Transcendental Club in the home of his mentor Ralph Waldo Emerson—specifically to discuss "the question of Mysticism." Thoreau had just returned to Concord from a trip to Maine, unsuccessfully seeking a teaching position, and perhaps he was too fatigued from his travels to attend. Yet the congregation, at this meeting and others, was germinal for Emerson, Bronson Alcott, Margaret Fuller, and others, who would go on to collect mystic literature. Emerson would in time write an essay in *Representative Men* (1850) on the Swedish polymath Emanuel Swedenborg, characterizing him as the preeminent mystic of his time; Fuller would describe herself as a budding mystic.[2] The ripples of the seminal meeting would hardly have been lost on Thoreau, even were he not in attendance that day.

The most recent and lengthy treatments of Thoreau's spirituality, by Alan D. Hodder and Malcolm Clemens Young, do not gloss his 1853 self-designation, nor does the more impressionistic and brief work of Paul

Hourihan.³ Two unpublished PhD dissertations, by Michael R. Keller and
Don Gervich, explicitly concern themselves with Thoreau's mysticism,
although both focus on his personal psychological development rather
than with his aesthetics, which are what primarily interests me here.⁴ Perhaps the mid-1970s *Thoreau: Mystic, Prophet, Ecologist* by the theologian
William J. Wolf set the tone for future scholars, specifically by his reductive reading of "mystic." Wolf takes it to connote a "dim consciousness of
the beyond," in other words, as a kind of raw-clay intuition underlying all
religions.⁵

But a mystic to mid-nineteenth-century ears was also something more
specific: it signified a theologically schooled interpreter, following on the
ancient Greek *mustikos*, or "initiated person." Thoreau's own well-thumbed
dictionaries indicate as much, beginning with Nathan Bailey's etymological lexicon and Samuel Johnson's vast glossary, which Thoreau owned in
a mid-eighteenth-century and 1828 edition, respectively. Here a cluster of
connotations around "mysterial," "mystery," and "mystagogue" emphasize
what is commonly found to be obscure or secret, in effect accessible only to
scriptural experts.⁶ In John Oswald's etymological dictionary of 1836 and
Noah Webster's comprehensive one of 1848, both also resting on Thoreau's
shelves, we find firm evidence that the earlier, mostly adjectival "mystic"
was by then also accorded the status of a noun or, in other words, of a
practitioner.⁷

To sharpen the focus a bit, I propose that Thoreau remained wary of
what he elsewhere styled a mysticism taken to extremes, perhaps most
memorably in relation to Thomas Carlyle (a sentiment Emerson would
echo in relation to Swedenborg, in chiding his subject for theological ped-
antry). In his 1847 essay on the Scotsman in *Graham's Magazine*, which was
in general quite appreciative of its subject, Thoreau opines that abstruse
prose such as he now and then encountered in Carlyle may be suspected of
"mysticism, fanaticism or insanity" if not leavened with a sense of humor,
which would impart what Thoreau calls "a pledge of sanity" to the whole
(*EEM* 235). Humor would indeed become his own preferred textual yeast
on many occasions, especially to make his reform-oriented compositions
more palatable and digestible. As the old rhetors are fond of pointing
out, humor is rhetorically disarming, whereas consistent obscurity will be
found off-putting and exclusionary.

As for Thoreau's own identification as a mystic, this arguably had less to do with anything specifically denominational or theological and more to do with exegetical practices until recently ascribed to the mystagogue. The word signified a learned initiate striving to recognize and revitalize the plural dimensions of mythological and scriptural language, seeking correspondences between the spiritual world and physical creation in all its forms. One of the famous mystagogues was the eponymous naturalist, or Physiologus, who commented deftly on natural creation in a long series of fable-like, moralizing vignettes in scrolls and manuscripts dating back to the third century AD. Here the cardinal idea was an admittedly simple binary, interpreting and dividing creation into such categories as evinced either good or evil, Christian or satanic tendencies. Translated over a vast range of languages, the *Physiologus* by several estimates ranked second only to the Bible in popularity during the Middle Ages.[8] In time it also came to form an important inspiration to the religious and philosophical concept of a "Book of Nature," as popularized during the Latin Middle Ages. This was a more ambitious and complex notion, whereby the natural world was seen as a legitimate and complementary "scripture" to the Bible, or "Book of Revelation." Its inherent appeal to the Transcendentalists, and to Thoreau in particular, is an evident, if to date neglected, subject, as their versions of environmental perception with a focus on symbolic and moral import had clear affinities with the general concept.[9]

While we cannot say with confidence whether Thoreau encountered the *Physiologus*, we do know that he read Alexander Ross's 1648 *Mystagogus Poeticus*, subtitled *The Muses' Interpreter*, with enthusiasm. Thoreau evidently relished Ross's dialogic structure, whereby bare-bones myths collected from Greek and Roman sources were juxtaposed with detailed, sometimes giddily multipronged commentary. With its dedicatory passages, the preface outlines how bees extract honey "from malignant weeds," thus pleasing the palate and nourishing the flesh and blood, while the mystagogus sucks his nectar from the high slopes of Parnassus, such as "delighteth the soul's tast[e], and doth it nourish to immortal bliss."[10] In his first book, *A Week on the Concord and Merrimack Rivers* (1849), Thoreau credits Ross for his "dateless benefits," and he was not alone in appreciating this kind of literature (*Wk* 58). Bronson Alcott owned a mid-seventeenth-century edition of the anonymously issued *Mundorum Explicatio*, purporting to explain the "mysteries of the external, internal, and eternal worlds" from hieroglyphic sources and showing the progress of a soul "from the Adamical fallen state to the regenerate and angelical."[11] Ralph Waldo Emerson, in turn, kept on his shelves an exclusive 1556 edition of Iamblichus's *De Mysteriis Aegyptiorum*, supplied with copious interpretive commentary by Nicolao Scutellio.[12]

As related more precisely to Christian traditions, the mystagogue harkened back to medieval concepts of the quadriga in comprehending scripture. According to this figure, which recalled a Roman chariot pulled by four horses, each Bible verse could be interpreted on four corresponding levels, commingling the symbolic and anagogical with the present and the past, the tangible and the historic. In a late 1854 addition to the "Conclusion" chapter of his *Walden* manuscript, while much engaged with establishing an *extra-vagant* form of writing and reading, Thoreau also tells us—by way of another tradition—that "the verses of Kabir have four different senses: illusion, spirit, intellect, and the exoteric doctrine of the Vedas," while "in this part of the world it is considered a ground for complaint if a man's writings admit of more than one interpretation" (*W* 325).[13]

We might say by way of analogy, then, that Thoreau enjoyed *quadruple entendre*, or something akin to this, when opportunity arose. Loading his literary tropes and image references to capacity was congenial to his persistent honing of awareness, whereby seeing well entailed writing well, and reading in turn demanded something more than mere recording to become fruitful, to come alive. Indeed reading—and, for that matter, listening—should to Thoreau ideally offer a continual unfolding, yielding ever more to those making an honest effort. We recall his many comments to such effect in the "Reading" chapter of *Walden*, while Thoreau gives his perhaps most vivid summing-up of the matter in a spring 1859 Journal entry, in which he states that he is poised to bring a cask of cider to his lecture audience, and even to open its tap, while they must suck their straws themselves (*J* XII:9). And so everything from abstinence to nourishment to intoxication, we infer, may follow. As always with Thoreau: caveat emptor.

But how did this challenging liberatory aesthetic work in practice? Well, among many enthusiastically planted homonyms, wide-ranging symbols, and images in *Walden*, we may recall here Thoreau's intricate turns on the concept of giving *account*; of his *liber*, or "shirt" which is simultaneously likened to bark, human skin, and the leaves of a book; of the "iron horse" and the enigmatic creatures of Thoreau's "New Mythology" as linked to a spectrum spanning from the tangible practice of painting mythological beasts on the flanks of locomotive tenders to the circumstance that Thoreau's "winged horse" and "fiery dragon" had their counterparts in his Journal, where he had them mark inspiration and creative despondency, respectively; furthermore the evocative "sleepers," at once raising railroad ties, dreamers, and philosophically dormant men: among these and many more, the "chanticleer" of Thoreau's title page motto, as well as its later reappearance in "Where I Lived, and What I Lived For," has received comparatively little attention.[14]

Thoreau's Chanticleer

John C. Broderick, writing in the mid-1950s, rightly credits Thoreau's clarion bird as a crucial, sustained symbol of awakening in *Walden*.[15] Yet many modern editions of *Walden*—including, remarkably, the standard Princeton—displace or omit the original title page and its motto. This fowl play dampens Thoreau's overture and renders his narrator's remark a bit into the book, "As I have said," followed by the chanticleer passage, utterly confusing. Chanticleer was a bird with rich connotations, as Thoreau was well aware. Indeed, it was so important to him that he drew it onto a late manuscript opening page of *Walden* to complement his words.[16]

What, then, does "chanticleer" convey beyond a calling for wakefulness, which trait, we might add, is already firmly ascribed to the cockerel in the Bible? Traditionally, the Latin *gallus* was linked to what the Romans called Gaul, that is, modern-day France. Thoreau's family was related on his father's side to French merchant stock, originally from the northwestern mainland but more recently based on the English Channel Islands, as Edwin Guillet has chronicled in detail.[17] The Thoreau family forebears were French Huguenots, in other words Protestants of Calvinist faith. They lived under the tenuous protection of the Edict of Nantes until the days of Louis XIV and his deputy Cardinal Richelieu, when under increasing persecution they were forced to flee the country and chose to settle on the English island of Jersey. The Gallic reputation for independence and resistance to oppression would have appealed to Thoreau, one would think—as would chanticleer's wider symbolism of French culture and especially literature. Also, as Thoreau's oldest grammarian Bailey points out, "chanticleer" came from the modern French "chanter," meaning "to sing," and "clair," that is, "clear" or "shrill."

But did "chanticleer" necessarily resonate among Anglo-Saxons? One clue surfaces with Thoreau's friend Daniel Ricketson, who on purchasing the newly published *Walden* annotated his copy profusely. To the chanticleer motto rendered in "Where I Lived," Ricketson added in the margins a dovetailing quatrain from a poem by John Cunningham, emphasizing how the powerful bird "perched on high, / Briskly crows, the Shepherd's clock / Jocund that the morning's nigh."[18] Supplying such related poetic verse as Ricketson did was perfectly in line with dictionary practice of the time, whereby word definitions were often complemented by the word's usage by canonized poets.

If we look to dictionaries we know Thoreau to have owned or can infer him to have consulted, including (beyond those already mentioned) Charles Richardson's compendious, two-volume *English Dictionary* of 1839, we find a handful of examples of chanticleer's poetic usage in the literature. Furthermore, Cornelius Matthews, the stylistic reformer and youth-book writer based in New York, brought out a popular sentimental novel called *Chanticleer: A Thanksgiving Story* in 1850.[19] Here an honorable but down-at-heel family saddened by the disappearance of their son is echoed by their barnyard bantam, symbolic as it becomes of tenacious hope and eventual rejuvenation. In the denouement the prodigal son returns, awaited by a loving wife and windfall inheritance.

In his Journal, Thoreau would also on occasion use "cockerel" or "cock," as well as the Americanism "rooster," noted by J. R. Bartlett in his idiomatic dictionary of 1848, which Thoreau also had on his desk.[20] But the former in particular would be risky for a connotation-sensitive writer such as Thoreau: "cock" was long established as a phallic vulgarism, and many inventive variations involving this word hinted well beyond a supposedly chaste masculine bravery and initiative.[21] The purely sexual, as we know, did not interest Thoreau in his wordplay, although he could on occasion champion the scatological and the frivolous as well as the irreverent.

So much for the literary and cultural connotations of "chanticleer." There was also, or so I propose, a deeper personal dimension to its deployment in *Walden*. This had to do with a boyhood friend of Henry's, named Charles Stearns Wheeler. Wheeler lived in the nearby village of Lincoln and joined Thoreau as his roommate at Harvard College. The by-all-accounts affable, diligent, and cheerful Wheeler is largely forgotten today. Yet his biographer, John Olin Eidson, stresses Thoreau's opinion of him as "a sort of connecting link between men and scholars of different walks and tastes."[22]

Wheeler was considered by Emerson to hold great promise as a Transcendentalist. The sunny youth embraced the divinity in man, lectured on self-reliance, kept a journal, and invited Thoreau to live with him for a carefree string of weeks in the summer of 1837, in a shanty above the shoreline of the idyllic Flint's Pond, somewhat east of Walden (some may also recall that Thoreau tried to gain permission to build his house there for his 1845–47 retreat, only to be snubbed by farmer Flint). Wheeler also edited and annotated an ambitious, two-volume edition of Herodotus's famous *History*, helped Emerson bring Carlyle and Tennyson to American audiences, and for a short time acted as *The Dial*'s German correspondent. What happened? In a cruel twist of fate, Wheeler was taken ill with a stomach ailment while visiting Germany in 1843, on a sabbatical of sorts, and died there at a mere 26 years of age. Emerson was shocked, and so were Wheeler's many friends, including Thoreau. The common feeling was one of a productive life cut mercilessly short.

There is a slight curiosity, however, to Thoreau's carefully pointing out a perceived fault of Wheeler's, close on the heels of the tragic news. In a letter to his sister Helen, written the same summer of 1843 from Staten Island, Thoreau says that "Stearns Wheeler has left a gap in the community not easy to be filled." Then, however, comes a qualification: "though he did not exhibit the highest qualities of the scholar" (*Corr* 1:211–12).[23] This may, of course, seem innocent enough. But it commingles with another noteworthy circumstance with Wheeler at its nucleus, namely, that Thoreau was nowhere represented in the ambitious undergraduate publication called *Harvardiana*, bound into handsome annual volumes during its run between 1835 and 1837. *Harvardiana*, though of modest circulation, collected essays, poetry, book reviews, and lectures written by the students themselves. And Stearns Wheeler was the journal's coeditor throughout. Whether Thoreau was not invited to contribute or opted out by his own choice is difficult to say. But the preface of the 1837 volume, where the *Harvardiana* editors finally sign off, is telling, if anything, for its un-Thoreauvian tenor: "Let no one then take up this volume, with the expectation of meeting with attempts at grave discussions, upon either Politics, Religion, or Philosophy. We have made no pretensions to the

names of Statesmen or Teachers. We have not striven to make louder with
our own voices that pitiful 'cock-crow of philosophy,' which is raised by
too many college chanticleers. We have not been ambitious of intruding
upon any one our religious or political common-places. In the prospectus
we stated, that it was our intention to fix upon this periodical, a *Collegiate*
character. This we have endeavored to do . . . To those, who have looked
upon our pastime with cold indifference, or shaken their wise heads at the
folly of our boyish play, we only ask, Would the sport have been made any
better, had you joined in it?"[24] This statement presents a disparaging view
of chanticleer and mocks the mission of philosophy, as well as of serious
writing, to which some students evidently adhered. It is not hard to imagine Thoreau having been one of them. Whatever its immediate impact on
him, Thoreau chooses to echo the Wheeler & Co. preface with his very
own twist several years later, in his 1851 lecture-essay "Walking": "Unless
our philosophy hears the cock crow in every barn-yard within our horizon,
it is belated. That sound commonly reminds us that we are growing rusty
and antique in our employments and habits of thought. His philosophy
comes down to a more recent time than ours. There is something suggested
by it not in Plato nor the New Testament. It is a newer testament—the
Gospel according to this moment . . . It is an expression of the health and
soundness of Nature, a brag for all the world-healthiness as of a spring
burst forth—a new fountain of the Muses, to celebrate this last instant of
time" (*Exc* 220–21). And in *Walden*, of course, Thoreau's identification with
chanticleer is unmistakable, a creature able to transcend the despondency
of Coleridge's famous ode, to grasp instead the joy that in counterpoint
"is the spirit and the power / Which wedding Nature to us gives in dower
/A new Earth and a new Heaven": "I do not propose to write an ode to
dejection, but to brag as lustily as chanticleer in the morning, standing on
his roost, if only to wake my neighbors up" (*W* 84).[25]

Thoreau's Shanty

With this I'd like to leave the connotations of Thoreau's clarion bird to
turn my attention to another aspect of *Walden*'s title page, namely, its
engraving of the author's abode. That the original sketch of Thoreau's sister
Sophia was not very strong is an old chestnut in the scholarly community.
Several eminent Thoreauvians through the years, ranging from William

Ellery Channing to Bradley P. Dean, have joined the debate: the former with disparagement, the latter with an attempt at digital tweaking of the house features, to better fit Thoreau's proof sheet comments on the engraving (I should add that these latter were evidently ignored by the publishers, Ticknor and Fields.[26]

Beyond the merits or not of Sophia's draftsmanship, however, no one seems to have considered the likelihood of the engravers, John Andrew and William J. Baker, themselves being the culprits after a fashion. First of all, if we are necessarily to find fault with the engraving, one oddity, in view of the title page's clearly stated theme of awakening, is that the dwelling by its shading seems rendered in midafternoon light rather than in a more fitting auroral ambience (see figures 8 and 9). What could explain such an anomaly? If we rule out sheer incompetence, more prosaic factors emerge as likely, and these work to contravene the intricate and independent authorial loading of imagery relating to Thoreau's chanticleer. Such factors would involve marketing and genre concerns, as well as limitations of costs where possible on the part of the publishers. A fairly exhaustive search of American antebellum title page wood engravings involving cabins, followed by a process of collating them against Thoreau's reading as well as available records from his publisher, Ticknor and Fields, points in this regard toward an interesting confluence.

Thoreau is known to have read Susanna Moodie's famous account of her family's adventurous quest to build a home in the 1840s wilds of New Brunswick, Canada, entitled *Roughing It in the Bush; or, Life in Canada.* Moodie's two-volume account was first published in North America by Putnam's of New York in 1852, and Thoreau copied from it in one of his Indian Notebooks circa 1853. Responsible for Moodie's title page engraving were James Richardson and Thomas Cox, like Andrew and Baker old hands in the business. From the "Cost Books" of Ticknor and Fields, we learn that Richardson and Cox became affiliated with the Boston publishers of Thoreau's *Walden; or, Life in the Woods*—as, again, the book was first titled—in the mid-1850s.[27] Did Andrew and Baker choose to copy a number of elements from their colleagues' earlier Moodie engraving in designing Thoreau's title page? Suffice it to say that there are a number of conspicuous parallels to ponder: the kindred, stylized depiction of the background trees; the similarly chosen portrait angle and relative size of the respective abodes; the gently tapering foregrounds shared by both images,

Figures 8 and 9. *The sun is but a morning star*. Diptych by British artist Ian Whittlesea (2011), adapted from *Walden*'s original title page, showing its house at dusk and at night. Giclée prints on Hahnemule photo rag, each measuring 29.7 x 21 cm. Photos copyright © 2017 Ian Whittlesea. Used with permission.

and the comparably fonted, reclining paring of the engravers' surnames in each lower right-hand corner (see figure 10).

My point in showing these pages side by side is not to suggest plagiarism or moonlighting by any of the parties involved. Rather, I see genre elements at work, including, for that matter, in the respective subtitles. Thoreau's chosen one echoed those of an 1844 *Dial* essay by Charles Lane, entitled simply "Life in the Woods," as well as an 1843 pioneer narrative by John S. Williams entitled *Our Cabin; or, Life in the Woods.*[28] Of course, it should be noted that Thoreau eventually wished for his original subtitle to be dropped, and in the second edition of *Walden*, issued in 1862, it was.[29] But from the outset in his first 1847 manuscript Thoreau *did* want the subtitle, conveying as he hoped (or so we may infer) *a life elsewhere*, forming an alternative to the common existential status quo as Thoreau saw it. For his publishers, the moniker may not have signified anything quite as exalted, yet it did inevitably signal a narrative account of something different from common expectations.

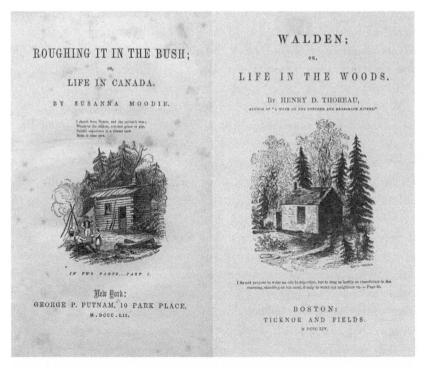

Figure 10. Engraved title pages of Moodie's (1852) and Thoreau's (1854) respective works. Photos copyright © 2017 Jesper Löfman. Used with permission.

Conclusion

What hope is there for an essay purporting to be about *Walden* that never ventures beyond an aspect of the work's paratext—its title page? If ever there was a surface reading, surely this would fit the bill. My rationale has been that Thoreau's entry page, with its declarative title, subtitle, engraving, and motto, proves itself richly indicative of the narrative to come. For one thing, as briefly touched on earlier, its engraving promises a full round of styles according to the classical *rota Virgilii*, or "Virgilian wheel." In other words, it announces that Thoreau's account will encompass the temporal and spatial purviews of the epic, georgic, and pastoral modes, based on the Roman's canonized works. The reader can then rightly expect to encounter linear time as related to a larger region or country; cyclic time revolving in a narrower tract; and blessed moments of *otium* at a chosen *locus amoenus*, "pleasant place" or "beloved spot." In these respects *Walden* also delivers. As related to human agency, the modes taken together further proclaim a dedication to heroism, to work, and to leisure—all rendered with Thoreau's distinctive slant, of course. For his heroism involves daring to strive for other ideals than those of the majority of his coevals; his work is that of rarefied enlightenment rather than conventional enrichment; and his leisure often emerges as active and engaging rather than drowsy and inert.

What then of the *mystic* Thoreau? Some may recall in this context Stanley Cavell's programmatic statement in *The Senses of Walden* regarding Thoreau's book, impressing upon us that "it means every word it says, and . . . is fully sensible of its mysteries and fully open about them."[30] This would ask the diligent reader to unpack all of *Walden*'s allusions and signifiers: a tall order, even for a prominent philosopher of language. Interestingly, in his 1981 expanded edition of *Senses*, Cavell slips in a mouse-that-roars qualifier: now *Walden* "means," as he tweaks his former phrase, "*in* every word that it says" (emphasis added). This sensible concession to the inherent plurality and alterity of words seems prudent in approaching a writer who as late as in his 1854 Journal lists the following as his personal "faults," at once aesthetic and moral: "paradoxes—saying just the opposite"; [being] "ingenious"; "playing with words" and finding himself "not always earnest" (*PJ* 8:403).[31] What Thoreau is acknowledging here could just as well be claimed of language itself, if raising a truism can be forgiven, namely, that it accommodates slipperiness as well as frankness, obscurity as readily as perspicuity. Thoreau simultaneously admits to being a demanding writer, whose narratives must be spied by the reader from different angles, pecked at accordingly, and digested with grit in one's gizzard.

Let us return at last to Thoreau's chanticleer in such hermeneutical spirit. How might the dawn-heralding bird of *Walden* fit into a mystical matrix such as the quadriga? Shoehorning the fowl into a strictly theological framework would be a mistake, of course, given Thoreau's proclivity for eclecticism. But we could still gainfully analyze it by way of expected multivalency. The literal level would then involve the bird itself; the allegorical, the common understanding of its championing of wakefulness; the tropological, its individual and moral radiance for the reader in question. We might again, assuming Thoreau to be his own first reader, point to the French connection, emphasizing the proud independence and self-reliance of Thoreau, his Huguenot forebears, and the Gallic *gallus*.

Finally, on the anagogical level—the most esoteric of the four, having to do with last days, ultimate fate, and the heavenly—we could point to Thoreau's chanticleer as at once a marker of defiance against Stearns Wheeler's brand of juvenile philosophy yet also a silent nod to him as a true, long-lost friend: a beloved neighbor whose spirit Thoreau would endeavor to wake with chanticleer's true call in *Walden*. (We may also recollect here that Thoreau had dedicated *A Week on the Concord and Merrimack Rivers* to the memory of his brother, John, some years earlier; John who had likewise died at 26, only a year earlier than Stearns, in 1842.) While Henry and Stearns may have interpreted chanticleer very differently, Henry nevertheless, in Ezekiel's prophetic tradition, chooses to mark his friend in order to preserve him—much as Cavell understands Thoreau to daub Emerson in the "Former Inhabitants; and Winter Visitors" chapter of *Walden*. The passage in question relates how Thoreau passed by Emerson's door in the village without mustering a call, yet, as he quietly comments of his mentor, he will "long . . . be remembered" (*W* 270).[32]

All this leaves us with keen expectations in delving into *Walden* proper, having girded ourselves as well as we could for the task. *Walden* is a demanding narrative in many respects, but among its plethora of yields is a generous and rewarding mysticism. William James, in his seminal 1902 study *Varieties of Religious Experience*, understood the concept to include ineffability, transiency, and passivity. Experiential mysticism would, in other words, involve a difficulty of translation; commonly be a fleeting

rather than sustained phenomenon; and often require a certain calm dis-
interestedness in whomsoever hopes at some interval to attract it. To these
marks, James adds another, possibly more surprising *noetic quality*: "mystical states seem to those who experience them to be also states of knowledge. They are states of insight into depths of truth unplumbed by the
discursive intellect. They are illuminations, revelations, full of significance
and importance, all inarticulate though they remain; and as a rule they
carry with them a curious sense of authority for after-time."[33]

A writer such as Thoreau, with the abiding ambition to pursue and convey such mystical states as occasioned, would inevitably run into hurdles:
some prosaic, such as having to cede a modicum of authorial control over
his title page engraving (possibly feeling the tug of genre expectations as
well), while others inhere to the considerable challenge of translating that
for which even carefully chosen words, regardless of their connotational
resonance, will be hard put to convey.[34] Yet Thoreau remained alive to
his epiphanies, spiritual and environmental, and primed his aesthetics to
match them as well as he could. One of his most memorable depictions of
a yearning for mystical experience occurs in "The Ponds" chapter of *Walden*
and as such will serve to close this essay with a quenching dip into the
book. Thoreau relates how he would spend gentle nocturnal hours gliding
over Walden's glassine surface, levitating between water and sky, effectu-
ally merging "you" and "I" in his little boat. He would hold his fishing
line absentmindedly in hand, when at once a tug from the depths would
reach his fingertips: "It was very queer, especially in dark nights, when your
thoughts had wandered to vast and cosmogonal themes in other spheres,
to feel this faint jerk, which came to interrupt your dreams and link you
to Nature again. It seemed as if I might next cast my line upward into the
air, as well as downward into this element which was scarcely more dense.
Thus I caught two fishes as it were with one hook" (*W* 175).

Notes

1. *W* 84 and illustration facing p. 357; see also Henry David Thoreau, *Walden*, facsimile
   reprint with introduction by Willard Thorp (Columbus, OH: Charles E. Merrill,
   1969).
2. See Leigh Eric Schmidt's valuable potted history of mysticism in the United States, in
   particular how the term changed its denominational connotations over time, in "The

Making of Modern 'Mysticism,'" *Journal of the American Academy of Religion* 71, no. 2 (June 2003): 284–87. I am gratefully indebted to William Rossi for this source.

3. See Alan D. Hodder, *Thoreau's Ecstatic Witness* (New Haven, CT: Yale University Press, 2001); Malcolm Clemens Young, *The Spiritual Journal of Henry David Thoreau* (Macon, GA: Mercer University Press, 2009); and Paul Hourihan, *Mysticism in American Literature: Thoreau's Quest and Whitman's Self* (Redding, CA: Vedantic Shores Press, 2004). More recently, in his avowedly spiritual biography of Thoreau, Kevin Dann likewise gives a cursory nod to Thoreau's self-designation, not developing it—or the concept of mysticism—further. Compare Dann's *Expect Great Things: The Life and Search of Henry David Thoreau* (New York: Tarcher Perigee, 2017), 227–28.

4. See Michael R. Keller, "Henry David Thoreau: Mystic" (PhD diss., Ball State University, 1977), 108–10, and Don Gervich, "The Writer and the Mystic: Henry David Thoreau" (PhD diss., Boston University School of Education, 1979), 40–42.

5. See William J. Wolf, *Thoreau: Mystic, Prophet, Ecologist* (Philadelphia: United Church Press, 1974), 109.

6. See Nathan Bailey, *An Universal Etymological English Dictionary . . . Seventeenth Edition* (London: T. Osborne et al., 1759), and Samuel Johnson, *A Dictionary of the English Language . . . Stereotyped Verbatim from the Last Folio Edition Corrected by the Doctor* (London: Joseph Ogle Robinson, 1828), 782. Compare Charles Richardson's more exclusionary definition of "mystic" as "one who pretends to *mysteries*, or doctrines and opinions that cannot be understood or comprehended," in his *A New Dictionary of the English Language*, vol. 2, L–Z (London: William Pickering, 1839), 1329. Thoreau was aware of Richardson's work, making a note to consult it, for instance, in preparing his *Cape Cod* texts. See *CC*, "Historical Introduction," 252. Validation of Thoreau's book holdings, readings, and references are taken from Robert Sattelmeyer's standard *Thoreau's Reading: A Study in Intellectual History with Bibliographical Catalogue* (Princeton, NJ: Princeton University Press, 1988).

7. See John Oswald, *An Etymological Dictionary of the English Language on a Plan Entirely New* (Philadelphia: Edward C. Biddle, 1836), 254, and Noah Webster, *An American Dictionary of the English Language . . . Revised and Enlarged by Chauncey A. Goodrich* (Springfield, MA: George and Charles Merriam, 1848), 741.

8. See Michael J. Curley, trans. and ed., *Physiologus* (Austin: University of Texas Press, 1979), ix–xliii.

9. For a lucid and concise overview of the background and history of this philosophical and religious concept, see Olaf Pedersen, *The Book of Nature* (Notre Dame, IN: University of Notre Dame Press, 1992).

10. See Alexander Ross, *Mystagogus Poeticus, or, The Muses' Interpreter* (London: Tomas Whitaker, 1648), 3.

11. Kenneth Walter Cameron, ed., *Transcendental Curriculum or Bronson Alcott's Library: The Inventory of 1858–1860 with Addenda to 1888* (Hartford, CT: Transcendental Books, 1984), 83.

12. See Walter Harding, ed., *Emerson's Library* (Charlottesville: University Press of Virginia, 1967), 150.

13. Miriam Alice Jeswine argues that four interdependent Vedic levels of interpretation held a stronger pull on Thoreau than did the medieval Christian ones, whereas I see Thoreau as eclectically embracing the general concept of multivalency, rather than

choosing a particular one as his lead. See Jeswine, "Henry David Thoreau: Apprentice to the Hindu Sages" (PhD diss., University of Oregon, 1971), 140–45.

14. For further commentary on these passages, see my "Alma Natura, Ars Severa: Expanses and Limits of Craft in Henry David Thoreau" (PhD diss., University of Gothenburg, 2014), esp. "Figuring Henry" (245–72) and "Tenth Muse Errant" (112–70).

15. See John C. Broderick, "Imagery in *Walden*," *University of Texas Studies in English* 33 (1954): 80–89.

16. For a reproduction of this drawing in its context, see *The Annotated Walden*, ed. Philip Van Doren Stern (New York: Clarkson N. Potter, 1970), 140.

17. See Edwin C. Guillet, *The Thoreau-Guillet Genealogy* (Toronto: University of Toronto Press, 1971), frontispiece Table 1, 7–11.

18. See Walter Harding, "Daniel Ricketson's Copy of *Walden*," *Harvard Library Bulletin* 15, no. 4 (October 1967): 407.

19. See Cornelius Matthews [commonly attributed], *Chanticleer: A Thanksgiving Story of the Peabody Family* (Boston: B. B. Mussey; New York: J. S. Redfield, 1850).

20. See John Russell Bartlett, *Dictionary of Americanisms: A Glossary of Words and Phrases Usually Regarded as Peculiar to the United States* (New York: Bartlett and Welford, 1848), 278.

21. See John S. Farmer, ed., *Slang and Its Analogues Past and Present: A Dictionary, Historical and Comparative, of the Heterodox Speech of All Classes of Society for More Than Three Hundred Years*, 7 vols. (1890; repr., New York: Kraus Reprint Corporation, 1965), 2:135–45.

22. See John Olin Eidson, *Charles Stearns Wheeler: Friend of Emerson* (Athens: University of Georgia Press, 1951), xi.

23. As it happens, this Thoreauvian sentiment was soon enough echoed by another of Wheeler's Harvard classmates, William A. Davis. See Davis's *Biographical Notice of Charles Stearns Wheeler, A.M., Who Died at Leipzig, June 13, 1843—Aged Twenty-Six Years* (Boston: James Munroe, 1843), 4–6.

24. See *Harvardiana: Volume III*, ed. Charles Stearns Wheeler et al. (Cambridge, MA: John Owen, 1837), iii.

25. Samuel Taylor Coleridge's "Dejection: An Ode," quoted from its eight-stanza version as given in Thoreau's personally owned edition of *The Poetical Works of Coleridge, Shelley, and Keats: Complete in One Volume. Stereotyped by John Howe* (Philadelphia: J. Grigg, 1832), 48–49.

26. For a transcription and photo of Channing's comment—"a feeble caricature of the true house"—on the title page of his personal copy of *Walden*, see the published auction catalog entitled *The Stephen H. Wakeman Collection of Books of Nineteenth Century American Writers [. . .]* (New York: American Art Association, 1924), Item no. 1005 (no pagination), and Bradley P. Dean, "The Title-Page Illustration of *Walden*," in *Thoreau Society Bulletin* 245 (Fall 2003): 7–8.

27. See Warren S. Tryon and William Charvat, eds., *The Cost Books of Ticknor and Fields and Their Predecessors, 1832–1858* (New York: Bibliographical Society of America, 1949), 289, 368, 477. See also James Dawson, "John Andrew, Wood Engraver," *Thoreau Society Bulletin* 250 (Winter 2005): 5.

28. I am indebted to Walter Harding for his findings regarding corresponding subtitles. See Harding, ed., *Walden: An Annotated Edition* (Boston: Houghton Mifflin, 1995), xiiin1.

29. See Raymond R. Borst, *Henry David Thoreau: A Descriptive Bibliography* (Pittsburgh, PA: University of Pittsburgh Press, 1982), 16–21. Thoreau subtitled his book "*or, Life in the Woods*" from his very first manuscript, version A, of 1847; see Ronald Earl Clapper, "The Making of Walden: A Genetic Text," 2 vols. (PhD diss., University of California, 1967), 1:39.

30. See Stanley Cavell, *The Senses of Walden* (New York: Viking Press, 1972), 3.

31. The quote is here stated as stemming from "the back paste-down endpaper of the manuscript volume from which *Journal 8* is edited." Cavell, *Senses of Walden*, 3.

32. See Stanley Cavell, *The Senses of Walden: An Expanded Edition* (1972; Chicago: University of Chicago Press, 1992), 31–32.

33. William James, "Mysticism," in *Varieties of Religious Experience: A Study in Human Nature, Being the Gifford Lectures on Natural Religion Delivered at Edinburgh in 1901–1902* (1902; London: Longmans, Green, 1908): 380–429. Evelyn Underhill, in her classic study of mysticism, also stresses as a cardinal threshold the point at which "supersensual experience ceases to be merely a practical and interesting extension of sensual experience—and passes over into that boundless life where Subject and Object, desirous and desired, are *one.*" See Underhill's *Mysticism: A Study in the Nature and Development of Man's Spiritual Consciousness*, 15th ed. (1911; London: Methuen, 1945), 72.

34. It is well to remember that Thoreau's self-designation as a mystic, as well as a transcendentalist and a natural philosopher, dates to 1853; his addition and editing of the chanticleer motto into the evolving *Walden* manuscript comes in versions D and F, dated to 1852–54, whereas all of the musings on extra-vagance and multivalency in the "Conclusion" chapter of *Walden* date to the F and G versions, that is, to 1853–54. Hence these are not gushing effusions of a supposedly Romantic, youthful Thoreau but very much part and parcel of the seasoned, mature writer.

7

MATERIALITIES OF THOUGHT

BOTANICAL GEOGRAPHY AND THE CURATION OF RESILIENCE IN SUSAN FENIMORE COOPER AND HENRY DAVID THOREAU

Rochelle L. Johnson

> Do not thoughts and men's lives enrich the earth and change the aspect of things as much as a new growth of wood?
>
> —Henry David Thoreau, Journal, July 3, 1840

This essay grows out of archival encounters with three artifacts of literary culture, each pertaining to the growth of ecological understanding in the mid-nineteenth century. Through my discussion, I hope to demonstrate how the work of the environmental humanities might help disrupt our present culture's troubling disregard for the findings of ecological science, which, as I note, emerged in part through mid-nineteenth-century literary-natural history. For my purposes, I reframe the environmental humanities as the *material* humanities, so as to emphasize these three artifacts of literary culture, as well as the intellectual history they represent, as themselves constitutive of "the entanglement of matter and meaning" that *is* earthly existence.[1] As Thoreau suggests in his Journal entry of July 3, 1840, thoughts and lives, as well as "a new growth of wood," inform landscapes as well as cultures (*PJ* 1:147). In the pages that follow, I perform an excavation of these artifacts of the intellectual history of ecological thought to explore their potential presence in our world today—here, at the boundaries of environmental renewal and environmental collapse, and at the borders of climate instability and climate catastrophe.

Scholars now widely recognize Henry David Thoreau's significance as a proto-ecological thinker, one key to the development of environmental thought in the United States. We acknowledge him as a skilled scientific collector, an early describer of the principles of forest succession, and a gifted natural historian whose phenological studies inform our own mapping of both nineteenth-century species distribution and contemporary climate change.[2] We tend, however, to treat Thoreau's prescient ecological insights as an anomaly in nineteenth-century literary naturalism. Especially in the popular-cultural imagination, but also within our scholarship, we figure Thoreau as a bit of an environmental eccentric, thereby suggesting that his pathbreaking ecological insights were isolated or even fortuitous. Yet when we look beyond the boundary of Thoreau's individual forays into ecological thought, we must reckon with a wider cultural concern over the impacts of nineteenth-century landscape alteration.

Just beyond the western border of Massachusetts, in eastern New York State, a contemporary of Thoreau observed her home landscape closely and also articulated now-recognized concepts in the science of ecology. By examining Thoreau's ecological expressions in relation to those of his New York contemporary, Susan Fenimore Cooper (1813–94), we confront the possibility of a more powerful and prevalent environmental consciousness in mid-nineteenth-century America. In Cooper and Thoreau, we encounter largely self-taught (albeit widely read) naturalists who lived 240 miles apart but expressed similar alarm over the increasingly compromised American landscape. I argue here that when we figure mid-nineteenth-century literary environmentalism as isolated and anomalous, we distort the wider prevalence of environmental concern in an era largely thought to lack environmental awareness. We also, however, reinforce a troubling history of building boundaries between the humanities and the sciences. Confronting this wider legacy of literary environmentalism not only demands recognizing the emergence of ecological principles through literary naturalism but also urges consideration of the effects of silencing this literary-scientific convergence in environmental history.

In the field of archaeology, artifacts are understood to reveal what members of a community value, how they engage with the physical world, and how they understand the place of humanity in the cosmos. Following this line of inquiry, I argue that three artifacts of literary culture—a journal fragment, a leaf from a book, and a newspaper advertisement—embody a materiality that informs ideation. They can be understood both as vestiges of the intellectual history of environmental understanding and as the ruins, as it were, of cultural possibility. Thoreau's and Cooper's insights into the limits of nature's capacity for replenishment might serve as thresholds between the presumed but artificial borders of materiality and intellectual history, of science and literature, and of their historical moment and our own.

The first artifact consists of a few leaves from Henry David Thoreau's Journal, in which we witness Thoreau working toward the idea that nature's apparent durability masks a fragility that requires human nurturing (figure 11).[3]

On November 25, 1860, winter rolled into Concord with a force no one could miss. During the night, a cold wind shook the houses, leaving sleepy inhabitants like Thoreau to note "a general deficiency of bed clothes." Morning brought "windows . . . as handsomely covered with frost as ever in winter" (JM 9). Even the crows were acting differently, gathering to feed and roost closer to the village; they "seem weary," a "cold gleam . . . reflected from the back & wings of each" (JM 10). "Winter weather," Thoreau notes, "has come suddenly this year" (JM 9).

In spite of the cold, Thoreau headed outdoors, where he counted, measured, and compared tree rings, using them as a tool to better understand tree growth rates, seed dispersal, and, ultimately, landscape history. While he spent most of his time observing trees, he also considered the relationships between new tree growth and landscape alteration and between wood chopping, agriculture, and reforestation. By the end of this cold day, he suggests that close observation of these altered landscapes can reveal their history of human use. If people would learn the signs of historical human presence in the landscape, they might better be able to preserve the health of those places. In other words, if Euro-Americans could observe their effects on the landscape more attentively, they might better curate nature's vitality.

Thoreau starts his outing by examining a "spruce plank from the RR [railroad] bridge." He finds that its rings measure five and a half inches from the center of the tree. He calculates each ring's approximate measurement, figuring the tree's annual growth rate. He then compares this specimen to that of another black spruce nearby, noting the variance in their growth rates. He observes that *other* species grow at considerably different rates. Certain trees grow higher and thicker than others in similar amounts of time: for instance, he explains, "The larch has made nearly 2ce [*sic*] as much wood as the spruce in the same time" (JM 9).

Figure 11. Henry D. Thoreau's Journal, November 25, 1860. The Morgan Library & Museum, New York, MA 1302.29, purchased by Pierpont Morgan with the Wakeman Collection, 1909.[4]

He then moves beyond comparative growth rates to the processes of tree reproduction. He examines a single species, noting its population density in relation to its new growth, and while doing so he gives thought to how

the land has been used by humans in recent times. For instance, the prox-
imity of some land formerly used as pasture to a large white pine wood
allows Thoreau to consider landscape use in relation to tree repopulation.
Seedlings grow more numerously, he observes, under less dense patches of
older trees. His conclusion: "White pines will spring up in the more open
parts of a white p[ine] wood—even under pines—though they are thin
and feeble—just in proportion to the density of the large pines—& when
the large trees are quite dense—they will not spring up at all" (JM 12).

At each step of his walk, Thoreau notes his location, often in terms of
who owns the property. His conception of space reflects both tree species
and human property rights, again signaling the relationship between nonhuman species and human inhabitation patterns. His observations on this
blustery day take him to several patches of land bearing nicknames or the
names of their owners: he observes trees at Ministerial Swamp (JM 9), in
"Hosmers [*sic*] Meadow just beyond Lupine Hill" (JM 10), "in the road
beyond Dennis'," "in the young woodland N of J. P. Bs cold pool" (JM 11),
"by Dugans [*sic*]," and "on the S side of the Tommy Wheeler hollow" (JM
13). In several locations, he notes that when a cleared pasture returns to
woods, "pitch pines—white pines & birches [fill] up" the formerly cleared
land, and that when those species reach approximately fifteen years of age,
"shrub and other oaks [begin] to show themselves," "gradually" engulfing
and obscuring introduced "apple trees & [stone] walls & fences" (JM 12).
One might notice these growth patterns and surmise when a patch of land
was first cleared. As he suggests, "the different condition & history of the
ground is very apparent" to one who takes time to look (JM 11).

Thoreau expresses particular satisfaction on this November day in two
things: first, that the physical world seems to operate according to "natural
laws" encouraging the regeneration of a wood (JM 12) and, second, that he
can be a participant in the vitality and processes he observes. At one point,
he expresses these satisfactions together, figuring himself as a beneficiary
of the natural laws he sees at work: as he walks through a former pasture
that is slowly returning to woods, he remarks, "I remember perhaps that
15 years ago there was not a single tree in this pasture— not a germinating
seed—of one—& now it is a pretty dense forest 10 feet high." Similarly, he
notices that plants are overtaking both rocks laid bare due to grazing cows
and paths formerly created by the cows: "The cow paths the hollows where
I slid in the winter—the rocks—are fast being enveloped & becoming

rabbit walks & hollows & rocks in the woods," He then follows this with an expression of gratitude for nature's capacity to re-wild and for his own ability to find pleasure in witnessing that reparation: "I confess," he writes, "that I love to be convinced of this inextinguishable vitality in Nature. I would rather that my body should be buried in a soil thus wide-awake—than in a mere inert & dead earth" (JM 12). The spirit finding comfort in the vital is one form of the entanglement of matter and meaning.

For Thoreau, this November day entails not only in-depth study of forest succession but also a study in discerning nature's healing following human landscape alteration. And as we know, November 25, 1860, was but one of many days when Thoreau worked to better understand how he might learn human and natural history through attentive observation. Yet observation—sight, seeing, witnessing, beholding—*was* essential to his growing knowledge concerning natural processes. Thoreau announces as much in his Journal when he asks, "How is any scientific discovery made? Why[,] the discoverer takes it into his head first— He must all but *see* it" (JM 10; emphasis added). In the familiar emphasis here on sight as primary to human perception, Thoreau also gestures to the relationship between witnessing and formulating an idea. He writes "He must all but see it" because his own hypotheses concerning tree growth and the re-wilding of cleared lands depend on the many things he views. Scientific theory springs forth from an observant amateur alert to the details of his world.

Through this literary artifact, we glimpse an important step in the history of science. Here we find a nascent ecology, emergent principles of forest succession and botanical distribution, and a building understanding of what we now call "cultural geography"—all the result of an attentive man's walk on a frosty November day.

The second artifact is the title page from the 1851 illustrated edition of Susan Fenimore Cooper's *Rural Hours*, which was first published in 1850. This illustrated edition testifies to the success of Cooper's book of nature observations; in fact, *Rural Hours* saw nine editions before 1887, when it was severely abridged for yet another issuing. Unlike Thoreau's best-known book of nature observations, *Walden*, Cooper's volume remained in print throughout most of her century. Like Thoreau's amateur science, however, Cooper's ecological insights also garnered the early notice of scientists (see figure 12).

RURAL HOURS,

BY a Lady

Red-Throated Humming Bird.

Endicott's Lith. N.Y.

NEW YORK

G. P. PUTNAM

1851.

Figure 12. Title page, Susan Fenimore Cooper's *Rural Hours* (1850), 1851 illustrated edition. Courtesy of the Fenimore Art Museum and Research Library, Cooperstown, New York.

We read in *Rural Hours* of a June afternoon when Cooper studied a hillside to discern its traces of human presence—much like Thoreau would in 1860. Like him, she expresses some degree of pleasure in having the skill to identify manifestations of human history within natural history. And also like Thoreau, who noted that "the different condition & history of the ground is very apparent" when one takes notice of it, Cooper "pick[s] out parcels of land in widely different conditions" as she walks along a hillside bordering her native village.⁵ Finally, just as Thoreau did, Cooper notes the manifest effects of human use of the area, pointing out that people must learn to *see* these evidences of human history and landscape alteration.

Cooper remarks that even standing in one place, she can make out four different stages of agricultural cultivation evident in the landscape, ranging from fields just recently cleared to land cleared but not tilled, and from patches plowed and seeded for the first time to land that has been in cultivation for over fifty years, since the early days of Euro-American settlement in her area. "To one familiar with the country," she writes, "there is a certain pleasure in thus beholding the agricultural history of the neighborhood unfolding before one, following upon the farms in sight these progressive steps in cultivation" (*RH* 89–90). Again, seeing—beholding—is key.

But even wilder-looking hillsides, she explains—those never having undergone tillage—reveal signs of their own history, including human presence and domestication. "Those wild pastures upon hill-sides, where the soil has never been ploughed, look very differently from other fallows. Here you observe a little hillock rounding over a decayed stump, there a petty hollow where some large tree has been uprooted by the storm." These hillsides "bear a kind of heaving, billowy character" (*RH* 91). Their grassy, hillocky contours mask the former roots of cleared trees. Cooper explains that these ghost-roots, along with soil erosion and wandering cows, contribute to the billowy effect that she describes: "These ridges are formed by the roots of old trees, and remain long after the wood has entirely decayed. Even on level ground there is always an elevation about the root of an old tree and upon a hill-side, these petty knolls show more clearly as they are thrown into relief by the light; they become much bolder, also, from the washing of the soil, which accumulates above, and is carried away from the lower side of the trunk, leaving, often, a portion of the root bare in that direction. Of course, the older a wood and the larger its trees, the more clearly will this billowy character be marked. The tracks of the cattle also make the formation more ridge-like, uniting one little knoll with another, for when feeding, they generally follow one another . . . and upon a hill-side they naturally take a horizontal course" (*RH* 91). The hillside geography, Cooper suggests, is a merging of human inhabitation (the wood chopper's stumps and grazing cows) and natural processes (the decaying root cavities and flow of rainwater).

Cooper points out to her reader the importance of seeing these traces of history in the landscape by claiming that, to the untrained eye, her region might appear less domesticated than it is. The signs of cultivation can be subtle, she says, but are still within sight: "there are softer touches also, telling the . . . story of recent cultivation." Rare, remnant patches of native wildflowers signal a displaced flora "surrounded on all sides by ripening crops of eastern grains and grasses" (*RH* 91). One particular channel seems to divide the nonnative, Old World flora from the remnant population of the native flora now decreasingly evident in the New World: "A path made by the workmen and cattle crosses the field, and one treads at every step upon plantain, that regular path-weed of the Old World; following this track, we come to a little runnel, which is dry and grassy now, though doubtless at one time the bed of a considerable spring; the banks are several feet high, and it is filled with native plants; on one side stands a thorn-tree, whose morning shadow falls upon grasses and clovers brought from beyond the seas, while in the afternoon, it lies on gyromias and moose-flowers, sarsaparillas and cahoshes, which bloomed here for ages, when the eye of the red man alone beheld them" (*RH* 91–92). The competing flora, then, also testifies to recent human activity in the area.

Whereas Thoreau traces human activity through pitch pine, Cooper does so through plantain. Both writers, however, recognize the relationship between plant distribution and the history of human clearing, just as they both value their abilities to discern how a landscape conveys its human history. Doing so requires the trained eye: observing, beholding, seeing.

The third artifact dates from June 1887, twenty-five years after the death of Thoreau, when an advertisement including both his and Cooper's names appeared in a local newspaper in Cooperstown, New York (see figure 13). The advertisement, issued by publisher Houghton Mifflin of Boston, alerted readers to the new, abridged edition of a book by the celebrated Cooperstown author Susan Fenimore Cooper: another edition of *Rural*

RURAL HOURS.

By Susan Fenimore Cooper. New edition, abridged. 1 vol., 16 mo., $1.25.

"Miss Cooper is the eldest daughter of the great novelist, and received her inspiration from the scenes she witnessed around her quiet country home at Cooperstown. She may have been said to have been the first American who wrote the impressions which the progress of the seasons make upon a cultured and poetic mind."—[Philadelphia Record.

No one, not excepting Thoreau, has written more delightfully of the charms of country life, of the advance of the seasons, and of the ways of birds and flowers. To those who live in the country this book is an education toward interest in common things.—[Christian Advocate, New York.

For sale by all Booksellers. Sent by mail, postpaid, on receipt of price by the publishers.

HOUGHTON, MIFFLIN & CO., Boston.

Figure 13. Advertisement for *Rural Hours*. The *Cooperstown (NY) Freeman's Journal*, June 17, 1887, p. 2 (enlarged). Courtesy of the Fenimore Art Museum and Research Library, Cooperstown, New York.

Hours, which had first appeared in print thirty-seven years earlier.[6] Strikingly, the advertisement links Cooper's work to Thoreau's because of its detailed attention to the landscape.[7]

The advertisement contains two endorsements for this new edition of Cooper's book. The first, taken from the *Philadelphia Record*, reads as follows: "Miss Cooper is the eldest daughter of the great novelist, and received her inspiration from the scenes she witnessed around her quiet country home at Cooperstown. She may have been said to have been the first American who wrote the impressions which the progress of the seasons make upon a cultured and poetic mind."[8] Indeed, Cooper's *Rural Hours* appeared four years before Thoreau's *Walden*, and some of her contemporaries viewed it as a signal national achievement in terms of landscape representation.[9]

For example, upon the book's first publication in 1850, scientist Spencer Fullerton Baird, then assistant secretary at the Smithsonian Institution, expressed his appreciation for Cooper's contribution to the nation's emerging literary natural history. He wrote her a letter of congratulations, suggesting that she was the first American who had written a certain kind of place-based book—a genre well established in British natural history but heretofore unknown, to his mind, in the United States (see figure 14).

His letter also, however, reveals that he considers Cooper's literary achievement to have a cultural-scientific importance, as well: "American naturalists, as well as simple lovers of nature have long been familiar with the works of [William] Howitt, Gilbert White, [John Leonard] Knapp, and other 'Old Country' writers in the field of literature which you so delightfully cultivate, but it has always been a subject of regret that nothing American was in our hands. It is true that [John James] Audubon, [Alexander] Wilson, [John] Godman, [William] Bartram, [Benjamin Smith] Barton, and some others have given us beautiful biographies of Nature and her works, but these have all been of a kind not well fitted to fill an evident void. May we not hope that your success will but stimulate you to further effort in this walk, sure as we may be that, like 'The Natural History of Selborne,' antiquity will but lend to our 'Rural Hours,' such charms. A book like yours is what we have needed."[10] Baird aligns Cooper's work most closely with established and respected natural historians and, specifically, Gilbert White, who pursued scientific theories through his close and repeated seasonal observations. In Baird's estimation, the new nation "needed" an author to attend closely to a region in order to represent—in literary form—the natural processes evident there. Cooper performed this cultural function.

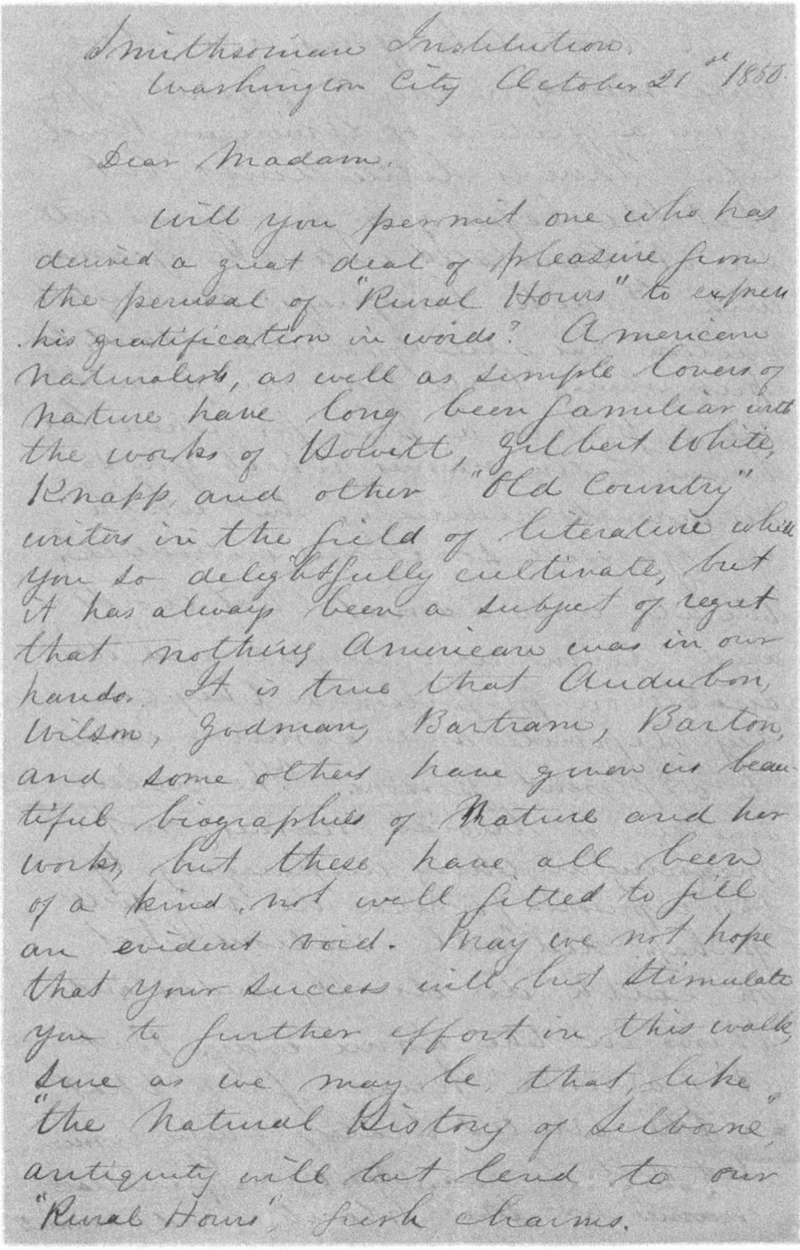

Smithsonian Institution,
Washington City October 21ˢᵗ 1850

Dear Madam,

Will you permit one who has derived a great deal of pleasure from the perusal of "Rural Hours" to express his gratification in words? American naturalists, as well as simple lovers of nature have long been familiar with the works of Howitt, Gilbert White, Knapp, and other "Old Country" writers in the field of literature which you so delightfully cultivate, but it has always been a subject of regret that nothing American was in our hands. It is true that Audubon, Wilson, Godman, Bartram, Barton, and some others have given us beautiful biographies of Nature and her works, but these have all been of a kind not well fitted to fill an evident void. May we not hope that your success will but stimulate you to further effort in this walk, sure as we may be that, like "the Natural History of Selborne", antiquity will but lend to our "Rural Hours" fresh charms.

Figure 14. Letter from Spencer Fullerton Baird to Susan Fenimore Cooper, October 21, 1850. Beinecke Library, YCAL MSS 415, box 13, folder 349, James Fenimore Cooper Collection, Series 1: Correspondence. Courtesy Yale Collection of American Literature, Beinecke Rare Book and Manuscript Library, New Haven, CT.

The second endorsement specifically mentions Thoreau as also a contributor to this important genre of literary natural history. Here, Cooper and Thoreau figure as educators of readers concerning what perhaps should have been common knowledge about natural phenomena: "No one, not excepting Thoreau, has written more delightfully of the charms of country life, of the advance of the seasons, and of the ways of birds and flowers. To those who live in the country this book is an education toward interest in common things."[11] In "delightfully" educating readers about "common things"—the "advance of the seasons," "the ways of the birds and flowers"—Cooper and Thoreau contributed something specific, something unique, to American culture. Like Gilbert White before them, they communicated ways of understanding a local landscape in a manner that we now call "ecological," with attention, that is, to seasonal processes and patterns, to the distribution and succession of plant species, and to the fact that the landscape attested to its manipulation by humanity.

Thoreau and Cooper often explored landscape as revelatory of a story of human habitation: a hillside might be read for its indications of past human use. Thoreau might observe a pattern of trees and surmise, on that basis, precisely when trees no longer standing were cut down. Similarly, Cooper might make out dead tree roots marking a hillside as an indication of recent agricultural use. One can read these certain signs in a patch of land and determine when it was last cultivated, when it was abandoned, and from whence the seeds of its current plants appeared, as well as why particular plants species now thrive there.

Both Thoreau and Cooper express satisfaction at their abilities to so clearly discern the settlement histories apparent in their surroundings, yet they both also indicate that not everyone sees this history. Even while they witness the seasonal vibrance of their natural surroundings, they express doubt at the human ability to nurture their surroundings such that they might endure the growing Euro-American presence. Their works contain their admissions of doubt that humanity can curb its appetite for landscape alteration, and both authors express apprehension concerning the possibility of long-term ecological health. As the *Freeman's Journal* advertisement suggests, these "common things" remained unknown to many readers, who required the "education" that these authors provide.

Indeed, Thoreau and Cooper both suggest that human ignorance of common things can impede what Thoreau called in his Journal "natural laws" (JM 12). On November 25, 1860, Thoreau argues, for example, that wood choppers should not cut down trees that are too young to send up new growth in the form of shoots. Yet they do, and in chopping down the twenty-five- to thirty-year-old oaks that originated as the shoots of oaks that are now merely nearby stumps, the choppers prevent healthy rejuvenation of a wood. He presumes that the choppers fail to notice that these shoots—which the choppers mistake as freestanding, fully fledged trees—grow next to the stumps of what were their parent trees. They cut the shoots, or sprouts, for their wood, thereby preventing future growth: "I see much oak wood cut at 30 years of age—sproutwood[.] Many stumps which have only 25 or 30 rings send up no shoots—because they are the sprouts from old stumps which you may still see by their sides—& so are really old trees & exhausted. The chopper should foresee this," Thoreau states, "when he cuts down a wood" (JM 13). The woodchopper might notice the varying sizes of tree width, recognize the shoots as the shoots of exhausted trees, and leave them to grow so as to replenish the wood. "The chopper should foresee this." The chopper *should* see this. The "history of the ground [*should be*] very apparent" through its "condition" (JM 11). But it was not, apparently, and in many of his writings, Thoreau, like Cooper, mourned this common inattention to common things.

We have no evidence that Cooper and Thoreau ever met and only a little evidence that he read—and then wrote—her name one day.[12] Yet as the example of Cooper and Thoreau attests, human beings sometimes have their closest affinities with people they never know—a haunting thought, but perhaps also a consoling one.[13] These affinities may emerge from shared physical experience or from shared ways of witnessing the world, perceiving, for example, that a hillside attests to its own modification through its botanical distribution, that the impact of a cut shoot differs from that of a hacked mother-tree, that a runnel highlights a threatened native flora, or that a landscape can reveal the limits of nature's proliferation. Taken together, these three artifacts suggest that Cooper and Thoreau worked toward an *idea* that might be phrased like this: a humanity attuned to the way in which a landscape reveals its history, human and otherwise, might be better equipped to understand nature's processes and its capacity—as well as its limits—for resilience. This idea now serves as the driving impetus behind the science of ecology, but in the nineteenth century, Cooper's and Thoreau's proto-ecological insights stood at the nearly imperceptible border between science and amateur nature observation and between science and literature.

As is well documented, the role of science shifted considerably in both Europe and the United States during this period, such that these writers' environmental insights might be said to exemplify the blurry boundaries between science and literature and between natural history as observation and ecological awareness as apprehension.[14] Historian of science Lorraine Daston describes the nineteenth century's growing boundary between a more objective, professional science and a more subjective, amateur knowledge as a distinction concerning the role of the imagination: in "the mid-nineteenth century, when new ideals and practices of scientific objectivity transformed the persona of the scientist and the sources of scientific authority," both scientific professionals and the general public began "opposing the imagination to science," seeing science and its hard facts as separate from the imaginative arts.[15] As the bifurcation deepened, science and the arts (such as literature) became increasingly divorced in practice as well as in the popular culture. The work of literary naturalists largely escaped "scientific" attention.[16]

Indeed, it would be years, and in some cases decades, before science would name these ecological principles that Cooper and Thoreau described.[17] Still, their conjectures became some of the central concepts in ecology: biodiversity loss, ecological exchange, mutualism or species interdependence, competitive exclusion, parasitism, biogeographic redistribution, ecosystem services, invasion ecology. In short, the boundary between what came to be considered professional science and their amateur observations resulted in science working for decades toward the ecological principles that Cooper and Thoreau had apprehended.

Beyond this, their work stands as evidence of an early, largely disregarded cultural-intellectual capacity to discern impending environmental collapse. Their prescient understandings now serve as a sort of archaeological ruin—the site of a nascent, but still fully unrealized, *idea*: widespread landscape alteration severely damages nature's resilience.

The word "idea" originates from the Greek ιδέα, meaning "look," "semblance," "form," and "species"; the stem word meaning is "to see." As the *Oxford English Dictionary* makes plain, the Greek word is thus analogous in derivation and original sense to the classical Latin *species*, from *specere*, "to see, behold." An idea, then, is a seeing, a species of thought emerging from a spectacle beheld, a model of understanding based on what is seen. A species of thought has, like every species, a certain valence in nature and culture that a collective civilization may never directly recognize or witness. Even if an idea remains unknown to most people, however, like any other species, it nonetheless contributes to the "entanglement of matter and meaning" that *is* the "nature we seek to understand."[18] Because, of course, in spite of the solidification of the science of ecology and, in 1973, the first formal use of the word "resilience" to indicate an essential quality of a healthy ecosystem, significant portions of the human population resist the very notion of ecosystems being under threat.[19] And even more basic, as recent articles attest, the amateur—and even *professional*—close study of the essential facts and phenomena of natural history is itself under threat.[20] Yet, as Thomas Pfau suggests, ideas have "agency."[21] Like a plant that will ever so slightly alter its growth direction to avoid potential danger or angle its emergence so as to capture the sun's maximum light or reach out slowly to its neighbors through its root structure to signal a nearby toxin, an idea may continue to perform its work in—and on—the world, whether the mass of men acknowledge its existence or can identify it by name.

Just as we might begin to curate the resilience of a growth of wood by understanding its botanical geography, so we might curate the resilience of historical thought by understanding its origins and distribution. When we realize that basic principles of ecology and environmental resilience emerged in the minds of common people who simply observed their changing home landscapes with regularity and thoughtfulness, we must also recognize these concepts as foundational to the culture of the United States—and not as contingent, academic, rarefied, or recent. As Pfau suggests, "If there is to be such a thing as responsible and responsive human understanding, its initial presumption has to be in favor of the substantive identity and temporal continuity of those phenomena with which the intellect takes itself to be engaged." Cooper's and Thoreau's notions of ecological resilience present us with evidence of an idea, a "charismatic presence within a social imaginary."[22] Given our own era's troubling disregard for ecological principles, we concede that Cooper's and Thoreau's concerns regarding ecological fecundity remain well warranted. Yet, a recovery of their idea might help us engage in "the cultural work that . . . is the process by which the unimaginable becomes, finally, the obvious."[23] That is, its recovery forces us to begin to grasp that environmental grief and ecological understanding are not modern-day experiences alone. We can reclaim these emotions, as well, as part of the nation's history.

If, as Wendy Wheeler argues, the material humanities "must mean a keen awareness of the layers and *the growth of meanings*," we will want to attend to the "substantive identity and temporal continuity" of Cooper's and Thoreau's ideas.[24] The material artifacts they left behind inform ecological understanding; they helped grow the meaning of that particular science. Their ideas certainly have, "themselves, agency," as Pfau claims; they indeed might be said to have served a "charismatic presence within a social imaginary."[25] "Ideologies," on the other hand, "are," in the words of James Engell, "often nothing more than the hardened cinders left by an extinguished fire of ideas."[26] Even as we dwell amid ideologies centered on endless growth and resource extraction, we may uncover a centuries-long presence in the social imaginary, name it as a species of thought, and begin again to manifest its meaning into matter. We might rekindle its fire, that seemingly inextinguishable vitality that lights the cold night sky from among the stumps and seedlings on a hillside.

Notes

1. The phrase is from Karen Barad's subtitle: *Meeting the Universe Halfway: Quantum Physics and the Entanglement of Meaning and Matter* (Durham, NC: Duke University Press, 2007).
2. This body of scholarship has emerged across the disciplines. On Thoreau as collector, see Laura Dassow Walls, *Seeing New World: Henry David Thoreau and Nineteenth-Century Natural Science* (Madison: University of Wisconsin Press, 1995); on Thoreau, forest succession, and ecology, see Daniel Botkin, *No Man's Garden: Thoreau and a New Vision for Civilization and Nature* (Washington, D.C.: Island Press, 2001), esp. 33–36, and David R. Foster, *Thoreau's Country: Journey through a Transformed Landscape* (Cambridge, MA: Harvard University Press, 1999); on Thoreau's phenological studies informing climate data, see Richard Primack, *Walden Warming: Climate Change Comes to Thoreau's Woods* (Chicago: University of Chicago Press, 2014). For Thoreau's contributions to environmental thought, see Robert Kuhn McGregor, *A Wider View of the Universe: Henry Thoreau's Study of Nature* (Chicago: University of Illinois Press, 1997). Lawrence Buell, *The Environmental Imagination: Thoreau, Nature Writing, and the Formation of American Culture* (Cambridge, MA: Harvard University Press, 1995), offers a note citing early studies that advocate for Thoreau as "a pioneer ecologist" (363): see 542n57. Walls's *Seeing New Worlds* remains the most thorough study of Thoreau's contributions to the science.

3. In the quotations from the Journal entry that follow in the text, I cite page numbers of the transcription of the entry at the Writings of Henry D. Thoreau website, Journal Manuscript vol. 33, http://thoreau.library.ucsb.edu/writings_journals33.html (hereafter cited in the text as JM).

4. Thoreau, Henry David, 1817–1862, Journal: autograph manuscript: [Concord], 1857 Apr. 2–July 31, page [8], entry dated 1860 Nov. 25, continued, "proobbably [*sic*] blown so far in the fall," MA 1302.29, Morgan Library & Museum, New York, NY.

5. Thoreau, Journal Manuscript 33, 11; Susan Fenimore Cooper, *Rural Hours* (1850), ed. Rochelle Johnson and Daniel Patterson (Athens: University of Georgia Press, 1998), 89 (hereafter cited in the text as *RH*).

6. Advertisement for Susan Fenimore Cooper's *Rural Hours, Cooperstown (NY) Freeman's Journal*, June 17, 1887, 2. This severely abridged 1887 edition followed nine earlier editions of the full text of *Rural Hours*.

7. The advertisement likely invokes Thoreau's *Walden* (1854); his Journal was not well known at this time.

8. Advertisement, 2.

9. On reviews of *Rural Hours*, see my *Passions for Nature: Nineteenth-Century America's Aesthetics of Alienation* (Athens: University of Georgia Press, 2009), 52–57, 143–44.

10. Spencer Fullerton Baird, ALS to Susan Fenimore Cooper, Beinecke Library, YCAL MSS 415, box 13, folder 349, James Fenimore Cooper Collection, Series 1: Correspondence, Yale Collection of American Literature, Beinecke Rare Book and Manuscript Library, New Haven, CT.

11. Advertisement, 2.

12. On Thoreau's reference to Cooper, see Johnson, *Passions for Nature*, 242n9.

13. My thanks to James Engell for planting the seed of this thought.

14. See Lorraine Daston, "Fear and Loathing of the Imagination in Science," *Daedalus* 127, no. 1 (Winter 1998): 73–95, and Daniel Goldstein, "'Yours for Science': The Smithsonian Institution's Correspondents and the Shape of Scientific Community in Nineteenth-Century America," *Isis* 85, no. 4 (December 1994): 573–99.

15. Daston, "Fear and Loathing," 74.

16. Rochelle L. Johnson, "Henry David Thoreau and the Literature of the Environment," in *A Companion to American Literature*, 3 vols., edited by Susan Belasco, Theresa Strouth Gaul, Linck Johnson, and Michael Soto (Hoboken, NJ: John Wiley & Sons, 2020), 2:86–101.

17. On the delay between Thoreau's findings and their recognition by scientists, see Foster, *Thoreau's Country*, 227–28.

18. Barad, *Meeting the Universe Halfway*, 67.

19. C. S. Holling, "Resilience and the Stability of Ecological Systems," *Annual Review of Ecology and Systematics* 4, no. 1 (1973): 14.

20. See John G. T. Anderson, "Why Ecology Needs Natural History," *American Scientist* 105, no. 5 (September/October 2017): 105, https://www.americanscientist.org/article/why-ecology-needs-natural-history; Richard Conniff, "Our Natural History, Endangered," *New York Times Sunday Review*, April 1, 2016, https://www.nytimes.com/2016/04/03/opinion/ournatural-history-endangered.html; and Ed Yong, "Natural History Museums Are Teeming with Undiscovered Species," *Atlantic*, February 8, 2016, https://www.theatlantic.com/science/archive/2016/02/the-unexplored-marvels-locked-away-in-our-natural-history-museums/459306/.

21. Thomas Pfau, *Minding the Modern: Human Agency, Intellectual Traditions, and Responsible Knowledge* (Notre Dame, IN: University of Notre Dame Press, 2013), 58.

22. Pfau, *Minding the Modern*, 60, 58.

23. Philip Fisher, *Hard Facts: Setting and Form in the American Novel* (New York: Oxford, 1987), 8.

24. Wendy Wheeler, "Natural Play, Natural Metaphor, and Natural Stories: Biosemiotic Realism," in *Material Ecocriticism*, ed. Serenella Iovino and Serpil Opperman (Bloomington: Indiana University Press, 2014), 78; Pfau, *Minding the Modern*, 60.

25. Pfau, *Minding the Modern*, 58. As Daegan Miller eloquently suggests, "Thought, when cared for, becomes immortal," in "On Care in Dark Times," *Edge Effects*, April 12, 2016, http://edgeeffects.net/care-dark-times/.

26. James Engell, "Romantic Poetry and the Culture of Modernity," *Literary Imagination: The Review of the Association of Literary Scholars and Critics* 3, no. 1 (2001): 96.

8

"A CRASH IS APT TO GRATE AGREEABLY ON OUR EARS"

THOREAU AND DISSONANCE

Danielle Follett

For Thoreau, music refers not only to material acoustic vibrations but also carries a metaphysical and moral significance. Thoreau's conception of sound is inextricable from his metaphysical views, and in his writings sonorous harmony resonates with overtones of spiritual harmony. Simultaneously, he expands his definition of musical harmony to include sounds conventionally considered to be dissonant and states that all sounds are musical. This essay investigates the philosophical implications of Thoreau's aesthetics of all-musicality and dissonant harmony, especially in the context of his spiritual and moral interpretation of sound. The discussion will necessarily take us by way of his views on violence.

In his earliest journal writings, under the rubrics of "harmony" and "sphere music," Thoreau sketches a theory of sound in which spiritual and acoustic harmony are intertwined. For example, in 1840 he writes: "[Music] is God's voice—the divine breath audible" (*PJ* 1:144).[1] Such thoughts are not unique to Thoreau's youth but are found throughout his writings, although the word "God" becomes less common. In 1853 he writes that "the strains of the æolian harp & of the wood thrush are the truest & loftiest preachers that I know now left on this earth" (*PJ* 7:216). And in "Higher Laws," Thoreau imagines John Farmer's experience of the sound of a flute which brought a moral message from a higher sphere (*W* 222). For Thoreau, just as for Emerson, the spiritual is inseparable from the sensory; Thoreau was no materialist, and although his idealist metaphysical views often remain implicit, they inform his writings from the first to the last.[2]

Harmony, for Thoreau, seems to refer to the holistic interrelatedness of existence, which is acoustically embodied in the physiological experience of resonance; it is physically manifested in natural law and spiritually in the moral principles he terms "higher laws." In *A Week*, Thoreau writes, "Music is the sound of the universal laws promulgated" (*Wk* 175). Historically, the concept of harmony also includes a political aspect, an idea of solidarity and justice, in the progressive uses of the word in eighteenth- and nineteenth-century America, such as in Robert Owen's New Harmony experiment and in Fourierist discourse. Encompassing these various dimensions—natural, spiritual, moral, aesthetic, political—the term *harmony* was widely used in Thoreau's time, and Thoreau's own uses of it are numerous.

Thoreau's association of the musical and the metaphysical participates in a longer philosophical history, to which it cannot be reduced, but nor can it be fully understood if seen outside this context. He offers a radical rewriting and modernization of the Neoplatonic idea of the music of the spheres by bringing cosmic music down to earth, hearing metaphysical harmony in all sounds, from the lowing of a cow to the squeaking of a pump. The idea of sphere music, associated with Pythagoras, was passed through the immanentist, idealist tradition of Plotinus, Iamblichus (quoted in *A Week*, in the context of sphere music), Ralph Cudworth (whom Thoreau read in the spring of 1840), and Emerson, among many others (*Wk* 176). However, although at times Thoreau maintains this metaphysics of quasimonistic immanence, at others he expresses a strong dualism between a higher and a lower sphere. On one hand, the sonorous and spiritual harmony he perceives is immanent and ubiquitous; for example, in 1851 he writes: "My profession is to be always on the alert to find God in nature—to know his lurking places. To attend all the oratorios—the operas in nature" (*PJ* 4:55). On the other, sometimes Thoreau says that literal sounds are hints of a higher harmony, thus introducing a form of dualism between the earthly and the heavenly. In his early poem, "Rumors from an Æolian Harp," sounds are "rumors" of an ideal place, a source of virtue. Similarly, in 1853, he writes that the ringing telegraph wire "is my redeemer— It always brings a special & a general message to me from the highest" (*PJ* 5:437). Thus, for Thoreau, sound is simultaneously the immediate and concrete embodiment of divine immanence and the hint or reminder of a higher spiritual realm. As Christopher A. Dustin concisely explains, "Thoreau's vision of God as immanent in nature is incomplete without the moment of transcendence that relates the natural and the human to a source lying beyond both."[3] The coexistence of these two spiritual views, immanence and dualism, will be important in the following.

The metaphysical value of sound is a constant throughout Thoreau's life; however, his writings on harmony evolve from the abstract, more overtly religious vocabulary of his youth toward the more sensorial, phenomenal descriptions of real sounds with spiritual overtones of the 1850s. This evolution accompanies the empirical turn in Thoreau's thought and practice around 1850; his metaphysical and spiritual views largely retreat to the background, but they remain present in a more subtle way. That sounds retain a metaphysical charge for Thoreau is clear, for example, in the following description of the song of a bobolink, written in 1857: "He is just touching the strings of his theorbo, his glassichord, his water organ, and one or two notes globe themselves and fall in liquid bubbles from his teeming throat. It is as if he touched his harp within a vase of liquid melody, and when he lifted it out, the notes fell like bubbles from the trembling strings. Methinks they are the most *liquidly* sweet and melodious sounds I ever heard . . . The very divinest part of his strain dropping from his overflowing breast *singultim*, in globes of melody. It is the foretaste of such strains as never fell on mortal ears, to hear which we should rush to our doors and contribute all that we possess and are. Or it seemed as if in that vase full of melody some notes sphered themselves, and from time to time bubbled up to the surface and were with difficulty repressed" (*J* IX:397–98; emphasis in original). Musical birdsong analogically slides into the language of liquidity and spherical shapes like bubbles that drop and burst. Thoreau's language mimes the singularity of the song by inventing new reflexive verbs (the notes "globe themselves," "sphere themselves"). The sound is vividly actual and yet it evokes the divine and the afterlife. We can hear the echoes of sphere music: "one or two notes *globe themselves* and fall in liquid *bubbles* from his teeming throat . . . The very divinest part of his strain dropping from his overflowing breast . . . in *globes* of melody . . . it seemed as if in that vase full of melody some notes *sphered themselves*, and from time to time *bubbled* up to the surface and were with difficulty repressed." Spheres, bubbles, globes: this is Thoreau's immanent and actual terrestrialization of the music of the spheres.

Thoreau heard metaphysical harmony not only in nature but also in the everyday sounds of human life. He desires to "hear a music in the rattling of the tool we work with," writes that "the squeaking of the pump sounds as necessary as the music of the spheres," and evokes "the hum of the shaft or other machinery of a steamboat which at length might become music in a divine hand" (*PJ* 1:213, 229; 4:302). He states several times that *all* varieties of sounds are musical and harmonious. In 1839, he writes: "All sounds, and more than all silence, do fife and drum for us"; in 1851: "Every sound is music now"; and in 1857: "Music is perpetual, and only hearing is intermittent" (*PJ* 1:96, 4:23; *J* IX:245). Based on Thoreau's view of thoroughgoing divine and harmonic immanence, we might name this idea of all-musicality his *panharmonium*.[4] This includes sounds often thought of as discordant, like the sound of a storm; under the rubric "Harmony," he writes in 1837: "Nature makes no noise. The howling storm—the rustling leaf—the pattering rain—are no disturbance, There is an essential and unexplored harmony in them" (*PJ* 1:13). The cosmic "sphere music" is called a "din": "The earth goes gyrating ahead amid such a din of sphere music" (*PJ* 1:34). Thoreau's panharmonium integrates cacophony into the category of harmony or aesthetically agreeable sound.[5] Indeed, even "a crash is apt to grate agreeably on our ears" (*PJ* 1:124).[6]

In 1840, in the first version of the different drummer trope, Thoreau writes: "A man's life should be a stately march to a sweet but unheard music, and when to his fellows it shall seem irregular and inharmonious, he will only be stepping to a livelier measure; or his nicer ear hurry him into a thousand symphonies and concordant variations" (*PJ* 1:146). Discord is only perceived as such by those who are not attuned to the universe's higher harmonies. In *Walden*, Thoreau describes the "harsh and tremendous voice" of a cat-owl: "*Boo-hoo, boo-hoo, boo-hoo!* It was one of the most thrilling discords I ever heard. And yet, if you had a discriminating ear, there were in it the elements of a concord such as these plains never saw nor heard" (*W* 272).[7] In nature there is no dissonance; all acoustic vibrations are ultimately harmonious as they are the sound of the promulgation of universal laws. Harmony, for Thoreau, does not exclude what is commonly considered discord.

However, hearing sphere music in the ruckus of our earth's activities may entail certain complications when we consider dissonance from a spiritual and moral point of view. Are the sounds of *all* earthly actions truly harmonious? As much as we may be tempted to divorce the sonorous from the moral when he starts talking about crashes and dins, that would be abandoning half of the radicality of Thoreau's thought. What does it mean to say that violent cacophony, understood now as music, "is the sound of the universal laws promulgated" (*Wk* 175)? Does a crash preach, like the thrush? What would John Farmer think if he were visited not by gentle flute music but by a wild clatter?

These questions reflect a larger one, concerning violence. The sonorous expression of violence is crashing and cacophony. Can violence, like dissonance, be subsumed within the larger notions of metaphysical harmony and higher law? What does Thoreau have to say about this complex question? We may begin to seek an answer in his recurrent, somewhat disturbing expressions in which violence is assimilated into what might be called an effective promulgation of higher laws. In a famous passage in "Spring," he writes: "I love to see that Nature is so rife with life that myriads can be afforded to be sacrificed and suffered to prey on one another; that tender organizations can be so serenely squashed out of existence like pulp,—tadpoles which herons gobble up, and tortoises and toads run over in the road; and that sometimes it has rained flesh and blood! With the liability to accident, we must see how little account is to be made of it. The impression made on a wise man is that of universal innocence. Poison is not poisonous after all, nor are any wounds fatal" (*W* 318). Thoreau knows that death, including violent death, is part of life: accident and predation are natural and ultimately innocent, just as crashes are harmonious and "there never was yet such a storm but it was Æolian music to the innocent ear" (*W* 131). The death of individuals does not adversely affect the life of the species and the health of nature in general. Commenting on this passage, David M. Robinson writes: "What, from a limited standpoint, may appear to be cruelty or ruthlessness Thoreau tries to understand instead as the process or mechanism that serves as a guarantor of nature's power and richness . . . Enormous loss, measured on a human scale, becomes less significant when seen from a higher and more comprehensive perspective."[8] Although discord exists among the parts, harmony still reigns on the level of the whole. The subsumption of natural violence into higher innocence is the metaphysical equivalent of the incorporation of dissonance into harmony; discord is not discordant after all, nor are any sounds unmusical.

Thoreau held this view from an early age. After his beloved brother, John, died tragically in 1842, Thoreau wrote the following words to Emerson: "The wind still roars in the wood, as if nothing had happened out of the course of nature . . . Nature is not ruffled by the rudest blast— The hurricane only snaps a few twigs in some nook of the forest . . . The old laws prevail in spite of pestilence and a famine . . . How plain that death is only the phenomenon of the individual or class— Nature does not recognize it, She finds her own again under new forms without loss. Yet death is beautiful when seen to be a law, and not an accident . . . One might as well go into mourning for every sere leaf—but the more innocent and wiser soul will snuff a fragrance in the gales of autumn, and congratulate nature upon her health" (*Corr* 1:105). The crashes and roaring of the storm do not interrupt nature's harmony. Death is one of the natural laws constantly promulgated and is beautiful even when tragic. This idea returns in *Cape Cod*, in a stoic description of the aftermath of a shipwreck: "I sympathized rather with the winds and waves, as if to toss and mangle these poor human bodies was the order of the day. If this was the law of Nature, why waste any time in awe or pity?" (*CC* 9). This is the crash, whose sound "grates agreeably" on his ears: the shipwreck. "I saw that the beauty of the shore itself was wrecked for many a lonely walker there, until he could perceive, at last, how its beauty was enhanced by wrecks like this, and it acquired thus a rarer and sublimer beauty still" (*CC* 10).[9] Paradoxically, the presence of death, or of dissonance, enhances aesthetic beauty, as it reveals the continuing vitality of nature despite the loss. According to higher laws, natural violence is an inescapable part of life, and no matter how grating the discord, it is still always subsumed into nature's harmony. The emphasis on natural law in these passages ("death is beautiful when seen to be a law," "If this was the law of Nature") shows that even as Thoreau embraces discord, such dissonance does not interrupt or displace his fundamental metaphysics of harmony, but expands it.

In his understanding of natural discord as harmonious, Thoreau is anticipating Darwin. At the same moment Thoreau was developing these ideas, Darwin was incubating his *Origin of Species*, in which he would argue that the death or nonreproduction of the weak is for the greater good of the species. In an epigraph to his work, Darwin quoted the natural theologian William Whewell. In the last paragraph he evokes the laws governing evolution, including that of natural selection, and expresses a view somewhat similar to Thoreau's philosophy of panharmonium: "Thus, from the war of nature, from famine and death, the most exalted object which we are capable of conceiving, namely, the production of the higher animals, directly follows. There is grandeur in this view of life."[10] Underlying the strife, a certain harmony is preserved.

One may reasonably wonder at this point what Thoreau means by a metaphysical harmony that is not always peaceful and sometimes involves violent crashes. It certainly does not mean static symmetry or perfect order, unless that last term also be redefined. Beyond the importance of natural law underpinning his idea of harmony, Thoreau seems to mean the unity of the dynamic universe-system and the relatedness of all of its parts with one another, which he designated with words like "sympathy," "resonance," and "relation," what today we might call "holistic interconnectedness and interdependence."[11] This holistic relatedness is not broken when there is conflict between the parts.[12] It includes particularity and difference and also means that there are no individuals who are absolutely other or foreign. It is characterized neither by pure homogeneity nor by radically heterogeneous particularity but rather by interdependent particularity. Discord and disorder for Thoreau seem to be related to the dynamic conflict between different entities within the whole and not to an ontology of objective chance.[13] Thoreau's conception of a dynamic and dissonant whole is based on the idea that spirit and natural law are immanent throughout all of nature, including its violence and discordance, and is related to Emerson's Neoplatonic and immanentist view of "Unity in Variety" (*CW* 1:27).[14] Although Thoreau places extra emphasis on variety, he does not neglect unity. One might also cite Alexander von Humboldt, who wrote in his *Cosmos*, "Nature . . . is a unity in diversity of phenomena, a harmony."[15] Thoreau's extension of the definition of harmony to include dissonance, difference, and discord occurs within the tradition of idealist metaphysics, rather than breaking with it. The incorporation of discord into a larger harmony might be seen as a Thoreauvian form of dialectics, comparable to Emerson's dialectics of "circles."

But we have not yet fully answered our question: Are all acoustic phenomena really harmonious? What about the sound of a gun? Does it, too, sound "as necessary as the music of the spheres"? In "Higher Laws," Thoreau is somewhat ambiguous about human predation: he says clearly that eating other animals is a lower stage of spiritual development, but he also admits that he "reverences" both the spiritual and the "savage" life and at times has been tempted to devour a woodchuck raw (*W* 210). He tends away from animal food because he finds it unclean and less spiritual, and "no human being, past the thoughtless age of boyhood, will wantonly murder any creature" (*W* 212). Yet if humanity is just another animal, as the nonanthropocentric worldview maintains, it should have no more qualms than other predators when it kills and eats other animals—as long as it takes only what it needs, as they do, and kills for food and not for wanton murder.[16] Nature is so "rife with life" that this local violence will not upset the universal balance. Thoreau seems to waver between these two spiritual perspectives: on one hand, the dualism of a lower, meat-eating stage versus a higher spiritual stage in which humans forgo eating other animals, and on the other, the immanentism of the universal innocence of all of nature's predation, including that of humans. In 1859, he writes:

> I hear these guns going to-day, and I must confess that they are to me a springlike and exhilarating sound, like the cock-crowing, though each one may report the death of a musquash. This, methinks, or the like of this, with whatever mixture of dross, is the real morning or evening hymn that goes up from these vales to-day, and which the stars echo. This is the best sort of glorifying of God and enjoying him that at all prevails here to-day, without any clarified butter or sacred ladles.
>
> As a mother loves to see her child imbibe nourishment and expand, so God loves to see his children thrive on the nutriment he has furnished them. In the musquash-hunters I see the Almouchicois still pushing swiftly over the dark stream in their canoes. These aboriginal men cannot be repressed, but under some guise or other they survive and reappear continually. Just as simply as the crow picks up the worms which all over the fields have been washed out by the thaw, these men pick up the musquash that have been washed out the banks. (*J* XI:424–25)

Although there is clearly some irony in the statement that there is no better hymn to God happening on that day than gunshots, it is surely not only ironic, as he goes on to say that this "springlike and exhilarating sound" is indeed a way of glorifying God, since God loves the natural processes of life including predation. In this passage, which recalls those cited above concerning natural violence, humanity is an animal among others, governed by the same laws of nature which require eating to maintain health, and therefore hunting is innocent. Strictly speaking, meat eating is compatible with the immanentist, nonanthropocentric view, whereas vegetarianism imposes a dualism between the ways of humans and those of other carni-vores. Thoreau's approach is thus ambiguous: at times he maintains a dual-istic view (higher/lower, clean/unclean, humans/other animals) according to which humans are held to a higher standard than other animals, and then at others he displays a monistic immanentism in which all predation, including that of human animals, accords with natural harmony. This tension between two spiritual views, immanence and dualism, seems to remain unresolved.[17]

The sound of the hunter's gun is thus somewhat ambiguous. What of the soldier's? The tension we have just seen reappears in this context in a slightly different form. In many early journal entries, as well as in his 1840 essay "The Service," Thoreau associates music with a soldier's bravery and heroism. He essentially argues that a soldier fighting for a just cause is act-ing in harmony with the universe. The essay seems to be written to inspire a spirit of "service" and a soldier's courage in its readers' everyday lives, rather than to advocate any concrete use of guns, though it also criticizes the "insincerity and sloth of peace" (*RP* 17). Rejected for publication in *The Dial* by Margaret Fuller, it may indeed seem rough terrain to read-ers because it juxtaposes two quite different registers, the highly abstract praise for spiritual courage and the evocation of the concrete practice of war, without offering the needed intermediary term—the particular moral justification for any historically situated use of violence, without which the violence is incomprehensible. Thoreau takes it for granted that the battle cry he praises is one in defense of justice and higher laws, such as John Brown's, and not, for example, that of the U.S. Army against the Semi-noles.[18] He states in "Slavery in Massachusetts," "Show me a free State, and a court truly of justice, and I will fight for them, if need be" (*RP* 9).

In this context, Thoreau believes that the universe has an immanent rhythm and music and that acting in sync with it inspires bravery and overcomes isolation. This helps explain the following passage: "Especially the soldier insists on agreement and harmony always . . . War is but the compelling of peace. If the soldier marches to the sack of a town, he must be preceded by drum and trumpet, which shall identify his cause with the accordant universe. All things thus echo back his own spirit, and thus the hostile territory is preoccupied for him. He is no longer insulated, but infinitely related and familiar" (*RP* 9). It is difficult to see how the sack of a town, which is very different from two armed forces meeting on a battlefield, could ever be considered to accord with the higher law of justice and make the sacker infinitely related to the rest of creation. This passage may perhaps be best understood as the overexcited froth of a young man who had not yet outgrown his guns, the process he recounts in "Higher Laws." At any rate, Thoreau's view here and elsewhere seems to be that through bold actions theoretically in accordance with higher principles, the soldier is not only related to his companions but also to the universe.[19] For Thoreau, the sound of a just war is harmonious because it resonates with the rhythm of the universe's immanent laws, and simultaneously, he states that the sound of all war is terribly dissonant: in 1840 he writes that "war is the sympathy of concussion" (*PJ* 1:124). It seems strange that sympathy, a romantic term related to harmony, could be found in the collision of battling bodies and the crash of concussion. But this idea reminds us again of the harmony he finds in storms and shipwrecks: the sympathy of concussion would be the accordance of discord or the harmony of dissonance. He continues: "Men do not peep into heaven but they see embattled hosts there. Miltons' [*sic*] heaven was a camp . . . The soldier is the practical idealist—he has no sympathy with matter, he revels in the annihilation of it. So do we all at times. When a freshet destroys the works of man—or a fire consumes them—or a Lisbon earthquake shakes them down—our sympathy with persons is swallowed up in a wider sympathy with the universe. A crash is apt to grate agreeably on our ears" (*PJ* 1:124). Even in heaven, where ultimate harmony should theoretically reign, the discord of war continues. This radical passage may be relatively incomprehensible if not seen in the context of the idea of a just war. The harmony of a just war's discord is thus related to the harmony of nature's violence, prefiguring the arguments cited above in the letter to Emerson and in "Spring": our sympathy with an individual is sacrificed to a sympathy with the whole. In the interest of higher ideals or the laws of nature, even "matter" may be destroyed; here we see a glimpse of Thoreau's dualism. Thoreau is not a simple sword-rattler; he prefers staying at home and braving the everyday experiences of life.[20] However, when necessary for a just cause, he supports the use of violence, for example, in rising up against slavery: "I do not wish to kill nor to be killed, but I can foresee circumstances in which both these things would be by me unavoidable . . . The question is not about the weapon, but the spirit in which you use it" (*RP* 133).

The discordant sound of a gun used in the spirit of justice thus "grates agreeably" on Thoreau's ears and is incorporated into the immanence of nature's harmony. But guns are not always used in this spirit, and this example shows that there are indeed some sounds that are not musical: if it is necessary to go to war for justice, then injustice exists, whose sound will always remain unbearable. Speaking of the execution of John Brown, he writes: "While these things are being done, beauty stands veiled and music is a screeching lie" (*RP* 136). And in "Slavery in Massachusetts": "Justice is sweet and musical; but injustice is harsh and discordant. The judge still sits grinding at his organ, but it yields no music, and we hear only the sound of the handle. He believes that all the music resides in the handle" (*RP* 105). The noise of this organ handle is evidently not as musical as the "rattling of the tool we work with" or "the squeaking of the pump" (*PJ* 1:213, 229). The image is quite evocative, as it vividly depicts the absence of harmony though not the absence of sound, just as true justice is not embodied in the "justice" of the court who sent Anthony Burns back to slavery. This truly harsh dissonance exists not only in metaphorical sounds: the rousing drumbeat that inspires the soldier in "The Service" is quite different from "this rub-a-dub" that Thoreau hears at night as soldiers, like those who executed the judge's decision, train in the street (*RP* 95). The immanence of divine harmony clearly does not extend so far as to include all forms of violence, in particular human acts of injustice. Here we see Thoreau's idealist dualism between higher principles and actual human society.[21] Thoreau's first writings on music sometimes express this view as well: "Some sounds seem to reverberate along the plain, and then settle to earth again like dust; such are Noise, Discord, Jargon. But such only as spring heavenward . . . are the true sphere music" (*PJ* 1:50). Thoreau's dualism thus enters into tension with, or overlaps, the immanentism of his panharmonium: not all sounds are musical after all. From the perspective of immanence, true discord does not exist; from that of dualism, some sounds are irretrievably dissonant. Whereas violence in nonhuman nature is harmonious (and we must stoically accept it), humans are capable of violently discordant injustice (and we should heroically combat it). Violence against other humans either perpetrates injustice or fights it in harmony with higher laws.

For Thoreau, in order to identify the difference between harmonious (though grating) and truly discordant sounds, or between a just and an unjust use of violence, spiritual or at least ethical principles are essential. In this sense it is impossible to disregard the religious and metaphysical aspects of his philosophy. And in keeping with this dualism between higher laws and many human actions, Thoreau does not extend his immanentist panharmonium to include all forms of human violence, thereby naturalizing social injustice. It would be hard to imagine Thoreau arguing alongside Herbert Spencer, in a debate he did not live to participate in, that the salutary violence of natural selection should be applied to human society or saying that he "love[s] to see that Nature is so rife with life" that the humans of London in 1854 "can be afforded to be sacrificed" and "serenely squashed out of existence" by malnutrition, overcrowding, disease, and unemployment (*W* 318). This reveals an essential distinction between nature's harmonious dissonance and humanity's unacceptably discordant injustice, and that a certain dualism thus inflects and qualifies Thoreau's immanentist panharmonium.

Notes

1. See also *PJ* 1:362.
2. I understand the term *materialism* as the ontological perspective that matter is the universe's fundamental substance (which may be dynamic), and *idealism* as the idea that spirit is prior to matter. The fact that Thoreau focused on particularity and did not often use metaphysical terminology after around 1850 does not mean that his philosophy did not continue to have a strong religious and idealist metaphysical orientation throughout his life. See Joseph Urbas's discussion of Thoreau's metaphysics in the context of Transcendentalist ontology in general in "'Being Is the Great Explainer': Thoreau and the Ontological Turn in American Thought," in *Thoreauvian Modernities: Transatlantic Conversations on an American Icon*, ed. François Specq, Laura Dassow Walls, and Michel Granger (Athens: University of Georgia Press, 2013), and Daniel S. Malachuk's analysis of the importance of the "City of God" for Thoreau in *Two Cities: The Political Thought of American Transcendentalism* (Lawrence: University Press of Kansas, 2016), as well as Christopher A. Dustin, "Thoreau's Religion," in *A Political Companion to Henry David Thoreau*, ed. Jack Turner (Lexington: University Press of Kentucky, 2009); Alan D. Hodder, "Thoreau and the New American Spirituality," in *Thoreau at 200: Essays and Reassessments*, ed. Kristen Case and K. P. Van Anglen (Cambridge: Cambridge University Press, 2016); and Alan D. Hodder, "The Religious Horizon," in *Henry David Thoreau in Context*, ed. James S. Finley (Cambridge: Cambridge University Press, 2017).
3. Dustin, "Thoreau's Religion," 284.
4. Many commentators have studied the ways in which Thoreau's panharmonium prefigures the aesthetics of John Cage; perhaps the most comprehensive study is Jannika

Bock, *Concord in Massachusetts, Discord in the World: The Writings of Henry Thoreau and John Cage* (Frankfurt: Peter Lang, 2008).

5. As a young man, Thoreau may have read William Gardiner's popular book *The Music of Nature; Or, an Attempt to Prove That What Is Passionate and Pleasing in the Art of Singing, Speaking and Performing upon Musical Instruments, Is Derived from the Sounds of the Animated World* (London: Longman, Rees, Orme, Brown, Green, and Longman, 1832). Gardiner offers descriptions of sounds such as storms, cataracts, and war (14–15) and musical transcriptions of animals, birds, insects, coughing, wheelbarrows creaking, children crying or playing, and "London cries." Emerson read Gardiner in late 1837, taking copious notes; see *The Journals and Miscellaneous Notebooks of Ralph Waldo Emerson*, ed. William Gilman et al., 16 vols. (Cambridge, MA: Harvard University Press, 1960–82), 5:432–33. Gardiner's book went through multiple editions in England and the United States. I have found no direct trace of Thoreau's reading it, but it is quite plausible given his friendship with Emerson and his strong interest in the music of nature at this time.

6. Branka Arsić states that Thoreau "proposes a listening that is attuned to cacophony and discord," in "What Music Shall We Have? Thoreau on the Aesthetics and Politics of Listening," in *American Impersonal: Essays with Sharon Cameron*, ed. Branka Arsić (New York: Bloomsbury, 2014), 177. She argues that dissonance is opposed to harmony (which she correctly associates with spirituality): "Harmony cancels dissonance by generating concord understood as the perfect essence hiding behind all discord" (174). I am claiming, rather, that Thoreau offers a radically inclusive definition of musical harmony, including what is normally perceived as discordant, rather than seeing concord and discord as opposites.

7. Kenneth W. Rhoads focuses on the link between music and wildness, as well as the spiritual dimension of sound for Thoreau, in "Thoreau: The Ear and the Music," *American Literature* 46, no. 3 (November 1974): 317–19, 323–27.

8. David M. Robinson, "Thoreau, Modernity and Nature's Seasons," in Specq, Walls, and Granger, *Thoreauvian Modernities*, 74.

9. See also Thoreau's reflections on the "strengthening sight" of a dead sucker (*PJ* 4:450).

10. Charles Darwin, *On the Origin of Species*, vol. 15 of *The Works of Charles Darwin*, ed. Paul H. Barrett and R. B. Freeman, 29 vols. (London: Pickering, 1986–89), 347.

11. Laura Dassow Walls introduces the useful concept of "empirical holism" to describe Thoreau's worldview, which coincides rather well with the vision I am suggesting; see Walls, *Seeing New Worlds: Henry David Thoreau and Nineteenth-Century Natural Science* (Madison: University of Wisconsin Press, 1995), 4. Jane Bennett, on the other hand, uses the term heteroverse in her analysis of Thoreau's perspective, which describes "how heterogeneous elements intersect or influence one another and how this ensemble of intersections does not form a unified or self-sufficient whole," in *Thoreau's Nature: Ethics, Politics, and the Wild* (Thousand Oaks, CA: Sage Publications, 1994), 53.

12. Branka Arsić argues that the objective state of the real is "dissonant, arhythmical, and indeed, asyntactical," which is "precisely what natural life is in the absence of a self to idealize it into prosodic coherence"; that is, the coherence of existence is only a human idealization projected onto it. See *Bird Relics: Grief and Vitalism in Thoreau* (Cambridge, MA: Harvard University Press, 2016), 101. However, Thoreau believed

that natural harmony and law exist objectively and immanently throughout reality, which thus coheres in a holistic ensemble of interconnections; its coherence is not only a human idealization.

13. As David M. Robinson writes, "Thoreau consistently tries to see a particular fact or event not as a random or unique occurrence but as indicative of a more comprehensive idea or law." See *Natural Life: Thoreau's Worldly Transcendentalism* (Ithaca, NY: Cornell University Press, 2004), 109. I have elsewhere argued that Thoreau's conceptions of chance and accident participate in his epistemology of surprise rather than constituting an ontology of indeterminacy and that his ontology remains anchored in natural law: "'Blue Berries Always Surprise Us': Thoreau, Happiness, and Accident," *Revue Française d'Études Américaines* 157, no. 4 (2018): 161–72.

14. It is theoretically possible to conceive of a unity that is materialist and not idealist, but there is no indication that this was Thoreau's view.

15. Quoted in Walls, *Seeing New Worlds*, 84.

16. Philip J. Cafaro states (though in the context of farming) that this is the "responsible answer": "Take what you need, but *only* what you need." See "In Wildness Is the Preservation of the World: Thoreau's Environmental Ethics," in *Thoreau's Importance for Philosophy*, ed. Rick Anthony Furtak, Jonathan Ellsworth, and James D. Reid (New York: Fordham University Press, 2012), 75.

17. Kathryn Cornell Dolan notes a similar ambiguity in a Journal entry that first condemns eating animals and then describes Eskimos hunting, in "Diet and Vegetarianism," in *Henry David Thoreau in Context*, ed. James S. Finley (Cambridge: Cambridge University Press, 2017), 222.

18. For Thoreau's views on war, see Larry J. Reynolds, "Warrior Culture," in Finley, *Henry David Thoreau in Context*. A number of commentators have observed that Thoreau advocated not only nonviolent resistance but also, when necessary, violent action against injustice; see, for example, Lance Newman, "Thoreau and Violence," *The Concord Saunterer* 23 (2015).

19. Branka Arsić understands this passage as a criticism of both harmony and war; she writes, "The accordant world is thus the effect of an arrangement that subjugates differences into harmony. In Thoreau's interpretation, the soldier's insistence on harmony is a function of his practice of subjugation" ("What Music," 206). She relates harmony to forced harmonization and colonization (207). However, far from intending to subjugate difference, Thoreau celebrates dissonance and difference in all their discordant particularity and finds them harmonious, thus redefining the term. Thoreau's soldier does not want to subjugate discord or difference but to conquer the foes of "Falsehood" and injustice, and in so doing he necessarily brings with him not only marching band music but the cacophony of war (*RP* 13). For Thoreau, the discord of a just war contains harmony because it aims to overcome injustice.

20. See, for example, *PJ* 1:91.

21. This dualism is well analyzed by Daniel S. Malachuk in his *Two Cities* in terms of the city of God and the city of man.

9

BEYOND TEMPORAL BORDERS

THE MUSIC OF THOREAU'S KALENDAR

Kristen Case

In the final years of his life, Thoreau began a work that was at once profoundly retrospective and singularly forward looking. In a purely formal sense, the charts of seasonal phenomena known as the Kalendar look back to the gardener's almanacs of John Evelyn and Gilbert White, to Virgil's *Eclogues*, and to the Roman agricultural writers Cato and Varro.[1] In their content they anticipate the twentieth-century developments of phenomenology, process philosophy, climate science, and ecology. But the Kalendar is polychromatic in another way as well. By organizing the experiences recorded in his Journal over a decade in charts of monthly seasonal phenomena, Thoreau transposed the records of particular moments in linear time into his emergent vision of seasonal time. That is, Thoreau spent the final two years of his life in part working toward a reconfiguration of his own temporal experience, a way of understanding lived time as fully integrated in natural or seasonal time.

Much of Thoreau's writing from *A Week* onward may be understood as responding to or managing loss, perhaps most notably the loss of his older brother and closest companion, John, in 1842.[2] The Journal itself, to which Thoreau devoted himself increasingly in his last decade, can be understood in part as a means of preserving experience against the linear passage of time. But for Thoreau, the function of the Journal was not essentially that of record keeping or documentation; rather, he sought to use the technology of writing as a means by which to live differently in time.

In Thoreau's Journal practices of the 1850s and early 1860s, every entry bears reference to at least three temporal points: the moment of observation, the moment of writing, and the moment of subsequent correction, gathering, and rearranging. But each of these modes must be further complicated: observation was not a single moment but a span of several hours of walking punctuated by the writing of field notes. Writing was in part a process of reading and arranging those notes, typically the following morning, and recasting them in the present tense. The retrospective Journal-work—the penciled corrections and deletions—was similarly ongoing and intermittent.[3] Each of these practices not only overlapped with but also helped constitute and sustain the others. Living intimately with both past and future, continually moving between them in the text that both recorded and, in an important sense, *was* his life, Thoreau discovered a way of being in time that more closely resembled the seasonal time he observed in nature: a temporal order in which experiences that are disparate in a chronological sense—say, two days in April, ten years apart—may nevertheless be understood, and finally *lived*, as part of the same experience.

When in Thoreau's final years list and chart making were added to the retrospective stage of this process, the orientation that had long been implicit in his Journal practices became more marked: these daily tasks of observation, recording, synthesizing, and transposing were aimed at the transfer of the discrete experiences of linear time into the (seemingly) lossless economy of natural time. In an 1857 Journal entry he observed, "These regular phenomena of the seasons get at last to be—they were *at first*, of course—simply and plainly phenomena or phases of my own life" (*J* X:127). The phrase "at last" bears particular significance for the late life work represented by the Kalendar. The form of the Kalendar charts, by means of which Thoreau could visualize all the individual phenomena recorded over the decade at a glance, can be understood as a kind of *musical* form, one in which individual notations must be understood as both discrete and simultaneous, both singular and parts of a larger pattern.

Following work on the centrality of grief to Thoreau's writing by H. Daniel Peck, Branka Arsić, and William Rossi, I want to suggest that the complex temporality reflected by the Kalendar represented a mechanism for both registering and recovering from loss—including the anticipated loss of his own life. As Rossi notes, "recovery," here, should not be understood in terms of the Freudian model of mourning, in which the mourner proceeds by stages to *let go* of the mourned object.[4] Rather, for Thoreau, recovery meant the retention of lost objects through the establishment of a temporality in which past, present, and future were experienced as deeply and vitally connected.

In a Journal entry written on January 8, 1842, just three days before John's painful death from lockjaw, Thoreau asks, "Of what manner of stuff is the web of time wove—when these consecutive sounds called a strain of music can be wafted down through the centuries from Homer to me— And Homer have been conversant with that same unfathomable mystery and charm, which so new tingles my ears . . . Am I so like thee my brother that the cadence of two notes affects us alike?" (*PJ* 1:361–62) Here, music seems to offer dissolution of the boundaries of both selves and historical moments, capable of crossing, Thoreau imagines, between Homer and himself, and also capable of affecting both himself and John in exactly the same way. As Arsić notes, Thoreau suggests that music can "counter the progression of time that would keep Homer at an insurmountable distance from him. Time becomes an embodied acoustic strain that, starting from Homer, 'wafts' into Thoreau's now, to put them in touch; it is as if sharing the same acoustic space, their existences were rendered simultaneous. The sound that reverberates through the room of the cosmos and enters Thoreau in his 'now' is thus assimilated to the same sound heard by Homer, and their respective presents encounter each other in the vast simultaneity of the universe."[5] Perhaps even more significant, the music unites Thoreau with his brother, who, though physically close, is already in the throes of dying and in doing so affecting a permanent separation. This momentary feeling of inner likeness to John will emerge again in the days following his death, when Thoreau will sympathetically experience the symptoms of his disease. But the first mechanism by which this impossible divide is crossed is music.

Shortly after John's death, Thoreau writes in a letter to Lucy Brown, "The memory of some past moments is more persuasive than the experience of present ones. There have been visions of such breadth and brightness that these motes were invisible in their light" (*Corr* 1:101–2). Worth attending to here is Thoreau's use of the present perfect "have been," which suggests a location between the present and the past. The deictic phrase "these motes" refers to present experiences, which are overlaid onto the past, capable, in ordinary experience, of blocking the past from view. But the brightness of memory here renders the present layer of experience "invisible." While in this passage Thoreau describes his experience of layered time in visual terms, the simultaneity of temporal positions he describes may more properly be called musical, and indeed in this letter as elsewhere, music acts as a palliative to the experience of loss.

April Music

Thoreau's process in producing the charts of General Phenomena reflects a logic akin to a hermeneutic circle: the whole of a month, they suggest, could be known by way of its parts, and the parts more fully understood in light of the whole. Perusing the years of his Journal and making lists of salient seasonal phenomena, Thoreau isolated certain meteorological categories as typical of the month in question. He then fleshed out his sense of these categories by providing instances of each in the squares of his chart corresponding to each year. The movement was thus from particular to the general and then back to the particular.

At the same time, Thoreau traversed, in his writing, from linear time—from the record of a single, already-completed day—to recurrent or seasonal time, of which his own picture was partial, local, and incomplete but which nevertheless offered a promise of ongoingness or return. By 1857 he had recognized that "the seasons and all their changes are in me. I see not a dead eel or floating snake, or a gull, but it rounds my life and is like a line or an accent in its poem . . . My moods are thus periodical, not two days in my year alike." Understanding the way his own seasonal phenomena fit within the general phenomena of the month enabled him to feel the "correspondence of Nature to man, so that he is at home in her," a sense that mitigated against the feelings of alienation he often felt in the wake of loss or in its anticipation (*J* X:127).[6]

Well before he began drawing up the charts of seasonal phenomena, Thoreau used the Journal as a means of layering temporal experience. On April 10, 1852, for example, he writes:

> 8 Am—Down river to ½ miles below carlisle Bridge, the river being high—yet not high for the spring . . .
>
> From Ball's Hill the Great Meadow looks more light—perhaps it is the medium between the dark and light above mentioned. Mem. Try this experiment again. *i.e.* look not toward nor from the sun but athwart this line. Seen from this hill in this direction—there are here and there

dark-shadows spreading rapidly over the surface . . . where the wind strikes the water. The water toward the sun seen from this height—shows not the broad silvery light but a myriad fine sparkles. The sky is full of light this morning—with different shades of blue—lighter below, darker above separated perhaps by a thin strip of white vapor.—Thicker in the east . . .

The aspect of the sky varies every hour about noon I observed it in the south, composed of . . . short clouds horizontal and parallel to one another, each straight & dark below with a slight cumulus resting on it. a little marsh-wise. Again, in the north, I see a light but rather watery looking flock of clouds at mid-afternoon slight wisps & thin veils of whitish clouds also. (*PJ* 4:430–32)

When we recall that Thoreau habitually wrote up the observations of his walks on the following day—that is, this passage would have been written *not* on April 10 but on April 11—his use of the present tense is striking: "The sky is full of light this morning." The present tense *is* and the deictic *this* are adopted here not as they might be in a finished literary work to affect a reader with a sense of immediacy but rather as a making-present, for the writer, of a lived past: a gathering of past experience into the present materiality of writing. In other words, Thoreau knew himself as the future reader of his Journal and used the Journal and its related projects as a means of bringing together seemingly disparate temporal moments. The instruction "Try this experiment again" projects a past and present self into the future by means of an imagined repetition, an *experiment*, that most Thoreauvian of modes. The notation "Mem" is a material *memorandum*, gerundive of *memorare*, literally "something to be brought to mind," the "to be" here signaling that the mind in question is located in the future: writing—the physical process and the material page—bridges the moment of seeing and the moment of seeing again, becomes a space in which each of these temporal points may be experienced simultaneously.

But if this entry works as a time machine aimed at the future, the Kalendar functions as a mechanism for reconstructing the past. Thoreau returns to the Journal entry for April 10, 1852, twice in the April charts of General Phenomena drawn up around 1861, once to note the height of the river on that date ("high—yet not high for the spring") and once to note the "dark barrel shaped clouds" he described and sketched that day. The category "River when highest in April," along with "River when Lowest in April" and "First leave off greatcoat," is filled in straight across the decade in the April chart, with copious annotation: a rare instance of a category being constantly observed across all the years of the Journal.[7] "High yet not high for the spring" informs us that by 1852, the height of the river had become a significant annual phenomenon, one that Thoreau understood in terms of its relation to other heights in that spring and other springs. By 1860, this sense is compounded by a decade's worth of such comparisons, and the April 10 entry has taken its place among a dense network of related observations. The Thoreau we must imagine to make sense of these relations is the Thoreau of April 10, but also the Thoreau of April 11, and finally the Thoreau of 1861 and all the Thoreaus in between.

The passage that follows is from the Journal entry of the following day, April 11, 1852, likely written up the morning of April 12 from field notes.

> The sight of Nut Meadow Brook in Brown's land—reminds me that the attractiveness of a brook depends much on the character of its bottom . . . I stop to look at the circular shadows of the dimples over the yellow sand—& the dark brown clams on their edges in the sand at the bottom. I hear the sound of the piano below as I write this and feel as if the winter in me were at length beginning to thaw—for my spring has been even more backward than nature's. For a month past life has been a thing incredible to me. None but the kind gods can make me sane— If only they will let their south winds blow on me. I ask to be melted. You can only ask of the metals that they be tender to the fire that *melts* them. To naught else can they be tender. The sweet flags are now starting up under water two inches high—& minnows dart. A pure brook is a very beautiful object to study minutely—it will bear the closest inspection— even to the fine air bubbles like minute globules of quicksilver that lie on its bottom . . .
>
> I see now the mosses in pastures bearing their lightcolored capsules on the top of red filaments. When I reach the bridge, it is become a serene evening, the broad waters are more and more smooth, and everything is more beautiful in the still light. (*PJ* 4:433–36)

Most arresting here is Thoreau's interruption of his present-tense recording of the previous afternoon's experiences with a real-time rendering of his thoughts while writing, each of these two senses of the present already estranged in the way words always are from the experiences they extend.

"For a month past life has been a thing incredible to me" is suggestive of particular and periodic bouts of practical skepticism: an inability to *credit* life, to grant it the value of his active investment. As H. Daniel Peck observes, the expression of this crisis as an estrangement from nature and especially from seasonal rhythms—"my spring has been even more backward than nature's"—reflects Thoreau's lifelong preoccupation with time as both linear (and so composed of continual loss) and circular (and so restorative).[8]

Thoreau returns to this entry in the April Kalendar charts as well, once to refer to the "placid eve[ning] reflecting water" that he observes minutely in the entry (figure 15) and once to note the quality of the evening light; he notes the date in a box corresponding to the category "Rain in pm followed by clear yellow light" (figure 16). In both the charts and the corresponding Journal entry, Thoreau is less interested in achieving an objective record of meteorological events than in recording his *perceptions* of natural phenomena, the way the world looks and feels to him in April. This orientation toward the intimate relatedness of the human to the nonhuman is pronounced in Thoreau's late work and can be understood both as a critique of emergent professional science and as an anticipation of twentieth-century philosophical developments.[9] "I think that the man of science makes this mistake and the mass of mankind along with him," he writes in November 1857, "that you should coolly give your chief attention to the phenomenon which excites you as something independent on you, and not as it is related to you" (*J* X:164–65). His own relatedness to the natural world was what Thoreau sought in recording his observations in the first place. This offered him, I want to suggest, a redefined sociality: a "friendship with the seasons" that could compensate for the loss or failure of human relations (*W* 131). The discrete strands of relation comprising Thoreau's sense of his correspondence to natural phenomena, a correspondence especially needful to him in moments of grief and loss, grew deeper and more complex as he discovered that they might be scored, like music, across multiple axes at once.

That it is Sophia's piano playing in the Journal entry of the April 11 that triggers the sensation of thaw seems not accidental to me. Thoreau associates music with restoration and healing throughout his writings, most notably, as we've already seen, in his descriptions of listening to the music box in the days leading up to his brother's death. Now again,

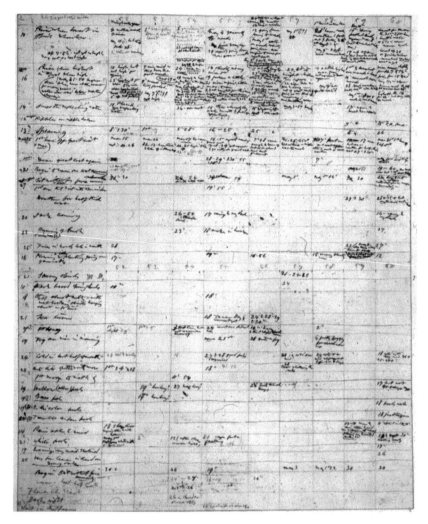

Figure 15. General Phenomena for April (2). MA 610. Courtesy of the Morgan Library & Museum, New York.

a decade later, music seems to offer Thoreau a kind of needed dissolution, a long-delayed thaw. The Journal entry of April 11, 1852, follows by just a few days the entry in which he registers a painful argument with a friend, almost certainly Emerson: "I have got to that pass with my friend—that our words do not pass with each other for what they are worth. We speak in vain—there is none to hear. He finds fault with me that I walk alone, when I pine for want of a companion—that I commit my thoughts to a

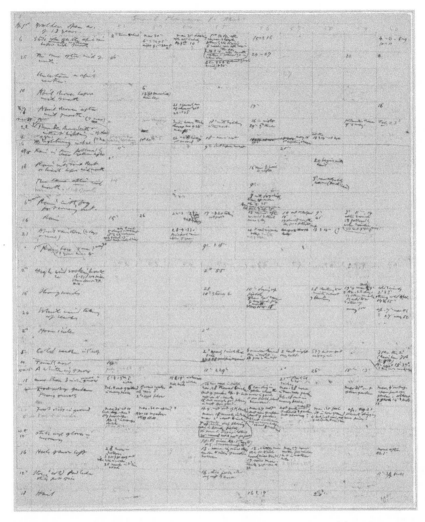

Figure 16. General Phenomena for April (1). MA 610. Courtesy of the Morgan Library & Museum, New York.

diary even on my walks instead of seeking to share them generously with a friend—curses my practice even— Awful as it is to contemplate I pray that if I am the cold intellectual skeptic whom he rebukes his curse may take effect—& wither & dry up those sources of my life—and my journal no longer yield me pleasure nor life" (*PJ* 4:426). As Mary Elkins Moller observes, the passage at once speaks to the centrality of the Journal practices to Thoreau's life and to the depth with which he feels his friend's "rebuke." Joel Porte describes the fall of 1851 as the season of Thoreau's "crisis with Emerson," and this passage, a few months later, is suggestive of such.[10] It is perhaps not surprising, then, that Thoreau complains that his "spring has been more backwards than nature's" and finds that his "life has been a thing incredible" to him. Perhaps most interesting, in asking to be "melted," Thoreau seems to have absorbed the terms of Emerson's rebuke. A few years later Thoreau would write that his friend (unnamed, but again almost certainly Emerson) "offered me friendship on such terms that I could not accept it without a sense of degradation. He would not meet me on equal terms but only be to some extent my patron. He would not come to see me, but was hurt if I did not visit him" (*J* VIII:199). But in April 1852, in the lingering winter after the crisis in their friendship, Thoreau took Emerson's charge of coldness seriously, perhaps even to the point of seeing that coldness as a kind of insanity, or at least unwellness. Prompted by the music of the piano a few days later, he interrupts his record of the previous day with a sort of prayer, which is also a sort of justification: "None but the kind gods can make me sane— If only they will let their south winds blow on me. I ask to be melted. You can only ask of the metals that they be tender to the fire that *melts* them. To naught else can they be tender" (*PJ* 4:434).

When, years later, Thoreau writes this day into his Kalendar, he retains his perceptions of the clear light and the calm, reflecting waters. The piano music, as well as the reflections about sanity, coldness, and thawing, have dropped out. The record of a crisis in human friendship seems to have given way to a record of deepening friendship with the nonhuman. In this sense the Kalendar may be understood to function as a particular kind of elegy, detailing not the loss itself (as recorded in the Journal) but rather the strategy by which the loss was "lived with and contained."[11]

December Music

The most complete of the Kalendar charts are the four that Thoreau drew up for the month of December. These charts are remarkable in several respects. First, they include December 1861, the month after Thoreau stopped keeping his regular Journal, and second, unlike the other monthly charts marked "General Phenomena," these are titled "*All* Phenomena for December" and suggest a more comprehensive picture of seasonal

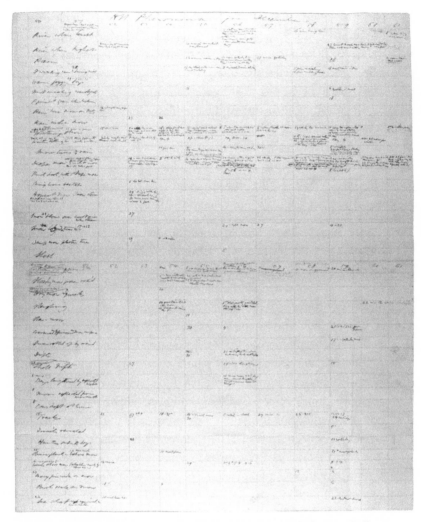

Figure 17. All Phenomena for December (1), Henry David Thoreau Collection. Courtesy Yale Collection of American Literature, Beinecke Rare Book & Manuscript Library, New Haven, CT.

phenomena, including bird and plant life, in addition to the weather-related phenomena he kept for other months.

The December charts thus present us with Thoreau's impressions of the month from an almost entirely retrospective view, and it is striking that the view is richer, fuller, more complete than those of the other months. No longer able to track in real time the unfolding of the December in which he is presently living, Thoreau uses the archive of his Journal to reconstruct a finely grained composite picture of the month, in which he may spend his days. Given these circumstances, the themes of the December Kalendar charts are especially interesting. Many of the categories are concerned with effects of visual contrast provided by the backdrop of snow and with signs of life in the midst of dormancy and barrenness. Thawing and freezing are recurrent themes here as well as in the spring charts.

Across from the category "Green in Winter" Thoreau marks the date December 7 in the column for 1853 and adds the note, "on forest floor." This note, scrawled almost illegibly sometime in 1861, points us to the Journal entry of nearly a decade prior, when he had observed his attraction to

> the numerous small evergreens on the forest floor—now most conspicuous.—Especially the very beautiful Lycopodium dendroideum (somewhat cylindrical,—& also *in this Grove*—the var *obscurum*) of various forms surmounted by the effoete spikes—some with a spiral or screw-like arrangement of the fan like leaves—some spreading & drooping— It is like looking down on evergreen trees— And the L. lucidulum of the swamps forming broad thick patches of a clear liquid-green with its curving fingers— Also the pretty little fingers of the cylindrical L. clavatum a clubmoss zigzagging amid the dry leaves not to mention the spreading openwork umbrellas of the L. complanatum or Flat club moss. all with spikes still Also the liquid wet glossy leaves of the Chimaphila— (winter or snow loving)—umbellata with its dry fruit. Not to mention the still green—Mitchella repens—& checquer berry in shelter, both with fruit—goldthread-goldthread—P. secunda with drooping curled back leaves. (*PJ* 7:193)

This striking passage, reminiscent of the famous "Deep Cut" passage of *Walden*, engages in a kind of syntactical participation in the energies of growth, each description spurring on the next, the rapid transformations linked by the connectives *and, also, not to mention* evoking the surplus and overflow of natural growth. As in the "Deep Cut" passage, the description is animated by a chain of present participles—"spreading," "drooping," "forming," "curving," "zigzagging"—emphasizing the continual becoming of these natural forms. Unlike the "Deep Cut" passage, however, this description is of evergreen plants in winter rather than thawing "sand foliage" in spring. And the presence of this spring-like vitality in the midst of the barren winter landscape is what Thoreau wishes in 1861 to call into presence.

The sudden perception of *life* in the midst of an apparently barren landscape is a recurrent theme throughout the Decembers of the 1850s. In an entry dated December 11, 1855, Thoreau anticipates the arrival of redpolls: "Standing there, though in this bare November landscape, I am reminded of the incredible phenomenon of small birds in winter. That ere long amid the cold powdery snow, as it were a fruit of the season, will come twittering a flock of delicate crimson tinged birds, lesser redpolls, to sport and feed on the seeds and buds now just ripe for them on the sunny side of a wood, shaking down the powdery snow there in their cheerful social feeding as if it were high midsummer to them." It is striking that the birds are not yet present—earlier in the entry he writes "I see no birds"—but as his description proceeds, the redpolls become a vivid reality. "The age of miracles is each moment thus returned. Now it is wild apples; now river reflections; now a flock of lesser redpolls. In winter, too, resides immortal youth and perennial summer." This passage takes on further temporal complexity when we consider that it was more than likely written on December 12, documenting a memory ("I am reminded") that is also an anticipation ("ere long"), both of which are reconstructed from his walk the day before (*J* VIII:42).

In this entry, as elsewhere, Thoreau's complex manipulations of temporal experience are tied both to grief and to music: "If any part of nature excites our pity, it is for ourselves we grieve, for there is eternal health and beauty. We get only transient and partial glimpses of the beauty of the world. Standing at the right angle we are dazzled by the colors of the rainbow in colorless ice. From the right point of view every storm and every drop in it is a rainbow. Beauty and music are not mere traits and exceptions. They are the rule and character" (*J* VIII:44–45). Music, here allied with both beauty and rainbow, stands for a fullness which our partial perspective denies us. Experienced properly, he suggests, the natural world is musical. The notes of April sound in December, the notes of successive Decembers harmonize with one another, and unity dissolves into multiplicity, as colorless ice into the colors of the rainbow.

Among the very few phenomena recorded in December 1861 are "radical leaves," noted on December 21. These tiny, close to the earth, root leaves are emblematic of the December phenomena Thoreau most loved to contemplate. His observation of them a few years earlier, in 1855, prompted this reflection, which he notes in the December chart: "Particularly are we attracted in the winter by greenness and signs of growth, as the green and white shoots of grass and weeds, pulled or floating on the water, and also by color as cockspur lichens and crimson birds, etc." (*J* VIII:63). As is suggested by this note and by other categories included on the chart, for example, "Notice colored things where snow," Thoreau's *attraction* to elements of the landscape that spoke to him of growth is as much a seasonal phenomenon as radical leaves or lesser redpolls: he, too, his own mind and body, was part of the seasonal music.

The winter of 1857 was a particularly difficult one for Thoreau. Two entries in the Journal for this month suggest that he battled both physical illness and a feeling he called "barrenness": "In sickness and barrenness it is encouraging to believe that our life is dammed and is coming to a head, so that there seems to be no loss, for what is lost in time is gained in power. All at once, unaccountably, as we are walking in the woods or sitting in our chamber, after a worthless fortnight, we cease to feel mean and barren" (*J* X:222). "Barrenness" is a telling descriptor, and Thoreau uses this word several times this winter. Describing the sight of new shoots of sweet fern, he writes, "Even this is a cheering and compensating discovery in my otherwise barren work" (*J* X:221). And, indeed, at least some of his sense of barrenness described in these entries seems to relate to the intensity of his surveying work at this time.

This description of barrenness in the December and January Journals corresponds with the near emptiness of the 1857 column on the four-page Kalendar chart for the month of December. In the entry above, as in the entry of April 11, 1852, when he heard the piano and suddenly felt "as if the winter in me were at length beginning to thaw," feelings of loss, alienation, barrenness, or coldness are addressed in the moment they are felt to give way to feelings of reintegration with the world, feelings prompted in both cases by a sound identified as musical. Shortly after the description of a barking dog in the December 27, 1857, entry, Thoreau writes that "we do not wonder that so many commit suicide, life is so barren and worthless; we only live on by an effort of the will. Suddenly our condition is ameliorated and even the barking of a dog is a pleasure to us" (*J* X:221). Music as an antidote to a suicidal instinct emerges in another entry, this one from the previous January:

What is there in music that it should so stir our deeps? We are all ordinarily in a state of desperation; such is our life; ofttimes it drives us to suicide. To how many, perhaps to most, life is barely tolerable, and if it were not for the fear of death or of dying, what a multitude would immediately commit suicide! But let us hear a strain of music, we are at once advertised of a life which no man had told us of, which no preacher preaches. Suppose I try to describe faithfully the prospect which a strain of music exhibits to me. The field of my life becomes a boundless plain, glorious to tread, with no death nor disappointment at the end of it. All meanness and trivialness disappear. I become adequate to any deed. No particulars survive this expansion; persons do not survive it. In the light of this strain there is no thou nor I. We are actually lifted above ourselves. (*J* IX:222)

Interestingly, the suicidal idea is not overcome but rather transformed; the self is abolished, as in suicide, but remains alive, merged into the sonic plain: "No particulars survive this expansion—persons do not survive it." The "boundless plain" in which Thoreau finds himself on hearing this strain of music is explicitly contrasted with life understood in terms of mortality and linear temporality. One senses in all of Thoreau's writings about sound that what he valued most was the feeling of being absorbed or surrounded.

Thoreau's perception of the contingency of his feelings of despair, the way they could be suddenly alleviated by something outside himself, is consistent with his 1852 declaration "none but the kind gods can make me sane . . . I ask to be melted." For Thoreau, cultivating openness to the more-than-human world was a strategy for counteracting the barrenness associated with linear time, with death, and with the loss of human friends. In the Kalendar charts, we see Thoreau working toward an openness that extended through time as well as across space, an ability to locate himself within cyclical time, surrounded by seasonal music, even in a barren present.

Notes

Some portions of this essay originally appeared in Kristen Case, "The Art of Losing: Thoreau's Journal Practices," *Thoreau Society Bulletin* 287 (Fall 2014): 5–6.

1. Robert D. Richardson, *Henry Thoreau: A Life of the Mind* (Oakland, CA: University of California Press, 1986), 305–8; Kristen Case, "Phenology," in *Henry David Thoreau in Context*, ed. James S. Finley (Cambridge: Cambridge University Press, 2017), 259–68.

2. See William Rossi, "Performing Loss, Elegy, and Transcendental Friendship," *New England Quarterly* 81, no. 2 (June 2008): 252–77; H. Daniel Peck, *Thoreau's Morning Work: Memory and Perception in* A Week on the Concord and Merrimack Rivers, *the Journal, and* Walden (New Haven, CT: Yale University Press, 1990); and Branka Arsić, *Bird Relics: Grief and Vitalism in Thoreau* (Cambridge, MA: Harvard University Press, 2016).

3. Leonard N. Neufelt and Nancy Craig Simmons, "Historical Introduction," *PJ* 4:631.

4. As Rossi notes, his reading of "Transcendental Friendship" "follows the recent work of Robert Neimeyer, Thomas Attig, and others . . . who have reexamined mourners' efforts to maintain the memory of the dead within a post-traumatic reconstruction of meaning. Although such efforts are commonly enough recognized as valuable in non-Western cultures, more often than not they have been pathologized as prolonged or 'unresolved' grieving in the traditional psychoanalytic model" ("Performing Loss," 257n14).

5. Arsić, *Bird Relics*, 52.

6. Kristen Case, "Phenology."

7. See Robert Thorson, *The Boatman: Henry David Thoreau's River Years* (Cambridge, MA: Harvard University Press, 2017), for a complete discussion of Thoreau's river-related phenology.

8. Peck, *Thoreau's Morning Work*.

9. See Laura Dassow Walls, *Seeing New Worlds: Henry David Thoreau and Nineteenth-Century Natural Science* (Madison: University of Wisconsin Press, 1995), and David M. Robinson, *Natural Life: Thoreau's Worldly Transcendentalism* (Ithaca, NY: Cornell University Press, 2004).

10. Mary Elkins Moller, *Thoreau in the Human Community* (Amherst, MA: University of Massachusetts Press, 1980), 35–37; Porte quoted on 35.

11. Rossi, "Performing Loss," 257.

PART III
WIDENING CIRCLES

10

"WIDER THAN OUR VIEWS OF IT"

THOREAU'S UNIVERSALISM

Daniel S. Malachuk

This essay concludes with recommendations for Thoreau's tricentennial in 2117, but I begin more modestly by comparing us—the bicentennial academic readers of Thoreau—to the centennial readers. How do we match up? On the one hand, we will never accomplish what they did: they canonized Thoreau. As Lawrence Buell has shown, around the start of the twentieth century, Thoreau was rescued from obscurity by a group of enterprising critics who praised him (along with Hawthorne, Whitman, and Melville) for challenging the genteel pieties that had once defined the American literary canon.[1] In contrast, on our watch over the last half century (at least according to one researcher's assessment of the Modern Language Association International Bibliography), while he still ranks among the twenty-five most-studied American authors, Thoreau has suffered the most significant decline in scholarly attention.[2]

On the other hand, perhaps we circa 2017 scholars have done something more important than those of 1917. For, back then, there was one piety they simply could not abide Thoreau opposing: patriotism. For the centennial scholars, all their newly canonized authors had to be, as Buell puts it, more "patriotic . . . than oppositional" in standing for "good old American individualism."[3] In contrast, if this volume's title and its contributors' affiliations are at all representative, Thoreau's bicentennial champions no longer read him as an American first and foremost, or even at all. Unlike our colleagues a century ago, that is, we take Thoreau seriously when he writes at the end of *Walden* that none of this was meant just for (in the shorthand then for generic English and American males) "John or Jonathan" (*W* 333).

Before congratulating ourselves too heartily on this crucial interpretive advance, however, we must acknowledge that in truth the real pioneers here were not academics but activists: the first readers to really push for a global Thoreau, that is, were not scholars but human rights leaders such as Leo Tolstoy, Mahatma Gandhi, and Martin Luther King Jr. and environmentalists such as John Muir, Aldo Leopold, and Rachel Carson. Long before us, they heard in "Civil Disobedience" a cry not for American liberties but for human rights; in 1945, for example, Roger Baldwin, a founder of the American Civil Liberties Union, recalled how "Thoreau's universalism was never more strikingly brought home to me than during a day I spent with Mr. Gandhi on a train trip through France in 1931," "the only visible book in his compartment [being] the 'Duty of Civil Disobedience.'"[4] Nor were we scholars the first to grasp Thoreau's significance as an environmentalist; rather, as Buell confessed in the very book that cemented Thoreau's standing among academics in this regard, we "professional Thoreauvians have by and large responded to rather than led this wave of reinterpretation."[5]

Most bicentennial readers, I imagine, would graciously acknowledge our belatedness on this score, join in praising the predecessor activists, and then consider the chapter closed. But this essay insists we reflect on a related failure on our part as academics vis-à-vis the activists, which has been our long-standing inability to reckon with the double-faceted nature of Thoreau's universalism. Yes, the academic consensus today is that Thoreau was, as the activists first argued, an ethical universalist, or (as a shorthand here) cosmopolitan: we trust that Thoreau valued all persons equally and sought to protect all of nature as much as possible. But the activists were also drawn to a second facet of Thoreau's universalism, one that we academics (with such exceptions as, for instance, George Shulman or Jeffrey Bilbro) cannot stomach: that Thoreau valued all persons and nature as part of a meaningful universe.[6] That is, for Thoreau as well as the activists, the human and nonhuman creation is of such precious value because, as divined in *Walden*, "*Next* to us the grandest laws are continually being executed," and "*Next* to us is . . . the workman whose work we are" (*W* 134; emphasis in original). That kind of universalism—not the ethical but the metaphysical kind—we academics have largely resisted acknowledging in Thoreau's work.

And so, when it comes to Thoreau's universalism, we bicentennial scholars have unfortunately not so much advanced our understanding beyond

1917 as taken one step forward and another step back. Yes, where the centennial scholars wrongly read Thoreau as a nationalist, we properly read him as a cosmopolitan, but where they properly read Thoreau as a capital-*T* Transcendentalist, we, on the other hand, stubbornly follow the modernists, say, like Romain Rolland, who purportedly declared, "Je hais les mots à majuscules."[7] We, too, hate words that are capitalized (or, in the case of the Thoreau quotation above, italicized). And so where we can clearly see now that the centennial scholars rather pathetically wished Thoreau to be a patriot just like themselves, we still cannot see that we, too, rather pathetically wish Thoreau to be just like us: to be (to recall yet another of Buell's helpful arguments) "de-Transcendentalize[d]."[8] De-Transcendentalism, or what I will here call "irony," is contemporary academia's genteel piety. Richard Rorty's definition is exemplary: "I use 'ironist' to name the sort of person who faces up to the contingency of his or her own most central beliefs and desires—someone sufficiently historicist and nominalist to have abandoned the idea that those central beliefs and desires refer back to something beyond the reach of time and chance."[9] So long as we are ironists like Rorty, we blind ourselves to the full significance of Thoreau's universalism for the future.

There's some talk in literary studies nowadays about our becoming "postcritical"; for instance, Rita Felski, in her 2015 *The Limits of Critique*, contends that, after forty years or so, we scholars of literature have finally had enough of the "hermeneutics of suspicion."[10] As I've argued elsewhere, though, scholars of Transcendentalism have long dispensed with suspicion in their assessments of these writers' intentions; most Transcendentalist studies scholars openly align themselves with their accounts of, say, Emerson's individualism, Fuller's feminism, or Thoreau's environmentalism.[11] And so, while it may now be à la mode in literary studies generally, postcritique has long been the dominant style of scholarship on Transcendentalism. Felski even suggests this: though without mentioning his prominence in our field of study, she identifies Stanley Cavell as part of "a substantial tradition of modern thought that has circumvented or challenged the logic of critique."[12]

So it is with this consensus in Transcendentalist studies in mind that I will appeal in what follows to my presumably postcritical colleagues to reconsider their one unexamined suspicion of Thoreau's program, a suspicion wholeheartedly shared by Cavell, incidentally: that of Thoreau's

Transcendentalism. In the last century, we scholars, taking our cue from the activists, have demonstrated over and over again how Thoreau's cosmopolitanism—his ethical universalism—makes him of the utmost contemporary as well as historical importance. As we enter a new century of Thoreauvian scholarship, shall we not at least consider the other lesson of the activists? Shall we not at least pause to note that Martin Luther King Jr.—who pointed to "the arc of the moral universe [bending] toward justice"—did not successfully defend human rights with the help of an *ironic* Thoreau?[13]

I will make this appeal below in two ways. First, I share evidence that we postcritical readers of Thoreau may already practically believe in his Transcendentalism; that is, despite ourselves, we intuit that, if not in the immediate present then at least in the future, Thoreau's Transcendentalism may indeed help us to better value all persons and nature. Second, I show some examples suggesting that Thoreau's universalism is undeniably metaphysical: not his moral and political claims on behalf of "higher law," which I have shown several times before, but rather his career-long portraits of a meaningful universe.[14]

Crypto-Transcendentalism

In 1992, Amanda Anderson argued that poststructuralist readers critique literature on behalf of norms the readers themselves deny holding, a style of critique she labeled "cryptonormativism."[15] In Thoreau studies, similarly, we often officially reject or more often look past Thoreau's god terms while nonetheless tacitly counting on their potency to bolster our claims for his contemporary relevance. This is generally true, I think, in our enthusiastic praise for Thoreau's abolitionism and environmentalism. We rarely go to the trouble of explicitly disavowing his appeals to "higher law" in defense of both, preferring instead to allow such rhetoric to render Thoreau all the more compelling in this regard: for example, we usually leave in place but also unremarked the capital W in his dictum that "in Wildness is the preservation of the world" (*Exc* 202). But here I'll show more precisely how crypto-Transcendentalism has been at work in the case of "planetarity."[16]

In 2003, Gayatri Spivak sought to bring together the movements for human rights and for environmental protection but without, of course, engaging in any kind of passé metaphysics. She described both the human rights and environmental movements as sharing an ethics of "planetarity," which entails the vigilant recognition of particular alterity (plant and animal).[17] In search of precedent ethics, two major scholars of American literature—Wai Chee Dimock in 2006 and Laura Dassow Walls in 2013—pointed to Thoreau's own protoplanetarity while still acknowledging some important differences from Spivak.[18] Most important among these differences was, as Walls put it, that Thoreau "forc[es us] to become . . . planetary thinker[s]" not just by scaling down to the particulars Spivak stressed but also by "scal[ing] up" so that we "never lose sight of the . . . extent of [our] relations."[19] Walls acknowledges here what a lot of ironist scholars of Thoreau will not: that Thoreau (as he wrote in his journal on Christmas Day in 1851) believed "we look upward for inspiration" (*PJ* 4:224).

Most of the time, ironist scholars like to avoid these upward-looking moments in Thoreau's writing and instead focus on the relatively few moments when Thoreau instead looks sideways or downwards, as if to liken him more to Aristotle than Plato (to recall the famous Raphael fresco). But even in these other directions Thoreau still reveals himself to be a Transcendentalist. Recall again the "next to us" moment in *Walden*, where he insists God is alongside us: "*Next* to us is . . . the workman whose work we are." The passage actually begins with Thoreau chastising us for dwelling on the particular rather than the universal: "For the most part we allow only outlying and transient circumstances to make our occasions. They are, in fact, the cause of our distraction. Nearest to all things is that power which fashions their being" (*W* 134). A single, universal power fashions the being of all "outlying and transient circumstances." Thoreau looks sideways to see it, yes, but only to confirm his intuition that this power holds the whole universe together. How about when he looks down? Well, consider also one of the rare—but oft-cited by ironists—downward-looking moments in *Walden* when Thoreau recalls the boy's joke to the men who sink deep into the bog before they reach the pond's "solid bottom" (*W* 330). Cavell is typical of such ironists in arguing Thoreau means here that "the bottom is [only] our construction of it": that, as Rorty stressed, we ironists "face up to the contingency of [our] most central beliefs [and] abandon the idea that those central beliefs . . . refer back to something beyond the reach of time and chance" like a solid bottom.[20] That's fine for Cavell and Rorty, but Thoreau actually begins the passage by insisting "Let us not play at kittly-benders"—fooling around on thin ice—for "there is a solid bottom everywhere." And he ends it by likening the men's bog/bottom confusion to the bad carpenter's putty/beam confusion. "Do not depend on the putty," he writes a sentence after the bog story; that is, don't depend on the stuff we make to hold things together. Rather, "Drive a nail home . . . So will help you God, and so only. Every nail driven should be as another rivet in the machine of the universe, you carrying on the work" (*W* 330): we carry on God's work by relying on the universe's original architecture. So, yes, Thoreau looks down and not up in this passage, but not to play around at kittly-benders. Instead, he urges us to see through the thin ice—the bog, the putty, the contingencies—all the way to the foundation, the solid bottom, "the machine of the universe."

But, again, most often Thoreau, like Plato, "scales up." Recommending in the "Higher Laws" chapter of *Walden* that we seek to live "in conformity to higher principles," Thoreau reminds us that by living in this "highest reality" (*W* 216), we enter a place where even "a little star-dust [is] caught" (*W* 217). In Thoreau's version of "planetarity," we cannot finally appreciate our planet of particulars without the grand overview of universal, higher laws. This is the final lesson of his experiment in *Walden*, as he writes at the end: "I learned this, at least, by my experiment; that if one advances confidently in the direction of his dreams, and endeavors to live the life which he has imagined, he will meet with a success unexpected in common hours. He will put some things behind, will pass an invisible boundary: new, universal, and more liberal laws will begin to establish themselves around and within him [that is, above, below, and to the side of him]; or the old laws be expanded, and interpreted in his favor in a more liberal sense, and he will live with the license of a higher order of beings" (*W* 323–24). In a more recent book edited by Rick Furtak, Jonathan Ellsworth, and James Reid, a number of ironist philosophers admire Thoreau's Socratic means while implying (in the Cavellian tradition) that this "perfectionism" was nonteleological (Stanley Bates) and devoid of Platonic ends (Ellsworth).[21] I see in these ironist philosophers' desires to associate Thoreau with Socrates examples of crypto-Transcendentalism, for in explicitly summoning Socrates they implicitly summon Plato and his "old laws" too (for we literally would not read Socrates today without Plato). We should instead be explicit about all of this. Perhaps we personally disagree—perhaps as trained ironists we are certain we must disagree—with Thoreau's Platonism. But, then again, perhaps we should not be so sure about that training; this is the contention of the next section.

The Great Silence

Crypto-Transcendentalism means endorsing Thoreau's ethical universalism without explicitly acknowledging how—for Thoreau at least—the "old laws" hold that universe together. Ethics aside, are we so certain today that we do not need something like those "old laws" just to understand the universe? Far from an insult to our pious ironism, that is, Thoreau's Transcendentalism may help us to grapple more seriously with the real possibility that our universe is meaningful.

To take seriously such claims about meaning in the universe is very difficult for many in the academic humanities, because we've been trained in what Paul Ricœur called "the hermeneutics of suspicion," his exemplary practitioners being Marx, Freud, and Nietzsche.[22] Nietzsche especially taught Cavell, Rorty, and all of us that whatever meaning is in this universe, we have made—rather than found—for ourselves. Perhaps the most influential version of this narrative (that our universe is devoid of meaning beyond what we have made for ourselves) is to be found in the opening paragraphs of his 1873 essay "On Truth and Lying in a Non-Moral Sense," the one that includes the electrifying claim that truths, after all, "are illusions of which we have forgotten that they are illusions."[23] Nietzsche sets the stage for such a claim with this captivating story about our meaningless universe: "In some remote corner of the universe . . . there was once a planet on which clever animals invented cognition. It was the most arrogant and mendacious minute in the 'history of the world'; but a minute was all it was. After nature had drawn just a few more breaths the planet froze and the clever animals had to die." We are clever animals, but we are deluded: we convince ourselves that our *made* truths are *found* truths: timeless, universal. This is a problem for all creatures, Nietzsche adds, and "if we could communicate with a midge we would hear that it too floats through the air with the very same pathos, feeling that it too contains within itself the flying centre of this world."[24]

As bewitching as Nietzsche's story has since become, we need to remember that he offers just one reading of what has come to be known as the "Great Silence." In physicist Enrico Fermi's 1950 formulation, the Great

Silence is the puzzle why, with the exception of Earth, such an ancient universe with, statistically, so many other worlds capable of life—many of them with a billion years or more of an evolutionary head start on us—has thus far proven lifeless. In the nearly seventy years since Fermi articulated it, "the problem remains," as Milan M. Ćirković puts it, "completely and irritatingly unsolved," despite multiplying efforts that have made this "the most complex multidisciplinary problem in contemporary science."[25] Nietzsche's rather innocent assumption was that the Great Silence simply proves the universe is meaningless, but many others since Fermi have interpreted that silence quite differently. Especially in recent decades, armed with ever more sophisticated versions of the 1961 Drake Equation (about the overwhelming likelihood of extraterrestrial life), philosophers have developed literally dozens of other explanations for the silence: sixty-six in one more recent publication, seventy-five in another.[26] These are in effect metaphysical solutions to a physical paradox, and the experts tend to sort them into different categories. Perhaps most compelling are those categories offered by Nick Bostrom of the Future of Humanity Institute at the University of Oxford. Bostrom contends the three most likely sets of explanations for the Great Silence each center on artificial intelligence (AI), a stage of technological advancement that here on Earth looks to bring great promise or peril. Bostrom's first set of explanations focuses on AI's perilous side, one taken quite seriously worldwide, as the January 2017 conference to hash out twenty-three principles to forestall such a catastrophe suggests. What if such peril has proven inescapable in the older worlds throughout the universe? That is, what if AI has served as a "Great Filter" that snuffs out extraterrestrial civilizations just as they reach the threshold of interstellar communication? Narratives along these lines constitute the first set of explanations. Bostrom's second and third sets of answers are, happily, more positive and quite intriguing: that other AI civilizations actually do abound in the universe and are either waiting for us to progress before bothering with us or mysteriously enabling our progress, effectively as our gods, we being to them like pets or computer games.[27]

What the Great Silence tells us, then, is not that our universe is meaningless, as Nietzsche assumed, but that our planet may be gliding in either of these directions spelled out by Bostrom, tragically "into the bin of extinction scenarios," as he explained in a 2015 *New Yorker* feature, or much more wonderfully "into the bin of technological maturity scenarios," wherein Earth is "in the center of this growing bubble of infrastructure"— Thoreau's "machine of the universe," if you will. Alluding to theories of planetary, stellar, and galactic civilization harnessing the power of stars for energy by Nikolai Kardashev, Carl Sagan, Freeman Dyson, and others, Bostrom hypothesizes that this infrastructure might support colonizing civilizations spreading out across the galaxy or that these are already under way by our godlike supervisors.[28]

For those postmodern academics who have forgotten that Nietzsche's fable about our meaningless universe is indeed just that, a fable, to listen anew to the Great Silence and hear in it such wildly different possibilities of meaningfulness as these can be overwhelming. Indeed, this is true for anyone, and in addition to scientists we will require artists with profound imaginations about the future to guide us. What kinds of artists? Well, in yet another recent article popularizing Bostrom's work, Ross Andersen points to one in particular. How can we begin to imagine a universe to whose mysterious workings we humans actively contribute? The first step, Andersen writes, is "to grasp the full scope of human potential, the enormity of the spatiotemporal canvas our species has to work with. You have to understand what Henry David Thoreau meant when he wrote, in *Walden* (1854), 'These may be but the spring months in the life of the race.' You have to step into deep time and look hard at the horizon, where you can glimpse human futures that extend for trillions of years."[29] Andersen directs our attention to a paragraph late in *Walden*'s "Conclusion" that readily invites direct contrast with Nietzsche's famous fable. Nietzsche and Thoreau begin their stories in remarkably similar ways: Nietzsche writes with disgust about the "stagnant self-complacency of mankind," while Thoreau sneers that "this generation inclines a little to congratulate itself on being the last of an illustrious line, and in Boston and London and Paris and Rome, thinking of its long descent, it speaks of its progress in art and science and literature with satisfaction." In all of this, Thoreau writes, we see merely the clever animal (though Thoreau calls him "the good Adam") "contemplating his own virtue," which again sounds much like Nietzsche's disdain for our self-satisfied conviction that we are the center of the universe (*W* 331).

But then Thoreau takes a very different turn. Nietzsche, recall, confidently asserts that if we could hear the midges they would be telling the same pathetic story we do about being the center of the universe. Thoreau, too, thinks of insects, but, listening more receptively to that Great Silence, concludes otherwise: "What youthful philosophers and experimentalists we are! There is not one of my readers who has yet lived a whole human life. These may be but the spring months in the life of the race . . . We are acquainted with a mere pellicle of the globe on which we live. Most have not delved six feet beneath the surface, nor leaped as many above it. We know not where we are. Beside, we are sound asleep nearly half our time. Yet we esteem ourselves wise, and have an established order on the surface [think of the kittly-benders] . . . As I stand over the insect crawling amid the pine needles on the forest floor, and endeavoring to conceal itself from my sight, and ask myself why it will cherish those humble thoughts, and hide its head from me who might perhaps be its benefactor, and impart to its race some cheering information, I am reminded of the greater Benefactor and Intelligence that stands over me the human insect" (*W* 331–32). For Thoreau, the Great Silence tells us not that we are alone but likely part of what Joseph Urbas calls an "ontological continuum" in Thoreau's thought, one that Thoreau here suggests may very well extend from insects, to us, to a capital-*B* Benefactor and a capital-*I* Intelligence across the universe.[30]

In many ways, this unflattering contrast of Nietzsche's and Thoreau's responses to the Great Silence is a reprise of their responses to Darwin's 1859 theory in *Origin of Species*. In 1860, Thoreau was introduced to that theory by a nephew of Asa Gray, the Harvard naturalist who admitted that same year to "feel[ing] most deeply that the whole subject is too profound for the human intellect. A dog might as well speculate on the mind of Newton."[31] Thoreau was similarly humbled in 1860: as "one of the first to apply Darwin's theories in the field," Walls explains, Thoreau "knew something even more powerful: there was more to learn, more he did not understand."[32] Nietzsche, in contrast, confidently and notoriously adopted the now debunked social Darwinist ideology (though with perhaps more nuance than scholars have allowed in the past).[33]

This essay began modestly but thus concludes quite differently. I've made a case to you, my presumably fellow postcritical readers of Thoreau, that if we want Thoreau's tricentennial in 2117 to be recognized, let alone celebrated, we ought to begin to read him more often as a universalist in both of the senses urged by the activists he inspired: that is, not only as an ethical universalist but as a Transcendentalist too. We have learned to bracket our suspicions so far as Thoreau's cosmopolitanism is concerned; we ought to learn to do the same with his Transcendentalism. In closing, consider quickly the clear limitations of the three alternatives to Thoreau the Transcendentalist cosmopolitan: the Transcendentalist nationalist, the ironic nationalist, and the ironic cosmopolitan.

First, there is Thoreau the Transcendentalist nationalist, which is effectively the 1917 Thoreau. It's not hard to imagine the quick demise of such a Thoreau today, and rightly so, for a Transcendentalist nationalist is a fancy phrase for a white supremacist. In *The History of White People*, Nell Irvin Painter concluded that Emerson's interests in metaphysics as well as Anglo-Saxon culture made him "the philosopher king of American white race theory."[34] One could fairly quickly sketch a similar portrait of Thoreau. Currently, at least, pace Painter, the mainstream position in Transcendentalist studies continues to be that Emerson's and Thoreau's interest in Anglo-Saxon culture is accidental rather than essential to their thought, but it is conceivable, in our increasingly heated culture war between nationalists and cosmopolitans, that we cosmopolitans might determine Thoreau and Emerson are just too much trouble, as, for example, we've already decided about a writer quite important to both, Carlyle. (Indeed, Carlyle's importance to Emerson is a key component of Painter's argument.)

The remaining alternatives are the ironic ones: the ironic nationalist and the ironic cosmopolitan. Thoreau as an ironic nationalist would be akin to the version of Walt Whitman offered by Rorty in his 1998 *Achieving Our Country*.[35] As a child of Nietzsche like us, Rorty recognized all metanarratives to be our pathetic midge-like constructions; but, as a pragmatist too, he nonetheless deemed the progressive nationalist metanarrative necessary for most people. Through some selective interpretations of his poetry, Rorty found such ironic nationalism in Whitman. Here again, though, I think any such nationalisms—even Rorty's progressive and ironic kind— will be deemed too problematic for most cosmopolitans. After all, the new alt-right nationalists are scary not least for being themselves quite capable ironists (e.g., Pepe the Frog).[36] We need to champion cosmopolitan authors from here out, not nationalists, ironic or otherwise.

That leaves the third alternative, Thoreau the ironic cosmopolitan, which I have posited to be today's reigning view among academics: the bicentennial Thoreau is an earnest, ethical universalist but also an ironist, not really a Transcendentalist. I've countered that, first, a lot of supposedly ironist academics show themselves to be—in their handling of Thoreau—crypto-Transcendentalists: they endorse Thoreau's ethical convictions about civil disobedience, abolition, and environmentalism while sidestepping, rather than renouncing, the "old laws" that ground these convictions. However, we really must be more candid and allow that Thoreau's planetary ethic works only when one "scales up," which Thoreau does by situating our planetary particulars within a grander "scheme of the universe" or "frame of the universe, and of such valor as God himself," as he put it early in his career in "A Walk to Wachusett" and "A Winter Walk," respectively (*Exc* 42, 59). Second, I argued that Thoreau was perhaps not so dated in hearing, in that Great Silence, evidence of such a universal scheme or frame or machine, or what Bostrom and the others call "infrastructure," and that it is, rather, us, with our quaint Nietzschean pieties about a meaningless universe, who cannot hear our chanticleer—the one who awoke two hundred years ago, to urge us to "thank Heaven, here is not all the world" and to recall that the universe is "wider than our views of it" (*W* 320).

We awoke to Thoreau's cosmopolitanism during this second century since his birth. In this upcoming third century, might we awake to his Transcendentalism? That is, are we prepared to listen not smugly but seriously to all of his earnest and often capitalized talk of the universe's "frame" or "scheme" (in those early writings just referenced) or the universe's "machine" in midcareer writings like *Walden* or—in his last book—"the shore yet further west"? I'll end with an example from *Cape Cod*. Near the close of the first chapter, "The Shipwreck," Thoreau begins to mourn persons lost when the *St. John* ran aground at Grampus Rock, but then concludes—on the basis of "more universal and convincing evidence . . . though it has not yet been discovered by science"—that their capital-S "Spirit" nonetheless endures beyond the rocks, metaphysically.

> Why care for these dead bodies? . . . Their owners [i.e., their souls] were coming to the New World . . . but, before they could reach it, they [the souls] emigrated to a newer world than ever Columbus dreamed of, yet one of whose existence we believe that there is far more universal and convincing evidence—though it has not yet been discovered by science—than Columbus had of this; not merely mariners' tales and some paltry drift-wood and sea-weed, but a continual drift and instinct to all our shores. I saw their empty hulks [that is, the dead bodies] that came to land; but they themselves [again, the souls], meanwhile, were

cast upon some shore yet further west, toward which we are all tending, and which we shall reach at last . . . All their plans and hopes burst like a bubble! Infants by the score dashed on the rocks by the enraged Atlantic Ocean! No, no! If the St. John did not make her port here, she has been telegraphed there. The strongest wind cannot stagger a Spirit; it is a Spirit's breath. A just man's purpose cannot be split on any Grampus or material rock, but itself will split rocks till it succeeds. (*CC* 10–11)

Notes

1. Lawrence Buell, "Henry Thoreau Enters the American Canon," in *New Essays on Walden*, ed. Robert F. Sayre (Cambridge: Cambridge University Press, 1999), 23–52.
2. D. G. Meyers, "MLA Rankings of American Writers," *Commentary*, March 26, 2012.
3. Buell, "Thoreau Enters the American Canon," 30.
4. Quoted in Mary King, *Mahatma Gandhi and Martin Luther King Jr: The Power of Nonviolent Action* (Paris: UNESCO Publishing, 1999), 22.
5. Lawrence Buell, *The Environmental Imagination: Thoreau, Nature Writing, and the Formation of American Culture* (Cambridge, MA.: Belknap Press of Harvard University Press, 1995), 368.
6. George M. Shulman, *American Prophecy: Race and Redemption in American Political Culture* (Minneapolis: University of Minnesota Press, 2008), and Jeffrey Bilbro, *Loving God's Wildness: The Christian Roots of Ecological Ethics in American Literature* (Tuscaloosa: University of Alabama Press, 2015).
7. Quoted in John Cruickshank, *Albert Camus and the Literature of Revolt* (Oxford: Oxford University Press, 1959), 5.
8. Lawrence Buell, "The Emerson Industry in the 1980s: A Survey of Trends and Achievements," *ESQ* 30, no. 2 (2d qtr. 1984): 117–36.
9. Richard Rorty, *Contingency, Irony, and Solidarity* (Cambridge: Cambridge University Press, 1989), xv.
10. Rita Felski, *The Limits of Critique* (Chicago: University of Chicago Press, 2015), 1.
11. Daniel S. Malachuk, "Transcendentalist and Gothic Intentions," in "Whither Transcendentalism?," special issue, *Revue Française d'Etudes Américaines* 140 (3d qtr. 2014): 52–64.
12. Felski, *Limits of Critique*, 150.
13. Quoted in King, *Mahatma Gandhi*, 127.
14. See Daniel S. Malachuk, *Two Cities: The Political Thought of American Transcendentalism* (Lawrence: University Press of Kansas, 2016).
15. Amanda Anderson, "Cryptonormativism and Double Gestures: The Politics of Post-Structuralism," *Cultural Critique* 21 (Spring 1992): 68.
16. I explore this case at length in "'The Sun Is But a Morning Star': Thoreau's Future," special Thoreau bicentennial issue, *Nineteenth-Century Prose* 44, no. 2 (Fall 2017): 13–36.
17. Gayatri Chakravorty Spivak, *Death of a Discipline* (New York: Oxford University Press, 2003).
18. See Wai Chee Dimock, *Through Other Continents: American Literature across Deep Time* (Princeton, NJ: Princeton University Press, 2006), and Laura Dassow Walls,

"Walking West, Gazing East: Planetarity on the Shores of Cape Cod," in *Thoreauvian Modernities: Transatlantic Conversations on an American Icon*, ed. François Specq, Laura Dassow Walls, and Michel Granger (Athens: University of Georgia Press, 2013), 21–42.

19. Wall, "Walking West, Gazing East," 26.

20. Stanley Cavell, *The Senses of Walden*, expanded ed. (Chicago: University of Chicago Press, 1992), 83.

21. Rick Anthony Furtak, Jonathan Ellsworth, and James D. Reid, eds., *Thoreau's Importance for Philosophy* (New York: Fordham University Press, 2012). See esp. Stanley Bates, "Thoreau and Emersonian Perfectionism," 14–30, and Ellsworth, "How *Walden* Works: Thoreau and the Socratic Art of Provocation," 143–58.

22. Quoted in Felski, *Limits of Critique*, 1.

23. Friedrich Nietzsche, "On Truth and Lying in a Non-Moral Sense," in *The Birth of Tragedy and Other Writings*, ed. Raymond Geuss and Ronald Speirs, trans. Ronald Speirs (Cambridge: Cambridge University Press, 1999), 146.

24. Nietzsche, "On Truth and Lying," 141.

25. Milan M. Ćirković, *The Great Silence: The Science and Philosophy of Fermi's Paradox* (Oxford: Oxford University Press, 2018), xiii, xv.

26. See Duncan Forgan, *Solving Fermi's Paradox* (Cambridge: Cambridge University Press, 2019), and Stephen Webb, *If the Universe Is Teeming with Aliens . . . WHERE IS EVERYBODY? Seventy-Five Solutions to the Fermi Paradox and the Problem of Extraterrestrial Life* (London: Springer, 2015).

27. Nick Bostrom, "Are You Living in a Computer Simulation?," *Philosophical Quarterly* 53, no. 211 (April 2003): 243–55.

28. Quoted in Raffi Khatchadourian, "The Doomsday Invention," *New Yorker*, November 23, 2015, 64–79.

29. Ross Andersen, "Omens," *Aeon*, February 25, 2013, https://aeon.co/.

30. Joseph Urbas, "'Being Is the Great Explainer': Thoreau and the Ontological Turn in American Thought," in Specq, Walls, and Granger, *Thoreauvian Modernities*, 120.

31. Quoted in Ćirković, *Great Silence*, 115. See also Laura Dassow Walls, *Henry David Thoreau: A Life* (Chicago: University of Chicago Press, 2017), 458.

32. Walls, *Henry David Thoreau*, 474.

33. See John Richardson, *Nietzsche's New Darwinism* (Oxford: Oxford University Press, 2004).

34. Nell Irvin Painter, *The History of White People* (New York: W. W. Norton, 2011), 151.

35. Richard Rorty, *Achieving Our Country: Leftist Thought in Twentieth-Century America* (Cambridge, MA: Harvard University Press, 1998).

36. See Angela Nagle, *Kill All Normies: Online Culture Wars from 4Chan and Tumblr to Trump and the Alt-Right* (Washington, D.C.: Zero Books, 2017).

11

CAPE COD, LITERATURE, AND THE ILLOCALITY OF THINKING ABOUT CAPITAL

Benjamin Pickford

> If the history of this beach could be written from beginning to end,
> it would be a thrilling page in the history of commerce.
> —Henry David Thoreau, "The Highland Light," *Cape Cod*

My purpose in this essay is to risk taking seriously my epigraph from Thoreau's *Cape Cod* and to propose that *Cape Cod* itself—which concludes with an effort to write the "history" of that sandy peninsula "from beginning to end," both in terms of its geologic idiosyncrasies and its human records—represents an attempt at this "thrilling page in the history of commerce" and therefore a uniquely focused economic study in Thoreau's oeuvre. *Cape Cod* is frequently open about its interest in economics. Thoreau remarks often on the tenuousness of economic survival on the Cape owing to its "doubtful soil," its "real and apparent barrenness" (*CC* 28–29). Weak agriculture and a dearth of timber force its inhabitants into the business of wrecking, an industry to which Thoreau dedicates much attention. In the book's notorious opening chapter, the cost in human suffering of the shipwreck of the *St. John* is obscured by the economic exigencies that continue indifferently, the seaweed collectors of Cohasset being "as serenely employed as if there had never been a wreck in the world" (*CC* 9). It is a scene that Thoreau describes as "affecting" not because of the mass of drowned bodies but because of the "sober dispatch of business" that went on uninterrupted in their midst (*CC* 5). As Thoreau muses, "This shipwreck had not produced a visible vibration in the fabric of society" (*CC* 7).

But lest such scenes be read as evidence of a commentary on the almost sublime indifference of economic necessity or a critique of an economic system in which individual agents can be so impassive in spite of the exceptionally *visible* damage inherent in this system, it is necessary to specify that my interest in Thoreau's study of economics in *Cape Cod* is only circumstantially and peripherally concerned with wrecking.[1] Instead, I am concerned with what defines and distinguishes a "thrilling" history of commerce, which is to say, given the time and context of *Cape Cod*'s composition, a thrilling history of capitalism. In the mid-nineteenth century, the form of vicarious pleasure now associated with the term *thrill* had not become distinct enough to obscure the word's etymological sense. Deriving from *thirl*, which relates to human-made holes or perforations, along with the tools used to produce them, the secondary, receptive, and passive forms of pleasure that appeal to the thrill seeker participate in this semantics of ecstasy, of being affected and pervaded by an external force.[2] When Thoreau writes of "walking along the shore of the resounding sea, determined to *get it into us*," therefore, he expresses his desire to be thrilled (*CC* 140; emphasis added). One is thrilled by good news or by a terrifying story; in either case, the verb describes an affective power that agitates or resonates in the emotions of its human subject, irrespective of the content of that which thrills. A thrilling history of capitalism would thus not be obliged to choose between commendation or critique of the economic system itself. Its obligation is only to engage its reader in a form of thinking that is coherent with the affective sense of the term. If the shipwreck of the *St. John* fails to produce a "visible vibration in the fabric of society," it is because this social consciousness is so determined by economic exigencies that the power of apprehension is forestalled. A thrilling page in the history of commerce should enliven and render visible that which is otherwise unavailable, but to do so, it must find a way to disengage economic thinking from the situated and cognitively determined economic subject.

There are two contextual parallels on which I draw in this essay and which make Thoreau a fascinating subject of analysis for the form of disengaged thinking just described. The first is the recent tendency of Thoreauvian scholarship to focus on his "extra-vagance," the meanings of "sauntering" and "excursions" in his work, and at last the effort Thoreau put into forms of desubjectification of perception, which Laura Dassow Walls calls "transjectivity," Meredith McGill describes as an "illocality" disengaged from "anchoring subjects or events," and Branka Arsić terms *literalization*, a nullification of the mediation of subjective experience toward an "actual . . . inhabit[ation of] of the perceived."[3] In such scholarship, and in a variety of ways, Thoreau literally aspires to a form of thinking "beyond borders" insofar as the boundaries of the personal constitute the borders that stymie critical insight. My contribution in this essay is to suggest that such interests align Thoreau with a second contextual parallel: his contemporary, Karl Marx, who—according to Louis Althusser's controversial but compelling thesis—underwent an "epistemological break" after 1845 that culminated in the forms of critique present in *Capital*. Althusser's claim is essentially that Marx was obliged to shed the epistemological conditions fixed by economic subjectivity, which are consistently characterized in the terms of localized and embedded perception. Althusser uses a narrow range of what he confesses are "important metaphors"; one is the "change of terrain," the imperative to deterritorialize and disengage from the foundation of economic thought provided by the edifice of political economy.[4] The second—and the more critical—is the imperative to reappraise the mechanisms of epistemological tropes that depend on sight, on the "fate of vision" (*RC* 17).

Both of Althusser's metaphorical categories have a peculiar resonance in *Cape Cod*. The barren, sandy terrain of Cape Cod unsettles Thoreau, to the extent that he often "look[ed] down to see if we were standing on terra firma" (*CC* 109). Thoreau makes this "change of terrain" the basis of the renewal of perspective he hopes to achieve. *Cape Cod* is intensely concerned with perspective; it announces this to the reader in its first line, where Thoreau expresses his wish to "get a better view than I had yet had of the ocean" for the sake of the unique, disembedded perspective it offers, since the ocean is that "of which a man who lives a few miles inland may never see any trace, more than of another world" (*CC* 3). The book's final line seems determined to leave this renunciation of embedded perspective as the text's lasting impression: "A man may stand there [on the shore of Cape Cod] and put all America behind him" (*CC* 215). The problem, however, is that these two metaphorical categories—a change of terrain and a disembedding of perspective—which Althusser suggests were simply inescapable in the nineteenth century and which so dominated the twentieth that he was incapable of posing his argument without them, provide the deceptive impression that critical subjectivity *is* possible. Indeed, Althusser

spends much of his time in "From *Capital* to Marx's Philosophy" commit-
ting rhetorical acts of violence on these metaphors, repeatedly emphasizing
that what is needed is "a real transformation of the means of production
of knowledge," a *real* epistemological break (*RC* 26). In the reading of
Cape Cod that follows, my objective is to reveal the text's dramatization
of a near-identical process, with Thoreau's "thrilling page in the history
of commerce" in the "Provincetown" chapter constituting his own highly
provisional attempt at a break that specifically addresses the apprehension
of capitalism's interpellation of consciousness and the impossibility of
attaining critical vantage in the second half of the nineteenth century.

Peripheral Vision

In Marx's era, America was rich enough in criticism of capitalism on moral,
religious, and—of course—paternalistic, proslavery grounds. As Marx
himself suggested in an 1852 letter, what was missing was systemic and
structural critique.[5] In 1876, as part of the centennial celebrations, Henry
Adams (as editor of the *North American Review*) commissioned a series of
articles to assess the intellectual and scientific state of the nation. Charles
Dunbar contributed an essay titled "Economic Science in America: 1776–
1876," the central concern of which was the absence of such a science in
nineteenth-century American culture: "Not only has no American school
of writers on political economy been established . . . but no recognized
contribution to the development of the science can be pointed out in any
way comparable to those made by the French writers, or to those which the
Germans are now making."[6] Seeking to account for this omission, Dunbar
revisited well-worn assumptions. "For the reason of the general sterility
of American thought upon [the subject of political economy] . . . and the
failure of our scholars as well as statesmen to contribute their share in the
progress made by the world," Yankee stereotypes provided an excuse: "Our
position as a nation charged with the business of subduing a new world,
and the rapid material development which has attended our success in this
work, have given to our life for the greater part of the century an intensely
practical aspect."[7] The American mind was, in other words, distracted.
Undoubtedly, the principal markers of the capitalist means of production
were absent or undeveloped in America until relatively late, and conse-
quently, the perception of economic structures by American writers was

inevitably stymied.[8] And vantage was critical: Marx confessed in the preface to the first German edition of *Capital* that he was capable of realizing the work only as a consequence of the vantage acquired through his political exile in England.[9] However, as Jacques Rancière has demonstrated in his statements of opposition to the reductive dichotomy of ignorance versus critical intelligence that he—and many others—perceive in Althusser's epistemological break, more subtle forms of provisional or incomplete epistemologies fill the gaps between pre-Marxist unconsciousness and Marxist critique.[10] Adams, who had commissioned Dunbar for his thoughts on American economic oversights in 1876, exemplifies in *The Education* a knowledge that is conscious of the form of the thing that it lacks. "No one, except Karl Marx, *foresaw* radical change," but nevertheless Adams was ready for the missing parts of the jigsaw these ideas represented. Marx was "standing there waiting for him"; the phenomenology of this encounter retrospectively appears to expose ignorance (Adams claims to have "had no idea" of what Marx would offer). But Adams self-deprecatingly overstates his unconsciousness; under conditions of *complete* ignorance, such ideas would inevitably lack the loam in which to take root.[11]

It is just such a premonition of critical awareness that motivates Thoreau's trip to Cape Cod. He wanted to go there, he says, "to *see* that seashore where man's works are wrecks" (*CC* 50; emphasis added). The expression of the search for a new vantage point evinces an effort of leverage on Thoreau's part. His desire to see "wrecks" is symptomatic of a perceiver enervated by the limits of embedded perception of the sort Thoreau characterizes as an "inlander's," overpowered by the heft of man's works in the American city, but it is also acute in terms of its potential to secure vantage on capital. A wrecking economy is peripheral to and a parasite of capitalism, one of two industries enabled by the contingent risks of maritime trade and the developing capitalist world-system of the mid-nineteenth century. The other was underwriting. In some ways, both wrecking and underwriting appear to exist outside of the nest of capital's influence and therefore possess the privilege of greater removal from its structural determination. Yet underwriting as an industry actually supports the program of capital's nonvisibility that is integral to its ability to become the structuring ideology of everyday life: whatever is insurable is necessarily reducible to capital's monetary valuation of the world, and through insurance, capital has one more tool to make such valuation appear normative. As Eric Wertheimer has written, underwriting may depend on capitalism's instabilities for its very existence, but it veils those instabilities through its reduction of all things to monetary value, a "socializ[ation] of capital."[12] Wrecking, on the other hand, renders starkly *visible* the contingencies of the global circulation of commodities and the human costs involved. It is the waterline of American capitalism, at which point its power to subdue the natural world abruptly ends.

The forms of vantage that a wrecking economy offers are therefore akin to those of the Cape itself by virtue of peripherality, disembeddedness, a form of minimal interest in and concern for the operation of social or economic systems elsewhere. "This sea-shore is a sort of neutral ground," Thoreau writes, "a most advantageous point from which to contemplate this world" (*CC* 147). If wrecking restores to the surface the sunken or buried realities of capital's risks, then it is notionally the material resource for a counterhistory of capital, a sphere in which to examine capital's contingencies in relative isolation, and a stark contrast to the secure quantifiability of capitalist accumulation in America's industrial cities. As Thoreau puts it, "the more barrels, the more Boston" (*CC* 211). But what is striking about Thoreau's leverage in traveling to the Cape to "get a better view" is its unraveling, to be gradually replaced by a sense of the failure of attempts to attain critical insight by simply taking up new vantage points. Early in the text, Thoreau describes his desire to clear obstacles to vision, and hence the interest in the Cape: "On studying the map, I saw that there must be an uninterrupted beach on the east or outside of the forearm of the Cape, more than thirty miles from the general line of the coast, which would afford a good sea view . . . and probably I could walk thence straight to Race Point, about twenty-eight miles, and not meet with any obstruction" (*CC* 4). But clearing the horizon does not inevitably enable the perceiver to lock eyes on whatever was sought. This simple concern with an open purview is unusual for Thoreau. In earlier works, his objectives are more clearly identifiable as the loci of new foundations, under which things might be "driven into corners," where they could be properly inspected. In "Resistance to Civil Government," the only *honest* spot in Concord is its jail, and so it is there that Thoreau must go; in *Walden*, mystery surrounds the depth of the pond, and so Thoreau must sound it. The fact that such efforts often evince a metaphysical delusion that Thoreau's writing then engages is well known, with Walter Benn Michaels's discussion of the antifoundationalist lesson of Walden's "false bottoms" being the key example.[13]

The difference with *Cape Cod* is that it reveals Thoreau's manifest consciousness that the pursuit of a new vantage point in and of itself will not resolve the issue. One needs to know *what* it is that one is looking for or, more important, *how* to go about the looking. By heading to the periphery or threshold point of economic life in the United States, all that Thoreau discovers is that the horizon lengthens again: "This peculiar open country, with here and there a patch of shrubbery, extends as much as seven miles, or from Pamet River on the south to High Head on the north, and from Ocean to Bay. To walk over it makes on a stranger such an impression as being at sea, and he finds it impossible to estimate distances in any weather . . . We shuddered at the thought of living there and taking our afternoon walks over those barren swells, where we could overlook every step of our walk before taking it, and would have to pray for a fog or a snow-storm to conceal our destiny. The walker there must soon eat his heart" (*CC* 105, 107). This passage is representative of the myriad discussions of mirages, of deceived perceptions, and of the failure of "the long wished for insight" present throughout *Cape Cod* (*CC* 60). It is exceptional only insofar as it foregrounds the existential unease that Thoreau's effort at leveraging his perspective creates. Being able to "overlook every step of our walk before taking it," Thoreau describes a condition of foreclosed possibilities that does not permit the walker (for which, in Thoreau, the word "thinker" is synonymous) to conceive of the possibility of an epistemological breakthrough. Thoreau's description thus evokes the hall of mirrors effect that curtails the emergence of authentically critical subjectivity under capitalism. Incapable of attaining an extrinsic perspective, the embedded subject can see no further than the obstacles presented by the most pressing economic exigencies. But even the aspirant Althusserian critical subject can go little further. Rancière described this enhanced vantage (and his problems with it) thus: "The Althusserian enterprise . . . explained that the place in which [the dominated] found themselves prevented them from understanding the laws of this domination: they were dominated because they did not understand, and they did not understand because they were dominated. Which meant that all the efforts they made to struggle against domination were themselves blind."[14] The problem is that although this mode of critique sees the totality of the effects of ideological domination, its totality constitutes a loop, a closed circuit, and in it lies the paradox of an epistemological topos of vision in the matter of capital. The critical subject must be capable of an overview that takes in the totality of this prospect, but—in the inevitable reinstantiation of the critical subject as an economic subject, embedded back within that prospect—the perspective enrobes her in what appears to be an infinite loop of foreclosed possibility.

It is striking, therefore, that in *Cape Cod*, Thoreau's conscious acknowledgment of the perils of an epistemology based on a topos of vision gives way to admissions of its inadequacy and attempts to formulate viable alternatives. The unraveling of an epistemological dependence on sight is given in terms that have a history for Thoreau: "As we looked off, and saw the water growing darker and darker and deeper and deeper the farther we looked, till it was awful to consider, and it appeared to have no relation to the friendly land, either as shore or bottom,—of what use is a bottom if it is out of sight, if it is two or three miles from the surface, and you are to be drowned so long before you get to it, though it were made of the same stuff with your native soil?" (*CC* 96). In these lines, Thoreau registers the pragmatic objections of his twentieth-century critics to the immanent realization of transcendental consciousness. In the sphere of economic thinking, transcendence of embedded perception would be extraordinarily "useful," if only it were possible. Its impossibility is the reason why "the protocols of *The German Ideology*'s philosophical rupture do not give us it in person" (*RC* 29); it is why a "thrilling page in the history of commerce" was necessary. Hence Thoreau then adds that when he stood looking "over that ocean, where, as the Veda says, 'there is nothing to give support, nothing to rest upon, nothing to cling to,' I felt that I was a land animal" (*CC* 96). Henry George—Thoreau's near contemporary and the most influential American economist of his era—was also a kind of "land animal," of course, but for Thoreau a retreat to land was simply a concession of his inadequacy to personally undertake the change of terrain that was necessary. George's remedy to capitalist inequality—the abolition of private property in land and thus the recovery of a stable foundation according to which accumulated wealth is redistributed—is anticipatively critiqued by Thoreau's observation that the shifting sands of the Cape delegitimize even this most fundamental of solid bottoms. As he writes, "All an inlander's notions of soil and fertility will be confounded by a visit to these parts, and he will not be able, for some time afterward, to distinguish soil from sand"

(*CC* 28). Firmly denied the "flattery" which might—in an etymological sense—provide the stable foundation for a new economic perspective (*CC* 147), the effects of Thoreau's perspectival leverage manifest themselves as the abandonment of an epistemology based on vision in favor of a radically different model.

A Thrilling Page in the History of Commerce

The alternative Thoreau pursues should not surprise us. A primary concern of Sharon Cameron in *Writing Nature* was to argue that Thoreau's Journal represented an undertaking in which textual leverage enlarges, enhances, and remedies the insufficiencies of human perception.[15] The perspectives which Thoreau is tasked with describing in *Cape Cod* rapidly exceed the adjectives available, and so—in seeking to depict the plains of Nauset—Thoreau adopts another form of textual leverage, in this case a lengthy excursion through the ecclesiastic history of the Cape that might "make the reader realize how wide and peculiar that plain was, and how long it took to traverse it" (*CC* 43). It is on precisely these terms that Thoreau's "thrilling page in the history of commerce" is to be constituted. Of course, Thoreau's potted history of Cape Cod Calvinism could not be described as "thrilling" in any sense, bar the etymological, according to which this history impresses the reader with affective qualities (textual expanse and peculiarity of detail) whose significance is to be realized in a kind of metonymic resonance rather than as coherent, informational material.

Hence, when the reader reaches the "Provincetown" chapter that closes the text, she has already served a brief apprenticeship in the hermeneutics of Thoreauvian textual excursions. Thoreau prepares his reader for what approaches in other ways as well. In the very last line of the penultimate chapter, he informs the reader that he and his companion "turned our weather-beaten faces toward Provincetown and the Bay again, having now more than doubled the Cape" (*CC* 166), thereby assuring that his account can be described as covering the Cape "from beginning to end" in a geographic sense. Once inside Provincetown, the largest and—in the opinion of its inhabitants—most "flourishing town" on the Cape (*CC* 170), Thoreau assumes for a final time the conventional position of economic vantage. Taking a seat "upon the highest sand-hill overlooking the town, in mid-air, on a long plank stretched between two hillocks of sand" (*CC* 171),

Thoreau offers a brief economic overview that calculatedly invokes the philosophical spectatorship extolled by Adam Smith: "From that elevation we could overlook the operations of the inhabitants almost as completely as if the roofs had been taken off. They were busily covering the wicker-worked flakes about their houses with salted fish, and we now saw that the back yards were improved for this purpose as much as the front . . . we saw that there was an art as well as a knack even in spreading fish, and that a division of labor was profitably practiced" (*CC* 173).[16] But to proceed far-ther the view must scale up incommensurably, and hence Thoreau embarks on the book's longest textual excursion which spans the Cape's history in an inconsistent reverse chronological order from the present, back through the accounts of the Puritans, through the documents of French explora-tion of the sixteenth and seventeenth centuries, to Icelandic manuscripts detailing possible Norse visitations as early as the tenth century, and from there backward to incredible assertions of Gallic fishing expeditions to the eastern seaboard before the birth of Christ (*CC* 196).

It is clearly, therefore, a history of the beach that spans "beginning to end," but it is not clear how it might be a "thrilling page in the history of commerce" until we read it for its metonymical resonances rather than for its manifest content. What is critical in "Provincetown" is its historiograph-ical method, which is distinctive on the basis of its overt rejection of any convention of historiographical method. First, the blatant issue of equiv-alence between the accounts Thoreau employs registers this history's indif-ference to the historiographical "solid bottom" of provenance. The "minute and faithful account[s]" of Samuel de Champlain's voyages are noted, but in the very next paragraph "probable" earlier voyages are given equal credence, and by the next page mere "rumors" are being added to the record (*CC* 187–88). Thoreau revels in the irregularity of his materials. A handful of mutually contradictory accounts of a French settlement on Sable Island, a sandbar off Nova Scotia, are assembled into a speculative discourse on whether its occupants survived on a diet of fish or on a stock of cattle left there by an earlier Portuguese expedition, or a combination of the two, or whether all such accounts are rumors. Thoreau's conclusion treats the sources indiffer-ently; his only interest is in the irregularity itself: "These are but a few of the instances which I might quote" (*CC* 190). In fact, at every opportunity, Thoreau exploits the uncertainty evoked by these materials and—in the form of his own prose—encourages that uncertainty to flourish. Joseph

Moldenhauer's textual notes in the Princeton edition of *Cape Cod* make an admirable and highly detailed effort to root Thoreau's excursions in their sources, but not without difficulty. One "passage is confusing," Moldenhauer notes, because Thoreau allows his pronouns to become entangled and sources to become obscure; elsewhere, a "citation of Belknap is misleading," another "citation of Bancroft . . . involves an obscurity." Many quotations in this section are misattributed or left unattributed.[17]

As other critics have noted, this is an extravagant, "unsettling" form of history.[18] It is also verifiably the last piece of *Cape Cod* to have come from its author's hand, since it was the focus of Thoreau's final efforts on the book as late as the spring of 1862, only weeks before his death.[19] Although this contributes to the inevitability that Thoreau's effort toward a new epistemological basis for economic critique will be incomplete, aspects of the text help to suggest the direction of his energies. A critical illustration comes in the form of a discourse on the sea, that which—at so many other points in the text—is represented as the type of an epistemology that undermines the security of human works, wrecks the products of human labor and (particularly in the case of the destruction of the Minot's Ledge lighthouse) the landmarks of human perspective:[20]

> Sir Thomas Browne (as quoted in Brand's *Popular Antiquities*, p. 372), on the subject of the tenth wave being "greater or more dangerous than any other," after quoting Ovid,—
>
> > "Qui venit hic fluctus, fluctus supereminet omnes
> > Posterior nono est, undecimoque prior,"—
>
> says, "Which, notwithstanding, is evidently false; nor can it be made out by observation either upon the shore or the ocean, as we have with diligence explored in both. And surely in vain we expect a regularity in the waves of the sea, or in the particular motions thereof, as we may in its general reciprocations, whose causes are constant, and effects therefore correspondent; whereas its fluctuations are but motions subservient, which winds, storms, shores, shelves, and *every interjacency irregulates*." (*CC* 124; emphasis added)

So Browne mocks Ovid's expectation that the sea should conform to human comprehension and thus command. But the critical aspect of this passage is not that the sea's irregularity defeats the epistemological desire to grasp its nature through pattern recognition but rather that "irregulating interjacencies" are a key feature of his decentralized history in "Provincetown." Indeed, they are a feature of this brief example, Thoreau choosing to foreground the fact that Browne's remarks—relying as they do on a quotation from Ovid—are quoted again by Brand before they are then quoted by Thoreau. The interjacencies of citational transference disengage *all* these quotations from their contexts, and Thoreau's decision to emphasize the scale of citationality alerts the reader to the potential contingencies engendered by this process.

Contingencies can happen to resolve questions in the mind of their observer, as they do in *Cape Cod*. A bleached whale bone evokes an Icelandic saga's account of Norse explorers who "cooked whales" on the New England coast, and hence, "it chanced that this was the most conclusive evidence which we met with to prove, what the Copenhagen antiquaries assert, that these shores were the *Furdustrandas*," the "wonderstrands" of Norse accounts of exploration (*CC* 147). But the enrichment of contingency is not secure in the way that Thoreau sometimes hopes. On multiple occasions, Thoreau seeks to validate the historical record through a recentralization, even a *reembodiment* of that history. His sickness after consuming the hen clam seems to "bring him nearer to the Pilgrims," who also sickened on eating Cape Cod's clams, but such reembodiment is deceptive, and he is too credulous in writing that this experience leaves him "prepared now to believe every word of *Mourt's Relation*" (*CC* 74). In "Provincetown," Thoreau closely compares *Mourt's Relation* with his own experience and finds little commensurability between what he reads and what he sees (*CC* 199–202). It goes without saying that the gratification of historical awareness should not lie in its validation of the conditions of the present; likewise, the use of Thoreau's history of the Cape is not to reassure the perspective of the embedded subject. What characterizes Thoreau's history, just as it characterizes the sequence of quotations noted in the excerpt from Browne just discussed, is instead an open associative hybridity, connections not founded by the legal dictates of historiographical verifiability but rather through contingency and resonance that may be thematic, intertextual, or simply linguistic. It is in literature—broadly conceived—rather than historiography that such associative hybridity is permitted to exist, according to which metonymic resonance becomes a relational paradigm as good as any other. Indeed, Thoreau openly tells us as much when he declines to cite a complete poem because certain lines happen to be "tied" or "yoked" to "unworthy companions by the rhyme" (*CC* 34). Literary provocations to ingrained or received structures of thought are enchanting, as Rita Felski has argued, and we might readily substitute "thrilling" for "enchanting" given the comparability of the two terms' semantic structure.[21]

As a means of thinking about capital, the potential benefit of the hybrid form sketched in "Provincetown" is multilayered. In thrilling its reader, it releases her from the conditions of embedded perception to which this text is manifestly opposed; as such, it releases her from the condition Althusser diagnosed in the young Marx, who "sought to know the essence of things" in the form of "a reading *at sight* . . . in the transparency of its 'concrete' existence" (*RC* 14). Indeed, to stay with Althusser, we find in "Provincetown" an echo of the structure of the epistemological break inasmuch as the form of Marx's critique is a self-deconstructing reading of classical political economy, *textual* rather than subjective in nature. Althusser phrases this as Marx's attempt "to *situate* himself with respect to the acknowledged masters of Political Economy," but the italicized "situate" (se *situer*) indicates that the verb is merely approximative (*RC* 16). This situation is fluid, non-situated, and never stable. In other words: "It is literally no longer the eye (the mind's eye) of a subject which *sees* what exists in the field defined by a theoretical problematic: it is this field itself which *sees itself* in the objects or problems it defines" (*RC* 24). The literariness of Thoreau's hybrid, associative history relentlessly extends the purview, dissolving bonds to context, something that is—as Fredric Jameson has noted—a manifestly capitalist propensity.[22] It illuminates the borderless interior of capital's structure that Thoreau's view from the beach evoked but—on the basis of the viewer's *real* situatedness on that beach—could not come to terms with.

No more than an inquiry into the architectonics of thinking about capital, Thoreau's proposition of literature's inherent illocality as a potential mechanism is, of course, limited. Yet glimmers appear to suggest where Thoreau's ideas *might* have gone, had the work of *Cape Cod* not been abruptly concluded by its author's death. *Cape Cod* is a travel book, like many of Thoreau's works, but this excursion narrative embodies the concept in a distinctive plurality of ways. John Lowney details the range of connotations of "excursion" that play out in *Cape Cod*, including the rhetorical *excursus*, of which "Provincetown" is unequivocally an example.[23]

Hence, if it is the case that in Thoreau's hands, and particularly in "Provincetown," an excursion narrative is *literally* a book that travels, it merely self-consciously embodies the condition of any text sent forth, on literary terms, to be read in any place, by any person, in any context, irrespective of its point or conditions of origin.[24] The extent to which this phenomenology of literature may offer the groundwork for a mode of excursive thinking on capital with more incisive results is perhaps a subject that Thoreau's thought would have taken; a similar model of excursive thinking certainly characterizes his musing on the irregular dissemination of cargoes lost at sea, which includes seeds. Reflecting on a Mr. Bell whose seedbank was lost in the recent wreck of the *Franklin*, Thoreau writes: "In ancient times some Mr. Bell was sailing this way in his ark with seeds of rocket, saltwort, sandwort, beach-grass, samphire, bayberry, poverty-grass, &c., all nicely labelled with directions, intending to establish a nursery somewhere; and did not a nursery get established, though he thought that he had failed?" (*CC* 131). *Cape Cod* itself remains an unsprouted relic in this respect. Given the lack of immanent critiques of capital in Thoreau's era, nineteenth-century American culture itself constitutes "a sort of neutral ground" in terms of its self-awareness of capitalism. But perhaps it would be better, in view of *Cape Cod*, to label it a neutralized ground, in which the dominance of Marx-derived critiques retrospectively applied to nineteenth-century American cultures may have had the unforeseen effect of scouring marginal or incipient forms of economic thinking like Thoreau's from the landscape.

Notes

1. There are, of course, many accounts of economic themes in Thoreau's work that emphasize his objections to capitalism. Here, I am concerned with the fact that *Cape Cod* dramatizes the complexity of the conditions that must exist—the architectonics and intellectual mechanisms required—*before* a critique can be undertaken.

2. For examples in Thoreau's other writing of the 1850s that illustrate how he uses the word to refer to experiences that produce an ecstatic sensation, see *J* IX:354, 355, 387, and X:54; *MW* 180, 224.

3. Laura Dassow Walls, "Walking West, Gazing East: Planetarity on the Shores of Cape Cod," in *Thoreauvian Modernities: Transatlantic Conversations on an American Icon*, ed. François Specq, Laura Dassow Walls, and Michel Granger (Athens: University of Georgia Press, 2013), 27; Meredith McGill, "Common Places: Poetry, Illocality, and Temporal Dislocation in Thoreau's *A Week on the Concord and Merrimack Rivers*,"

American Literary History 19, no. 2 (Summer 2007): 362; Branka Arsić. *Bird Relics: Grief and Vitalism in Thoreau* (Cambridge, MA: Harvard University Press, 2017), 8–9.

4. Louis Althusser, "Elements of Self-Criticism" (1974), in *Essays in Self-Criticism*, trans. Grahame Lock (London: NLB, 1976), 110. See also Louis Althusser, "From *Capital* to Marx's Philosophy" (1965), in Althusser, Étienne Balibar, Roger Establet, Pierre Macherey, and Jacques Rancière, *Reading Capital: The Complete Edition*, trans. Ben Brewster (London: Verso, 2015), 26; hereafter cited in the text as *RC*.

5. Marx mocked Henry Carey in this letter, noting nevertheless that he was "the only North American economist of any note." *Letters, 1852–55*, vol. 39 of *Karl Marx and Friedrich Engels: Collected Works*, ed. E. J. Hobsbawm et al. (London: Lawrence and Wishart, 1983), 62.

6. Charles F. Dunbar, "Economic Science in America: 1776–1876," *North American Review* 122, no. 250 (January 1876): 137.

7. Dunbar, "Economic Science," 145–46.

8. Charles Post offers an efficient summary of the myriad social and economic conditions that made early and antebellum America starkly different from industrialized Britain, France, and Germany: "The existence of unoccupied lands, available at little or no cost . . . made the establishment of capitalistic social property relations impossible"; chattel slavery "*set up barriers*" to labor-saving technological changes, specialization, and the production relations of wage labor; finally, most small landowners in antebellum America "marketed no more than 40–50% of their total output" until well into the nineteenth century, permitting the extended existence of precapitalist "webs of kinship and communal relations" and preventing the emergence of commodity relations. Post, "The American Road to Capitalism," in *Case Studies in the Origins of Capitalism*, ed. Xavier Lafrance and Charles Post (Cham, Switzerland: Palgrave Macmillan, 2019), 166, 168–69, 170–71.

9. "The physicist either observes physical phenomena where they occur in their most typical form and most free from disturbing influence, or, wherever possible, he makes experiments under conditions that assure the occurrence of the phenomenon in its normality. In this work I have to examine the capitalist mode of production, and the conditions of production and exchange corresponding to that mode. Up to the present time, their classic ground is England." Karl Marx, *Capital, Vol. I*, vol. 35 of *Karl Marx and Friedrich Engels: Collected Works*, ed. Alexander Chepurenko (London: Lawrence and Wishart, 1996), 8.

10. See, in particular, Rancière's preface to the new English edition of Jacques Rancière, *Proletarian Nights: The Workers' Dream in Nineteenth-Century France*, trans. John Drury (London: Verso, 2012), vii–xii.

11. Henry Adams, *The Education* (1907), in *Novels, Mont St. Michel, The Education* (New York: Library of America, 1983), 750, 786.

12. Eric Wertheimer, *Underwriting: The Poetics of Insurance in America, 1722–1872* (Stanford, CA: Stanford University Press, 2006), 11.

13. Walter Benn Michaels, "*Walden*'s False Bottoms," *Glyph* 1 (1977): 132–49.

14. Rancière, *Proletarian Nights*, vii.

15. Sharon Cameron, *Writing Nature: Henry Thoreau's Journal* (New York: Oxford University Press, 1985), esp. 10, 14, and 49–50. Laura Dassow Walls also discusses how Thoreau's Journal constitutes a "tool for seeing" in *Seeing New Worlds: Henry David*

Thoreau and Nineteenth-Century Natural Science (Madison: University of Wisconsin Press, 1995), 122–26.

16. For Smith, the ability to bring the entirety of the industrial process into the view of the overseer was the illustrative virtue of his example of the pin factory: "In those trifling manufactures which are destined to supply the small wants of but a small number of people, the whole number of workmen must necessarily be small; and those employed in every different branch of the work can often be collected into the same workhouse, and placed at once under the view of the spectator." Adam Smith, *An Inquiry into the Nature and Causes of the Wealth of Nations*, ed. R. H. Campbell and A. S. Skinner (1776; Oxford: Clarendon Press, 1979), 14.

17. See Moldenhauer's textual notes to the historical excursion in "Provincetown" in the Princeton edition (*CC* 403–23). The quoted sections come from 409–10.

18. John Lowney describes Thoreau's account of the long history of failures to settle the Cape and the New England coast as an "'unsettlement' narrative." Lowney, "Thoreau's *Cape Cod*: The Unsettling Art of the Wrecker," *American Literature* 64, no. 2 (June 1992): 242. Mitchell Robert Breitwieser notes, "Compared even with *Walden* then . . . *Cape Cod* is truly *extravagant* and peripatetic, partly because [Thoreau] died" before the book was published. Breitwieser, "Thoreau and the Wrecks on Cape Cod," *Studies in Romanticism* 20, no. 1 (Spring 1981): 16. Both Lowney and Breitwieser link the peculiar style of Thoreau's history to an assemblage of textual wrecks, a compelling reading which informs my own but which does not explain by itself how this is a "thrilling page in the history of commerce."

19. Moldenhauer, introduction to *CC* 278–83.

20. As Thoreau notes, "This light-house was the cynosure of all eyes," but its existence was short lived: "This light-house, as is well known, was swept away in a storm in April, 1851, and the two men in it, and the next morning not a vestige of it was to be seen from the shore" (*CC* 207).

21. Rita Felski, *Uses of Literature* (Malden: Blackwell, 2008), 51–76.

22. Describing finance capital, itself the logical extension of the money form in Marx's critique, Jameson writes: "Capital itself becomes free floating. It separates itself from the concrete context of its productive geography . . . it separates itself from that concrete breeding ground and prepares to take flight." Fredric Jameson, "Culture and Finance Capital," *Critical Inquiry* 24, no. 1 (Autumn 1997): 251.

23. Lowney, "Thoreau's *Cape Cod*," 244. Some versions of *Cape Cod* remove both the history of Cape Cod Calvinism and the "Provincetown" history to appendixes, rendering them instances of excursus in the most literal sense. See, for instance, the 1951 Bramhall House edition, where the appendicization of the historical parts of *Cape Cod* is justified on the basis that "in their context these passages interrupt the account of Thoreau's excursions." Thoreau, *Cape Cod*, arranged with notes by Dudley C. Lunt (New York: Bramhall House, 1951), 277.

24. For more on Thoreau's "traveling" books, see Michaels, "*Walden*'s False Bottoms," 144, and Walls, "Walking West, Gazing East," 22–23.

12

BETWEEN "THAT FARTHEREST WESTERN WAY" AND "THE UNIVERSITY OF THE WEST"

THOREAU'S DIALECTIC OF REFORM

Sandra Harbert Petrulionis

No celebrant of his bicentennial can remember a time when the political identity of Henry David Thoreau did not share equal billing with his stature as nature writer, proto-environmentalist, and philosopher. On his one hundredth birthday in 1917, however, it was zealous reformers across the Atlantic, like Leo Tolstoy and Emma Goldman, who drew inspiration from Thoreau's provocative charge to "let your life be a counter friction to stop the machine" (*RP* 73–74). With some exceptions, U.S. commemorations at that time typically appeared in "Today in History" news blurbs, a few of these mistaken about even the basic facts of Thoreau's life. It took World War I as well as increasing labor and other social and political unrest of the 1910s before Americans began to appreciate the profound words of their dissenting native son's critical energy. Later, as first Mohandas Gandhi and then Martin Luther King Jr. drew on his example of "civil disobedience," Thoreau's reputation as an inspiring and universal political figure was fixed.[1]

But like the U.S. Constitution itself, the subversive Thoreau is frequently quoted, often misunderstood, and far too little read. Especially mistaken has been the frequent alignment of Thoreau with Gandhi and King, whose committed pacifism he never shared. Rather, in confronting the most distressing national crisis of his time, the institution of slavery, Henry Thoreau ranged widely in considering how to oppose this massive injustice. Experts across the disciplines have long debated the contradictions in Thoreau's reform writings, particularly the loaded subject of violence. One camp blasts Thoreau for being "radically inconsistent" in advocating nonviolence and then later endorsing the militant extremist John Brown. The other side prefers to see Thoreau's antislavery politics as evolving rather than contradictory, which is by far the more persuasive view.[2] Like all good Transcendentalists, Thoreau contradicts himself—not only from one essay to the next but within the same essay—and indeed he becomes more combative in both his rhetoric and his actions over the turbulent 1850s.

In addition to the central issue of violence, in forging his antislavery identity, Thoreau addresses other vital concerns, especially the role of a reform-minded individual. Is political reform best facilitated by an individual or by an organization? How can an individual best pursue ethical reform action? For Thoreau, these questions are subsumed by a more personally vexing one: Should a philosopher's inward repose be transformed into direct action?

As Thoreau grapples with these questions over twenty years, an intriguing and even profound "idea of the West" animates his reform continuum. Across his literary canon, Thoreau conceives of "the West" as an unbounded plain, where freedom of the mind and body coexist; it is this conception of the geographic terrain that bookends his deliberations on reform. At one end of the spectrum resides the individual burrowing deep in his own mind, on a figurative path to self-discovery that in both an early essay as well as in the concluding chapter of *Walden* Thoreau calls "that fartherest western way" (*RP* 197). At the other end lies the raucous American frontier, where in "A Plea for Captain John Brown," Thoreau tells us that Brown studied "Liberty" and commenced "the public practice of Humanity" at the "great university of the West" (*RP* 113). My purpose here is to trace the ongoing tensions and oppositions of Thoreau's antislavery politics as they align on a western trajectory modeled after what eighteenth- and early nineteenth-century German idealist philosophers such as Johann Fichte, Georg Friedrich Hegel, and others laid out as a "dialectic." Hegel proposes that in a dialectic process, an individual initiates a claim that becomes one side of an issue. The opposite view emerges, setting up a contradiction. Ideally, the process of pivoting back and forth between these oppositions will forge a tentative synthesis between the adversarial perspectives. Transcendentalists on both sides of the Atlantic were influenced by Hegel's assertion that intellectual progress could result from a dialectical model, especially as its method "emphasizes development through conflict."[3]

Thoreau's earliest writings suggest his striving for various forms of synthesis. As a recent Harvard graduate just starting to keep a journal, he affirms that "when any real progress is made, we unlearn and learn anew, what we thought we knew before" (*PJ* 1:24). He asserts that "truth is always paradoxical" (*PJ* 1:143). Added to which, he recognizes his own battling sides. Ironically, just three months before the most famous political act of his life (a night in jail), Thoreau acknowledges the uneasy fit "between a love of contemplation and a love of action—the life of a philosopher & of a hero" (*PJ* 2:240). In addition to his stated preference for "the poetic & philosophic," he judges that the heroic life "unfits me" for the philosophic (*PJ* 2:240). A few years earlier, his opinion had differed: "What I began by reading I must finish by acting" (*PJ* 1:268).

Whether Thoreau consciously employed a philosophical dialectic in formulating and reformulating his response to slavery is not my concern here. What interests me is the usefulness of this model in helping us understand the constant flux of Thoreau's antislavery politics. Over a lifetime of weighing diverse tactics, ethical underpinnings, and personal action, when it came to slavery, Thoreau could not achieve Hegel's hoped-for synthesis. Like many Americans, as the nation careened toward civil war, he confronted a political maelstrom that ultimately displaced him from the unbounded West of his imagination onto the bloody western plains of Kansas-Nebraska.

Along with other Transcendentalists, Thoreau has been called a "radical abolitionist," that is, an antislavery activist, especially one who adhered to the tenets of Boston abolitionist and pacifist William Lloyd Garrison. Like most unqualified characterizations of Thoreau, this is not quite right. More accurate, Thoreau was consistently antislavery in principle and occasionally an abolitionist extremist, as were his three major writings on the subject: "Resistance to Civil Government," better known as "Civil Disobedience" (1849); "Slavery in Massachusetts" (1854); and "A Plea for Captain John Brown" (1859). He put action behind these words many times, not only to protest the Mexican War and in his services to the Underground Railroad but also to break federal law by aiding a fugitive from so-called justice. But more about that later.

Thoreau first addressed the subject early in the 1840s, with brief tributes to outspoken abolitionists Nathaniel Rogers and Wendell Phillips.

He admired both men's sharp tone and equally strident condemnations of clergymen who kept mum about slavery. Like Emerson at this time, Thoreau advocated inward self-reform over collective action. Individuals should heed the call to improve society, he believed, but only after perfecting themselves. Moreover, he insists, it is extreme individual action, not organizations, that brings about genuine change, although he finds few reformers who are "radical enough" (*RP* 182). Whence comes such an individual? In this early example of his thinking on the subject, Thoreau counsels that the source of reform is "inward . . . a direction which no traveller has taken" (*RP* 193), a path he beckons us toward: "Shall we not stretch our legs?—Why shall we pause this side of sundown? We will not then be immigrants still further into our native country. Let us start now on that fartherest western way which does not pause at the Mississippi or the Pacific, pushing on by day and night, sun down—moon down—stars down—and at last earth down too" (*RP* 197). That these lines from an 1844 lecture also appear a decade later in the "Conclusion" chapter of *Walden* attests to their ongoing value to Thoreau.

From this inward contemplative West, the pendulum also swings in Thoreau's early writings to encompass violent engagement in the world. He honors Puritan saints and other military figures for their patriotic bombast and courage, the same ideals he will later equate with the education that abolitionist martyr John Brown receives at "the university of the West." As a young man, Thoreau also argues against the pacifist doctrine of the leaders of the new Non-Resistance Society, whom he directly counters in his essay "The Service": "Let not our Peace be proclaimed by the rust on our swords, or our inability to draw them from their scabbards, but . . . keep those swords bright and sharp" (*RP* 13). In two Concord Lyceum debates in 1841, he and his brother, John, argued the affirmative in sparring with Bronson Alcott on the question of whether forcible resistance is ever permissible.[4] However serene the travels may have been along "that fartherest western way" of inward reform, the outward journey, for Thoreau, was not necessarily a passive one.

Through the example of his mother, sisters, aunts, and other Concord abolitionists, Thoreau as a young man began to appreciate concerted collective action as a useful reform strategy. In 1837, Concord women had formed an antislavery society through which they fostered community activism for the next thirty-plus years. In addition to petition drives and fundraising venues, they brought a steady stream of militant voices, including that of Frederick Douglass, to speak in Concord. Ten years ahead of Henry's radicalization, Cynthia, Helen, and Sophia Thoreau attended national conventions and signed public resolutions endorsing an extremist antislavery agenda, including abolitionist leader William Lloyd Garrison's call for "disunion," or northern secession from the slave-holding states.

As war with Mexico broke out in 1846, his sisters, Sophia and Helen Thoreau, were among Concord residents who signed a public "Anti-War Pledge." During his routine visits home from Walden that summer, Henry and his family surely talked about this unprovoked military aggression, which was obliging him to reconsider his notion of political reform in a new light. In such a context, the self-improvement of the inward "fartherest western way" now seemed a tame and ineffective strategy.[5] The pendulum of his reform dialectic swung rapidly. As Thoreau noted in his Journal two days after settling in to his cabin at Walden, "in all studies we go not forward but rather backward with redoubled pauses" (*PJ* 2:156).

Inspired at least in part by the vocal activism of his family, Thoreau's next action is legendary. Like his friend Bronson Alcott, Thoreau had not paid his poll tax for several years, a largely silent protest against a proslavery government.[6] When waylaid by the tax collector one summer evening in 1846 and told to pay up, he refused and was promptly hauled off to spend his now-heralded night in jail. Courtesy of this isolated happenstance, Thoreau's antislavery identity expanded from a Transcendentalist ethos of self-improvement to a principled, rebellious activism. For us, of course, his action set off alarm bells still tolling loudly in our ears today. In defending his jail stint to his neighbors—an act of resistance that Emerson considered "mean and skulking, and in bad taste"—Thoreau formulated an ethical reform treatise, centered on the monstrosity of slavery.[7] Many prefer its original title of "Resistance to Civil Government," but the essay is best known by the title of its later republication as "Civil Disobedience." Although Thoreau's refusal to pay his poll tax and his willingness to go to jail are responsible for his subsequent branding as a pacifist, nowhere in this essay does Thoreau claim his nonviolent example as the sole or even the best method of resisting injustice. Both the ambiguity of the word "civil" as well as the nouns it modifies from one title to the other feed vigorous debates. Does "civil" convey the decorum with which one disobeys or the type of government being resisted? How does resistance differ from disobedience?

Opening with his bold anarchist pronouncement—"that government is best which governs not at all" (*RP* 63)—Thoreau moves quickly to his purpose, which is to deplore the war on Mexico and to lay out an ethical postulate that demands "action from principle" from all citizens (*RP* 72). Individual Americans are *obligated* to resist unjust laws: "This people must cease to hold slaves, and to make war on Mexico, though it cost them their existence as a people" (*RP* 68). There is no middle ground here. To Thoreau, no man can "without disgrace be associated with" the current proslavery government (*RP* 67). His own night in jail may have been a solitary act, but "under a government which imprisons any unjustly, the true place for a just man is also a prison" (*RP* 76). Thoreau indicts all who share his views for not being in jail too: "If ten *honest* men only,—aye, if *one* HONEST man, in this State of Massachusetts, *ceasing to hold slaves*, were actually to withdraw from this copartnership, and be locked up in the county jail," the revolution would succeed—since faced with "keep[ing] all just men in prison, or giv[ing] up war and slavery, the State will not hesitate which to choose" (*RP* 75–76). In what he calls a "peaceable revolution" (*RP* 76), Thoreau expands his reform spectrum by bridging individual with collective action. Moreover, he also primes the pump for the curriculum offered at the "university of the West": "Honest men [should] rebel and revolutionize," he insists; they should "break the law" (*RP* 67, 73).

Also important is the essay's wider historical moment. Not only was the United States at war with Mexico in the late 1840s, but in 1848, the first woman's rights convention was held in Seneca Falls, New York; a slim pamphlet entitled the *Communist Manifesto* was published in England; and across Europe—in Hungary, Poland, Italy, Austria, and over forty other countries—it was a year of unprecedented social uprisings. As Thoreau assuredly knew, political upheaval, with social justice at the forefront, was in the air, east as well as west. In the United States, the political West had become problematic. According to Thoreau's rosy view, "This government . . . does not keep the country free. *It* does not settle the West . . . the character inherent in the American people has done all this" (*RP* 64). Yet by the time "Civil Disobedience" was published in 1849, this "settl[ing of] the West" had doubled the geographic footprint of slavery, setting the scene for conflict to escalate there over the next decade.

Examples of Thoreau's fraught deliberations appear throughout "Civil Disobedience." Though negative toward democratic politics in general,

Thoreau nevertheless wants to be a responsible citizen and appreciates the government when it works on his and others' behalf. He advises us to "rebel and revolutionize" but claims to be disinterested in "the sudden revolution of these times and this generation" (*PJ* 1:360). "The definition of a peaceable revolution" is followed by the proviso "if any such is possible" (*RP* 76). To his suggestion that "even suppose blood should flow?" Thoreau adds, "Is there not a sort of blood shed when the conscience is wounded?" (*RP* 77). And although he "quietly declare[s] war with the State," he does so "after my fashion" and "will still make what use and get what advantage of her I can." For a wordsmith like Henry Thoreau, these are deliberate rhetorical choices—"revolutionize," "war," "blood shed." But in true Transcendentalist fashion, he reserves the right to change his mind and wraps up with what may seem an absurdly weak finish to this terribly earnest essay: "This, then, is my position at present" (*RP* 84). In this first urgent call to action, Thoreau's political ethos is a work in progress. But as an antislavery activist, he's just getting started.

What about this famous essay so disturbed Senator Joseph McCarthy in 1953 that he included "Civil Disobedience" among the literary works he wanted to ban from U.S.-sponsored libraries abroad? It wasn't so much Thoreau's anarchist sentiments and certainly no potential communism that worried McCarthy. Instead, it was something far more disturbing— Thoreau's direct attack on the principle of democracy itself, coupled with the unwavering belief that each individual must resist until we get the government we deserve. A decade ahead of John Stuart Mill's renowned treatise on the liberty of the sovereign individual, Thoreau affirms that one person acting from the higher law of conscience is as legitimate a political actor as the democratic majority. In his view, a democratic tyranny of the majority empowered a system of domestic terrorism to enslave millions of fellow Americans. We can imagine the panic these lines induced in the likes of Senator McCarthy: "If the [government's] injustice . . . is of such a nature that it requires you to be the agent of injustice to another, then, I say, *break the law*. Let your life be a counter friction to stop the machine" (*RP* 73–74; emphasis added).[8]

Some recent critics have lamented what they see as the mainstreaming of "civil disobedience." In an excellent counter to this concerning trend, James Finley examines the explosive power of Thoreau's essay for today's social justice movements that are led by people who understand that what

Thoreau has in mind is a resistance that will "shock, unsettle, and fracture the status quo." From Bree Newsome scaling a flagpole in front of the state-house in Columbia, South Carolina, to Dakota Access Pipeline protestors David Archambault and Iyuskin American Horse setting up resistance camps, to climate activist Tim DeChristopher's twenty-one months in prison, to civil rights veteran the Honorable John Lewis still speaking truth to power—America yet produces courageous individuals willing to throw sand in the machine. Nor must we go back to the McCarthy era to find politicians threatened by Thoreau's legacy. Legislators in over thirty states have recently put forward bills, including some directly benefitting energy companies and cloaked as "critical infrastructure" laws, to "criminalize and increase penalties on peaceful protesting," one even "allowing motorists to run over and kill protesters so long as the collision was accidental." As Finley observes, today's Black Lives Matter and other activists know well the historical power they're marshaling. When encouraged to "do civil disobedience" "the *right way*," the "civil" way, they understand they're being misdirected and often purposefully derailed.[9]

A year after "Civil Disobedience" appeared in print, the crisis over slavery entered its final and most volatile decade. The Fugitive Slave Law, enacted in 1850, led thousands to flee northern cities for Canada to avoid being reenslaved—in scenes not terribly unlike our recent exodus of desperate refugees crossing the same northern border when the promise of DACA (Deferred Action for Childhood Arrivals) has, for the Trump administration, become the method of their identification and arrest. With the 1850 statute, the federal government threw its enforcement arm to assist enslavers in recovering their human "property," many of whom had been living as free people in free states for decades. Northern citizens could also be conscripted to aid in the recapture process, making Thoreau's hypothetical scenarios in "Civil Disobedience" suddenly quite real.

Early in 1851, two young men didn't make it out of Boston before being arrested and charged as fugitive slaves under the new legislation. The first, Virginian Shadrach Minkins, eventually reached Canada, courtesy of Black abolitionists who liberated him out of the courthouse itself and then conveyed him west along the Underground Railroad to Concord, where a few of Thoreau's neighbors helped plan the next stages of the escape route. Although Minkins's presence in Concord those few hours remained secret for years to come, Thoreau opens his Journal the next day with a volley that leaves little doubt he'd heard the news: "Do we call this the land of the free?" (*PJ* 3:194).[10]

Some weeks later, Thomas Sims did not fare as well. After a brief trial, Boston officials returned him to his Georgia enslaver. During these days, Thoreau began writing the first of several sustained critiques of slavery in his Journal, the literary record that presents the most immediate testament to Thoreau's reform dialectic, as it documents the mounting tension between the inward "western way" and the impinging chaos of the political west. Thoreau hurls his anger at city and state officials who had handed over Thomas Sims: "There is such an office if not such a man as the Governor of Massachusetts— . . . He has probably had as much as he could do to keep on the fence during this moral earthquake" (*PJ* 3:203). As did many abolitionists at this time, Thoreau invokes the local revolutionary spirit: "In [17]75 2 or 300s of the inhabitants of Concord assembled at one of the bridges with arms in their hands to assert the right of 3 millions to tax themselves . . . About a week ago the authorities of Boston . . . assisted by a still larger armed force—sen[t] back a perfectly innocent man . . . into a slavery as complete as the world ever knew" (*PJ* 3:203). He tries to recover his solitude: "Mouse-ear in blossom for a week—observed the crowfoot on the cliff in abundance & the saxifrage / The wind last Wednesday . . . blew down a hundred pines on Fair Haven Hill" (*PJ* 3:208). But each day the Journal evidences his distress. After observing "a Dandelion in blossom," Thoreau follows, "Could slavery suggest a more complete servility? Is there any dust which such conduct does not lick and make fouler still with its slime?" (*PJ* 3:208). As he will do in antislavery tirades to come, Thoreau hoists "Jesus christ [*sic*]" himself: "Do you think *he* would have stayed here in *liberty* and let the black man go into slavery in his stead?" (*PJ* 3:203). And on it goes, page after Journal page.

When Henry Williams sought refuge in Concord later that year, it was Thoreau and his family who this time served the Underground Railroad. In an uncharacteristically detailed Journal entry, Thoreau relates their conversation; he was especially intrigued to hear the navigational methods used by Williams and others who fled their enslavement (*PJ* 4:113). A similar scenario played out two years later when the Thoreaus assisted an unidentified man who, like Williams, had also escaped from Virginia. Not long after, a free Black woman stayed a day or more with the Thoreaus. Thoreau records her "errand . . . to get money to buy her husband who is a slave" (*PJ* 7:134–35).[11] Undoubtedly, these encounters and others not yet recovered in the historical record furthered Thoreau's sense of the degrading and horrific injustice of slavery.

By the mid-1850s, the literal west of the Kansas frontier monopolized abolitionists' attention. In the spring of 1854, Anthony Burns was arrested as a fugitive slave in Boston. As historical serendipity would have it, Burns went on trial the same week as the city hosted the state antislavery society's annual meeting and the same week the U.S. Congress debated yet another proslavery law, the Kansas-Nebraska Act. Instead of new states entering the union as slave or free according to their southern or northern geography, as had been the case for the past quarter century, the Kansas-Nebraska Act overturned that compromise and left this key decision to be decided by popular vote. What ensued presaged the Civil War, as southerners raced with their enslaved human property to outnumber northern abolitionist émigrés also heading to settle this western territory.[12]

It was an incendiary time in Boston. When abolitionists failed to free him, Anthony Burns was remanded to his enslaver's custody. To prevent further rescue attempts, martial law was effectively declared in the city, where an artillery regiment and three platoons of U.S. Marines joined federal marshals and city police (ordered to "fire upon the crowd" as necessary) in "escorting" Burns to the Virginia-bound boat waiting in the harbor.[13]

Thoreau erupted. His Journal entries for June 1854 present a wildly tilting reform pendulum, as summer days display his rage toward northern complicity with the Slave Power alongside bird sightings, berries ripening, flowers blooming. In a remarkable use of this rhetoric, Thoreau appeared on the public antislavery stage on the Fourth of July to deliver a speech in Framingham, Massachusetts, later known as "Slavery in Massachusetts," the only time in his life he spoke at an organized abolitionist rally. He preached to the choir that day, the scene filled with stalwart reformers, there to mourn Burns and vent their hostility to the Kansas-Nebraska Act.

Draping the lecture podium, an inverted American flag signaled the nation's distress. After William Lloyd Garrison opened the morning festivities with a prayer, he set fire to a copy of the U.S. Constitution, brandishing it aloft as "a covenant with death, and an agreement with hell." By the time Thoreau followed Sojourner Truth to the platform in the afternoon, the summer heat rivalled Garrison's extraordinary act. Shocked at abolitionists' distress about slavery in Nebraska and Kansas, Thoreau pulls attention back to the millions of figurative slaves in his own state—the municipal leaders and state legislators implicated in reenslaving Anthony Burns. Thoreau reminds the crowd that men make the law free, not the other way around. Gone from this speech are the equivocations, the theoretical queries of "Civil Disobedience." Gone, too, is noncooperation with injustice, as "thoughts [that] are murder to the State" replace Thoreau's former "quiet declar[ation of] war" (*RP* 108).

The Journal lays bare the ceaseless shifts of Thoreau's reform dialectic at this time. Not only one day to the next, but one line and midline to the next, these pages pivot from contemplation to social activism and back again. Political events had so interrupted his usual pursuits that Thoreau felt bound to write about them; he could not shake the distraction. No longer is this "an era of repose," he laments (*RP* 108). "The state has fatally interfered with my just & proper business" (*PJ* 8:198–99); "the

Figure 18. A perennial symbol of Thoreau's Transcendentalist hope, the white water lily still reminds us each summer that beauty rises from the bottom river muck, just as justice can emerge from our darkest American moments. Photo courtesy of the author.

remembrance of the baseness of politicians spoils my walks" (*PJ* 8:200). A Transcendentalist to the core, however, he recovers, his stability achieved at the "chance" sighting of "a white water-lily" emerging from the muck of the river bottom (figure 18), representing to him the potential for justice to be derived from the foul stench of slavery: "What confirmation of our hopes is in the fragrance of this flower! I shall not so soon despair of the world for it, notwithstanding slavery" (*PJ* 8:200; *RP* 108). Throughout July and into August 1854 (*Walden* hit bookstores in August), "Slavery in Massachusetts" positioned Thoreau as an impassioned new abolitionist voice. But the fever pitch of the reform pendulum took an emotional toll: "Methinks I have spent a rather unprofitable summer thus far," he confided to a friend. Quoting William Wordsworth, he follows, "I have been too much with the world" (*Corr* 2:221).

Five years went by before Thoreau again spoke publicly on the subject of slavery. During this time, he basked in the limited but generally positive attention paid to *Walden*; he lectured on "Walking," "The Wild," and his excursions to Cape Cod and to Canada. His Journal shows his delight in painted tortoises, varieties of driftwood, "the fungus called spunk," the "crisp and shriveled" leaves and stems of the water smartweed (*J* IX:117, VIII:13). The Journal also reveals that Thoreau kept up with the news from Kansas, where the *idea* of the West had given way wholly to a very real and violent rampage. His reform pendulum veers even to the point of desiring civil war five years ahead of its outbreak: "There has not been anything which you could call union between the North and South in this country for many years, and there cannot be so long as slavery is in the way. I only wish . . . that the north had more spirit and would settle the question at once, and here instead of struggling feebly and protractedly away off on the plains of Kansas" (*Corr* 2:471). If civil war would at last abolish America's founding compromise over slavery, Thoreau staked his support for it.

The Boston and New York papers reported daily the gruesome news from the West. Since it competed with headlines of other outrages in Kansas at the same time, however, a particularly horrific preemptive strike in May 1856 at Pottawatomie Creek received little coverage in the eastern press. The guerrilla who led his loyal fighters to execute five unarmed men as their families looked on was the most famous alumnus of the University of the West: abolitionist John Brown.

Shortly after these atrocities, Brown traveled east, holding audiences in Concord and other towns spellbound as he related wild west skirmishes, including a few where he and his men had liberated enslaved men and women and where one of his sons had been killed. Unlike Emerson and Bronson Alcott, Thoreau did not record his impression of Brown at this time, despite talking with him for much of an afternoon. Two years later, Brown visited there again, spending his fifty-ninth and last birthday with Concord friends before heading south to lay plans for what would be his final abolitionist maneuver. When news of the attack on the federal arsenal at Harpers Ferry, Virginia, reached Concord in mid-October 1859, abolitionists there reacted with awe, dread, and more than a touch of local pride. One of Brown's secret conspirators for the raid was none other than their own schoolmaster, Franklin Benjamin Sanborn, the neighbor and friend who had first introduced Brown to Thoreau.[14]

On the rainy autumn day of October 18, 1859, Thoreau penned a characteristic give-and-take in his Journal as to the transcendent purpose of human endeavor: "A man's experience and life" should have an "essential fragrance," like "going a-huckleberrying in the fields of thought." Instead of "flee[ing] . . . to the theatres, lecture-rooms, and museums of the city," his neighbors ought to "stay here awhile . . . walk on water; all these brooks and rivers and ponds shall be your highway"—a pastoral route reminiscent of Thoreau's "fartherest western way." The next day's multiple-page entry opens in medias res: "When a government puts forth its strength on the side of injustice, as ours (especially to-day) to maintain slavery and kill the liberators of the slave, what a merely brute, or worse than brute, force it is seen to be!" (*J* XII:399–400). From the "the fields of thought" to the aftermath of Harpers Ferry, the reform pendulum swerved abruptly. Journal entries over the next several weeks stay squarely on John Brown, the "heroic liberator" of "fettered four millions" whose "action from principle" seemed a page from Thoreau's own script (*J* XII:402, *RP* 72).

Within weeks, Thoreau became one of the first in the country to champion Brown, who by then had been convicted and sentenced to hang. Once more, as with "Slavery in Massachusetts," Thoreau crafted his private rant into a public address, delivering it three times in almost as many days. Its eventual title, "A Plea for Captain John Brown," sets forth the primary objective: to lobby for Brown's character more than deal with his specific deeds, whether in Kansas or Harpers Ferry. For Thoreau, Brown's noble end justified his violent means. At last, the guns "were employed in a righteous cause. The tools were in the hands of one who could use them" (*J* XII:422). Thoreau's reform dialectic had made its farthest arc yet in the activist direction.

Thoreau casts Brown as a political actor who prepared for his dramatic role by "study[ing] Liberty" at the "great university of the West." As he explains, "Having taken many degrees," Brown then "commenced the practice of Humanity" (*J* XII:420–21). Thoreau affirms the militance with which Brown enacted these humanitarian studies but demurs from judging: Only "they who are continually shocked by slavery have some right to be shocked by the violent death of the slaveholder," a fact he emphasizes repeatedly (*J* XII:418). Thoreau castigates the press and insists that any report of Brown's violence must give equal time to the domestic terror that enslaves four million Americans. Thoreau refuses to judge "any tactics that are effective of good, whether one wields the quill or the sword" (*J* XII:417). Far better, he argued, was Brown's "philanthropy" than that "which neither shoots me nor liberates me" (*J* XII:425). In John Brown, Thoreau recognizes the "man of ideas and principle" for whom he had called in vain a decade earlier, an authentic American hero "such . . . as it takes ages to make" (*J* XII:424). Not content merely to throw sand in the machine, Brown gave his life as a counter friction to stop it. "You don't know your testament when you see it," Thoreau mocked (*RP* 138).

Paper and pencil kept under his pillow during these weeks, on and on Thoreau writes. Occasionally, the pendulum moderates as he remembers "a man may have other affairs to attend to" (*RP* 133). But Brown won't let him go. Admiring the "delicately rippled" clouds of the mid-November chill, he finds "it hard . . . to see its beauty then, when my mind was filled with Captain Brown. So great a wrong as his fate implied overshadowed all beauty in the world" (*J* XII:443). A few days later he is likewise surprised, "hav[ing] been so absorbed of late in Captain Brown's fate," to find "the old routine running still," neighbors still going about their business, "the little dipper . . . still diving in the river as of yore." "I meet him at every turn," Thoreau confesses (*RP* 153). Seemingly for the first extended time in his life, Thoreau cannot retreat to the "fartherest western way."

The day after Brown was hanged in early December, Thoreau moved from words to action, in a west by southwest line. For a few hours, we might even say that he, too, attended the "university of the West," though one much closer to home than Kansas. Thoreau renders the scene rather cryptically in his Journal, but when added to details later provided by Franklin Sanborn, the story emerges. Among the few of Brown's men who escaped from Harpers Ferry was a frail and very wealthy young abolitionist named Francis Jackson Meriam, whom Sanborn had directed to John Brown just a day ahead of the Harpers Ferry raid. Elated by the six hundred dollars in gold that Meriam provided for purchasing remaining supplies, Brown took one look at this unlikely combatant and decided to post him behind with two others to guard the weapons stockpile while Brown and the remaining men set off on foot to seize the federal arsenal.

Learning from passersby of the outcome at Harpers Ferry—fourteen dead, several wounded, Brown and five men captured—a panic-stricken Meriam headed north with four others over the Appalachian scrub, while a reward of five hundred dollars was offered for the capture of each in all the papers. Almost incredibly, he safely reached Canada within a few days, only to return distraught and frantic to Boston on the day of Brown's hanging. Anxious family and friends prevailed on him to return to Canada, but Meriam mistakenly took a train that ended in Concord rather than Fitchburg, where he would have made a northbound connection. Realizing what he'd done and where he was, Meriam made for Sanborn's home, not far from the train depot. Sanborn says in later accounts that he turned immediately for help to Emerson and Thoreau, giving them no specifics. Early the next morning, Emerson's horse and wagon stood waiting for Thoreau, who drove as prearranged to Sanborn's home to pick up "Mr. Lockwood," the name he'd been given. Thoreau kept his frantic passenger covered in the wagon during their drive west to the nearby South Acton station.[15] His Journal adds another layer of secrecy, as he refers to his passenger as "X."

Can we be sure that Thoreau understood his morning's errand to be connected to the Harpers Ferry raid? If so, was he therefore consciously an "accessory after the fact" to this ongoing national sensation? Yes, and surely yes. Not only Concord residents but everyone in the country knew of Sanborn's widely publicized connection to John Brown; in recent weeks he had fled to Canada twice himself for fear of arrest. Added to which is Thoreau's poetic ending of this Journal entry: "When I hear of John Brown and his wife weeping at length, it is as if the rocks sweated" (*J* XIII:4).

Had he been caught aiding and abetting this fugitive from justice, Thoreau could conceivably have shared the same fate as the six men, including Brown, executed for their role at Harpers Ferry. Indeed, as Thoreau and "X" headed out of Concord that morning, one of those who had initially escaped with Meriam but was later captured, John Cook, sat in a Charlestown, Virginia, prison awaiting hanging.[16]

Thoreau's 1846 night in jail is *the* example on which his popular political reputation has rested. This nonviolent action from principle has been more palatable than his elevation of Brown as an "Angel of Light." At the very least, many wish that Thoreau had denounced Brown's carnage in Kansas. How could Henry David Thoreau, they ask with alarm, regard an executioner of unarmed men as a "superior man?" (*RP* 137). One of these critics explains that he "part[s] company with Thoreau when it comes to John Brown."[17] I don't know how to do this. In an America where buying and selling human beings were legal and hugely profitable ventures, Thoreau refuses to condemn a man who died trying to end this practice. By this late moment in the nation's crisis over slavery, Thoreau had come to accept that the ethical life sometimes puts forward incompatible choices, that the repose of "that fartherest western way" could be supplanted by the brutal reality of the literal West.

What would a discussion of Thoreau's politics be if it remained safely fixed on the distant past? For like Thoreau, we are also attuned to a dialectic process of social justice and social reform. Whether on demilitarizing the police, prison abolition, climate change, immigration and the criminal separation of refugee families, environmental justice, corporate hijacking of electoral politics, universal health care, or perpetual for-profit warfare (and the list goes on), we well understand taking small steps forward and giant leaps back. If Thoreau had been with us to blow out the candles during his bicentennial, he would, I'm nearly certain, deliberate the pros and cons of these issues. He would also just as surely hold many of us accountable for our predicament—for talking mostly to the like-minded, for indulging our consumerist lifestyle on the backs of abused and even enslaved laborers in the global economy, and, with apologies to Pink Floyd, here I charge myself and my academic peers most of all, for "hav[ing] become comfortably numb." Self-satisfied in our dens of tenured security, we have ignored the gathering storms of increasing police brutality, systemic racism, mounting student debt, economic disparity, and disaffection on both our rural campuses and urban centers. One recent critic calls us "to be a counter friction to academia itself," and I couldn't agree more.[18]

For us, as for Thoreau, a synthesis seems nowhere to be found. But because we are teachers of young adults whose tomorrow is at risk, we cannot give way to despair. Empowering them with Thoreau's reminder that "revolutions are never sudden," we forge an ethical compass by which together we will take the actions from principle essential to confront today's injustices (*PJ* 1:23). And on we must plod—inward along our "fartherest western way," and ready, when the urgency demands, to apply our studies from the "great university of the West."

Notes

1. Gandhi also acknowledged that "Thoreau was not perhaps an out and out champion of non-violence," in *Non-Violent Resistance (Satyagraha)* (New York: Schocken Books, 1961), 3; King, *Stride toward Freedom: The Montgomery Story* (1958; repr., San Francisco, CA: HarperCollins, 1986), 51.

2. Michael Meyer, *Several More Lives to Live: Thoreau's Political Reputation in America* (Westport, CT: Greenwood Press, 1977), 165; Lawrence Buell, "Disaffiliation as Engagement," in *Thoreau at Two Hundred: Essays and Reassessments*, ed. Kristen Case and K. P. Van Anglen (Cambridge: Cambridge University Press, 2016), 200–215; Raffaele Laudani, *Disobedience in Western Political Thought: A Genealogy* (Cambridge: Cambridge University Press, 2013), 92–93.

3. Joe Pellegrino, "Georg Wilhelm Friedrich Hegel," *Biographical Dictionary of Transcendentalism*, ed. Wesley T. Mott (Westport, CT: Greenwood Press, 1996), 134–36.

4. See, for example, "Sir Walter Raleigh" in *EEM* 180–218; Sandra Harbert Petrulionis, *To Set This World Right: The Antislavery Movement in Thoreau's Concord* (Ithaca, NY: Cornell University Press, 2006), 69.

5. Petrulionis, *Set This World Right*, 58.

6. Thoreau acknowledges in "Resistance to Civil Government" that this local tax of $1.50 did not go to support the war or slavery: "I do not care to trace the course of my dollar, if I could, till it buys a man" (*RP* 84).

7. *The Journals of Bronson Alcott*, ed. Odell Shepard (Boston: Little, Brown, 1938), 183.

8. Richard T. Arndt, *The First Resort of Kings: American Cultural Diplomacy in the Twentieth Century* (Dulles, VA: Potomac Books, 2011), 155; Walter Harding and Michael Meyer, *The New Thoreau Handbook* (New York: New York University Press, 1980), 209–10.

9. Jane Bennett, *Thoreau's Nature: Ethics, Politics, and the Wild* (Lanham, MD: Rowman & Littlefield, 2002), 82; James Finley, "#ReclaimThoreau," *The Concord Saunterer*, n.s., 23 (2015): 127, 124, 123; Nicholas Kusnetz, "How Energy Companies and Allies Are Turning the Law against Protesters," Inside Climate News, August 22, 2018, https://inside climatenews.org/news/22082018/pipeline-protest-laws-felony-free-speech-arrests-first

-amendment-oklahoma-iowa-louisiana; Eliza Newlin Carney, "Spate of Anti-Protest Bills Target Social Justice Infrastructure," Sunlight Foundation, June 18, 2018, https://sun lightfoundation.com/2018/06/18/spate-of-anti-protest-bills-target-social-justice-infra structure/; Spencer Woodman, "Update: Lawmakers in Ten States Have Proposed Legislation Criminalizing Peaceful Protest," *Intercept*, January 23, 2017, https://the intercept. com/2017/01/23/lawmakers-in-eight-states-have-proposed-laws-criminalizing -peaceful-protest/.

10. See Gary Collison, *Shadrach Minkins: From Fugitive Slave to Citizen* (Cambridge, MA: Harvard University Press, 1997).

11. Moncure Daniel Conway, *Autobiography: Memories and Experiences of Moncure Daniel Conway*, 2 vols. (Boston: Houghton, Mifflin, 1904), 1:141.

12. Petrulionis, *Set This World Right*, 97–100.

13. Petrulionis, 99.

14. Petrulionis, 130.

15. Petrulionis, 142–45.

16. Steven Lubet, *John Brown's Spy: The Adventurous Life and Tragic Confession of John E. Cook* (New Haven, CT: Yale University Press, 2012), 205.

17. Lewis Hyde, introduction to *The Essays of Henry D. Thoreau*, ed. Lewis Hyde (New York: North Point, 2002), xlvi.

18. Jean Lee Cole, "An Accidental Activist," *The Concord Saunterer*, n.s., 23 (2015): 119.

13

THOREAU
CROSSING TO THE SACRED

David M. Robinson

"It is not when I am going to meet him, but when I am just turning away and leaving him alone, that I discover that God is" (*Corr* 2:55). Thoreau offered his friend H. G. O. Blake this wry account of his encounters with an elusive God in an 1853 letter. He suggested to Blake that God may be elusive, but only because spiritual seekers are not prepared to recognize the divine when it appears. Thoreau's observation suggests that an ongoing quest for the transcendent is an important element in his many nature excursions. Those moments when Thoreau crosses into the sacred, or realizes later that he has already done so, are the focus of this essay.[1]

Thoreau faced one of his most profound encounters with holiness in his 1846 excursion into the Maine wilderness, in which he reached the summit of Mount Ktaadn (known now as Katahdin) and returned through a strange, isolated, and treeless wilderness. Reaching the mountain's summit, Thoreau confronted an utterly blinding fog, denying him the vision that he sought. It is as if he had been imprisoned in darkness or deemed unworthy of the sacred. Not until his descent, when he crossed an uncannily familiar landscape, was he unexpectedly staggered by the holiness of ordinary objects.

Thoreau described a quite different form of sacred experience in a series of 1852 Journal entries devoted to a celebration for the coming of spring. Naming and describing the plants, blossoms, birds, and frogs in the woods around Fairhaven Bay, he depicted a heaven-saturated locale, the reverse of Ktaadn's fierce majesty. His search for the signs of spring took him beyond the season itself. Much less dramatic than the experiences on Ktaadn, Thoreau's composed enchantment in the spring countryside nevertheless evokes the elusive God he spoke of in his letter to Blake. "I say, God," he explained to Blake. "I am not sure that that is the name. You will know whom I mean" (*Corr* 2:55).

"Vast, Titanic"

Awakened deep in the night at his campsite below the summit, Thoreau stood mesmerized by this moonlit vision of the mountain that he had trekked for days to see. "There stood Ktaadn with distinct and cloudless outline in the moonlight; and the rippling of the rapids was the only sound to break the stillness" (*MW* 55). He had been envisioning it for much longer, we can surmise, in his imagination. Thoreau had abandoned his Walden cabin to make this trip, an excursion from his pastoral retreat deeper into the wildest area he could reach. The man encamped in his small cabin just outside Concord had now seen the mountain itself, his greatest aspiration in this challenging expedition. By the time that Thoreau and his companions neared the summit of Ktaadn, the weather had dramatically changed, and the peak was engulfed in a sea of dense clouds that blocked any sight of the summit itself or the view beyond. Thoreau first attempted to reach the summit in the afternoon, eagerly leaving his companions behind while they were pitching camp. He was stopped, after some effort, by the heavy cloud cover. The next morning he outdistanced his companions toward the top, only to be met again with impermeable mist. His descriptions of these attempts to climb to the peak make Ktaadn a military objective rather than the symbol of splendor or divinity. This willful and determined Thoreau reminds us of Emerson's portrayal of a combative friend. "There was somewhat military in his nature not to be subdued, always manly and able, but rarely tender, as if he did not feel himself except in opposition" (*CW* 10:415). In language increasingly laden with religious implications, Thoreau transformed his own fruitless ascent into a parable of the debilitated human condition, from which some crucial element has been drained. As he neared Ktaadn's peak, he began to lose the energy and intensity that had sustained his ascent. "Some part of the beholder," he acknowledged, "even some vital part, seems to escape through the loose grating of his ribs as he ascends. He is more alone than you can imagine" (*MW* 64).

Thoreau's description of the impact of the failed ascent is striking. He depicts a climber draining away through a porous rib cage, as if the body had been entirely deflated. Was this enervation the cause of a physical injury or a spiritual failure? He cannot quite explain the source of this feeling of emptiness, and in the aftermath of his failed struggle to reach the summit, the reader is left with a would-be mountain conqueror who now seems a helpless castaway. Thoreau did approach the peak, as he was determined to do, but he was not able to attain the revelation, visual and spiritual, that he expected.[2] The ascent of Ktaadn had wiped away the celebratory mood of his moonlit vision of the mountain. His evident disappointment that he had failed in his urgent drive to reach the mountain's peak accentuates the idea that he regarded his effort not only as the achievement of a personal goal but also some form of transcendent breakthrough. This had been more than a challenging climb. Thoreau remained diligent in providing his reader with the details of the landscape and the tactics of overland hiking and camping but was unable to offer deeper insight into Ktaadn's peak beyond its continuing mystery.

Thoreau is now regarded as a champion of wilderness. He stands as a prophetic seer who realized the destructiveness of the new industrial era. Although his three journeys to Maine were his deepest explorations of wilderness, this experience on the peak of Ktaadn, as Laura Dassow Walls wrote, "turned out to be his worst nightmare."[3] Thoreau speaks of the experience in the voice of human frailty, a quite unusual role for him. His account of the climb ends, therefore, in a dark meditation on the daunting vastness of the cosmos. "It reminded me of the creations of the old epic and dramatic poets, of Atlas, Vulcan, the Cyclops, and Prometheus. Such was Caucasus and the rock where Prometheus was bound. Æschylus had no doubt visited such scenery as this. It was vast, Titanic, and such as man never inhabits" (*MW* 64). The value of wilderness, its sacredness, is that it must remain uninhabited and undisturbed. Thoreau knew that, but to be turned away from the place that represented the quintessence of the wild nevertheless dismayed him. The next phase of the trip, descending the mountain, would bring a deeper and more complicated experience. His account of it continues to resonate as we read it now.

"With Awe"

The dispiriting ascent of Ktaadn foreshadows a much different encounter with the mountain on the descent. "What is most striking about the Maine wilderness," Thoreau wrote, "is the continuousness of the forest." With the exception of "the bare tops of the high mountains, and the lakes and streams, the forest is uninterrupted" (*MW* 80). This was one of the many descriptive observations that Thoreau provided, hoping to be informative to others who might travel to the Maine woods. His description also carries a hint of marvel at a landscape that could be so completely undisturbed and unspoiled. This building sense of the forest's astonishing comprehensiveness helps explain why Thoreau and his companions felt such impact when they unexpectedly entered a place of "Burnt Lands," a large treeless area ignited in the past by lightning strikes. The land, now green, resembled "a natural pasture for the moose and deer," Thoreau wrote (*MW* 70). His surprise and curiosity about this unusual place is a major shift from the dark bewilderment he felt on the mountain peak. As he explores it, he is compelled to an ardent expression of wonder, a crucial moment in the understanding of his spiritual perspective. When he entered the Burnt Lands, he noticed "no recent marks of fire, hardly so much as a charred stump." There was no evidence of ruin except the curious absence of trees. Even though this place was "exceedingly wild and desolate," Thoreau called it "some pasture run to waste," depicting the clearing as a relic of previous human life (*MW* 70).

Thoreau's instinctive transformation of this weirdly isolated place into something familiar or "ordinary" is the key to its impact on him. "I looked with awe at the ground I trod on," he wrote, stunned by "that Earth of which we have heard, made out of Chaos and Old Night. Here was no man's garden, but the unhandselled globe" (*MW* 70). He had imaginatively tamed the wild for an instant by seeing it as a pasture, but in doing so, he evoked the strangeness or "uncanniness" of the ordinary earth.[4] He had recognized the miraculous by seeing it as the familiar. "We walked over it with a certain awe," he wrote, "stopping, from time to time, to pick the blueberries that grew there, and had a smart and spicy taste" (*MW* 70). A wild blueberry is, of course, an awesome thing, but Thoreau and his companions are testifying to the wonder of the earth itself as they walk over this unusual yet familiar place.

The recognition of the ordinary as the yet undetected wondrous, which this scene depicts, is what drew Stanley Cavell so strongly to Thoreau.[5] In *The Claim of Reason*, he wrote, "One can think of Romanticism as the discovery that the everyday is an exceptional achievement."[6] This observation on the everyday or the ordinary was, for both Cavell and Thoreau, closely connected with the idea of the "present," in both the sense of time and of nearness. Cavell cited Thoreau's statement that "God himself culminates in the present moment" (*W* 97), commenting that "the present is his experiment, the discovery of the present, the meeting of two eternities."[7] Cavell regarded Thoreau's "discovery of the present" as a holy event, the interlocking of the human with the divine. The imperative to be awake and fully aware in each moment was, in this sense, Thoreau's central message in *Walden*. This responsibility necessarily requires a familiarity with our surroundings and social interactions, a closeness to things and events that was consciously developed and nurtured through the course of each day. As Cavell put it, "The present is a task and a discovery."[8] He described *Walden* as a book intensely focused on the ever-renewing effort to find the creative possibility of the place in which we find ourselves. Responding to Thoreau's observation in the "Spring" chapter that "the phenomena of the year take place every day in a pond on a small scale" (*W* 301), Cavell emphasized the moment and its call as the means by which the ordinary can be sanctified. "And what is sacred about a day? The experiment is the present—to make himself present to each circumstance, at every eventuality."[9]

Cavell's association of the present with "discovery" and "experiment" makes it clear that sustained attention to the ordinary is neither submissive nor detached. Of particular note is the way Cavell read *Walden* with the recognition that Thoreau's account of his task in writing the book shadows the narrative it presents. This resulted in a book that could not be easily categorized as literary or philosophical but was best described as "genuine Scripture," an epistle of instruction on the moment and its value.[10] Cavell emphasized the importance of this exegetic approach to *Walden*, seeing Thoreau's praise of the classics and world scriptures as the framework for the kind of writing that is discovered or overheard, rather than created, by the author (*W* 103–4). "This writer [Thoreau] is writing a sacred text. This commits him, from a religious point of view, to the claim that its words are revealed, received, and not merely mused."[11] Cavell's characterization of *Walden* as sacred text is not, of course, a declaration of his discipleship, but it emphasizes his (and Thoreau's) belief that a bond of truth must be kept between writer and reader. An ordinary language, accessible to all earnest learners, was crucial.

Thoreau's description of the daily happenings of pond life represented for Cavell a gesture toward this repair of the loss of both self and community that signified a caustic skepticism in human interaction. Cavell's attention to Thoreau's detailed descriptive passages of birds and their behaviors, or his perceptive discussions of the importance of being a neighbor and self-consciousness, suggest the ways that Thoreau's "scripture" provided an alternative mindset.[12] Thoreau's discovery of the earth itself in the Burnt Lands is a similar event and one of Thoreau's most momentous hymns to the ordinary. The scene portrays a thirst for the recovery of a lost sense of the sacred, and its highest moment, the declaration of "*Contact! Contact! Who* are we? *where* are we?" expresses a rapture that is one of Thoreau's deepest spiritual avowals (*MW* 71). His exclamation might be seen as an alternative to Emerson's "transparent eyeball" passage in *Nature* as the defining statement of transcendentalist spirituality (*CW* 1:10). Thoreau reaches longingly for contact with the earth, whereas Emerson releases the earth around him and drifts mistily away.

Thoreau's "contact" passage, however, becomes entangling in its complexity when followed closely. The phrases seem to waver between a celebration of "contact" attained and a yearning for "contact" not yet fully realized. Thoreau seems to *have* contact, but also *not to have* it. "I stand in awe of my body," he tells us. "This matter to which I am bound has become so strange to me" (*MW* 71). This feeling of alienation brings into question both his sense of belonging and his reverence for the ordinary. He is "in awe" of his body but also declares it "strange." Thoreau reveals this estrangement to suggest the mystifying duality of physical experience. "I fear bodies, I tremble to meet them," he writes (*MW* 71). Is this the trembling of fear or of desire? In either case, the statement leads directly to a celebration of what he terms "our life in nature," the daily experience of "rocks, trees, wind on our cheeks! The *solid* earth! the *actual* world! the *common sense!*" At this point Thoreau proclaims, "*Contact! Contact!*" with ecstatic conviction (*MW* 71).

Ah, but only if the passage ended there. The outburst continues, not in ecstasy, but into uncertainty. "*Who* are we? *where* are we?" (*MW* 71). In posing these questions immediately after his declarations of contact,

Thoreau steps back from his witness to the power and magnetism of "the *solid* earth" (*MW* 71). Perhaps the questions could be read as expressions of wonderment, but the shadow of uncertainty remains in them, as if doubt and perplexity continued to follow Thoreau from Ktaadn's peak. "What is this Titan that has possession of me?" he asks (*MW* 71). The Titan is the body and also the "*solid* earth" and the totality of things that are called "matter"—all of which remain enigmatic, somehow distanced from our full knowing. These questions remind us of the rich nineteenth-century scientific inquiry into the nature of matter, an inquiry still alive in modern physics.[13] In a time in which material evidence of the evolution of life on the planet was expanding and the phenomenon of electricity was pushing toward new conceptions of matter itself, Thoreau's questions seem particularly profound and resonant. His praise of "the *actual* world" is a crucial episode in his search for the elusive God, but not, as he realized, an absolute and unchanging creed (*MW* 71).

"The Dream Frog"

Thoreau's excursion to Mount Ktaadn was an encounter with nature in the wild. Even though he hoped for experience that went beyond him, he left the mountain with feelings of stunned disappointment near the summit and what we might call "elated perplexity" in the Burnt Lands. Though he was drawn toward these extreme borders of earth's natural power, he was also engrossed in the recurring seasonal processes of nature in the countryside around him. In late April and early May of 1852, Thoreau carefully recorded the coming of spring in Fairhaven Bay and the hills nearby, describing in his Journal the events of emerging new life with his own reactions and appraisals.[14] That this particular coming of spring echoed the original creation of the world is the central motif in this series of Journal entries. Drawn by the rapid unfolding of new plant life, Thoreau recorded predawn, midafternoon, and evening saunters in which he was able to trace returning birds, emerging frogs and turtles, and the first of the area's blossoming wildflowers. "Are not the flowers which appear earliest in the spring the most primitive & simplest?" he asked. He followed that query with a dated record of the seventeen types of blossoms he had observed over the past two weeks, using "Grays names" to list them "in the order in which I think they should be named" (*PJ* 5:3). Carefully recording his observations, he searched the spring for a sense of form or order, pursuing evidence that plants do not blossom randomly but through a comprehensible process. These Journal entries show us a developing naturalist gathering the records that will help understand the progression of seasonal change in this climate. They also show a remarkable alertness to the day and the moment and a sense of the miraculous ordinary that would inform *Walden*. Here was a seeker of spiritual insight, who saw in the early blossoms and leafing plants the assurance of the world being created anew.

Despite his wariness of churches and theological dogma, Thoreau was a deeply religious man who searched for the governing laws of natural change and development in both his omnivorous reading and in his extensive naturalist studies. His daily saunters were signs of his calling, his urge to fulfill a deeply felt mission. As Emerson wrote, "His determination on Natural History was organic" (*CW* 10:424). Thoreau's careful manuscript records of his nature excursions have turned out to be valuable scientific data in our century, notably in Richard B. Primack's use of Thoreau's records as a baseline for the study of climate change in New England.[15] Perhaps Thoreau had a scientist's inkling that his identifications and lists would prove to be of future value, but that was by no means the driving motivation of his observations. He craved the rapidly emerging information in botany, zoology, geology, and other sciences of his day, but his naturalist interests were more than scientific in character. His study of these natural processes and seasonal patterns was also worshipful. His attitude was less that of the detective than of the saint.

In his Journal entry for April 28, 1852, Thoreau summarized his ongoing observations of early blossoming, noting that "the first six [of the blossoms he saw] are decidedly water or water-loving plants & the 10, 13th, & 14th were found in the water—& are equally if not more confined to that element." He added that later blossoms appeared in drier and warmer patches of soil, places "like the earth first made dry land." It was less the flowers themselves than the order of their emerging into light that fascinated Thoreau. "This may perhaps," he wrote, "be nearly the order of the world's creation" (*PJ* 5:4). As he was viewing the coming of a new spring, beautiful and fascinating in itself, Thoreau was also seeing a confirmation of the ordered characteristics of original creation itself. "The Peterboro hills are in sun shine and unexpectedly are white with snow," he wrote of one of his walks around Fairhaven Bay. Struck by the contrast of the snow with the budding and blooming area around him, he felt as if the reflected light had somehow reversed time. "I never saw [the hills] appear so near. It is startling thus to look into winter" (*PJ* 5:5). The ability to look back at the winter just passed, as well as to see the strikingly different spring around him, intensified his feeling of the cycle of change. "How suddenly the flowers bloom," he responded. "The spring flowers wait not to perfect their leaves before they expand their blossoms" (*PJ* 5:5).

The quickened urge to bloom that he noted, the vital energy of renewing nature, exemplified his own desire to blossom creatively through language. "The blossom in so many cases precedes the leaf so in poetry?—they flash out" (*PJ* 5:5). In this and many other comments, Thoreau showed himself to be not only an observer of spring but also an active participant in it, a human in conscious renewal, taking in the atmosphere of revitalization just as the plants and animals of the region were doing. The Journal's patterns of close observation, naming, and recording disclose Thoreau's effort to merge himself, body and mind, into his natural surroundings. The idea that his poems come to him suddenly with little preparation, and "flash out" like a blossom ahead of the plant leaves, was his assurance that he shared the vitality of the wildflower. He responded to the creation's music as an interpreter, taking particular interest in the developing sounds of the songs of birds and the peeping of frogs. These notations, important for his growing scientific attention to the location and identification of the new spring inhabitants, were also the texts of his hymns and scriptures.

Entering a shady part of the woods where his vision was reduced, he described "the fine metallic ring" of the "wood-thrush." The quality of the sound interested him because it "most adequately expresses the immortal beauty & wildness of the woods." Thirsting for that virtuosity of expression, Thoreau went "in search of him," and after some effort found the bird "on a low branch of a small maple near the brook in the swamp." The wood thrush still sang, but perhaps because of Thoreau's pursuit, it now sang "more low or with less power—as it were ventriloquizing" in a way that made him seem "further off than ever" (*PJ* 5:13). Thoreau sees himself within this scene, not merely as an observer of it. His tracking revealed the thrush's wide awareness of its surroundings, its quickness and agility in hiding, and its interesting capability of shifting the tone of its song in order to baffle its potential pursuers. This cunning bird, with its multifaceted song, was in Thoreau's eyes the ever-receding wild itself, the elusive God.

While the bird kept a distance from him, he was able to reach, and eventually touch and hold, other creatures that embodied nature's creative power. "Caught 3 little peeping frogs," he wrote, and as he moved closer to the water, his shadow set off a chorus of frog peeping which had a "peculiarly trilled & more rapidly vibrated note" that signaled a "note of alarm" (*PJ* 5:13). It was, as he found, also a love song. Reaching to find another frog and study it more closely, he "caught one," only to find it was "two coupled. They remained together in my hand" (*PJ* 5:13). These copulating frogs that the surprised Thoreau held gently in his hand were the soul of the new spring that he had tracked. They exemplified nature's vibrant creativity, the persistence of life and its inexorable renewal, and, most important, its bonding and fusion. The two frogs are one in Thoreau's hand, a merging of lives that ensures life's continuance. This mildly amusing "capture" scene seems far removed from the thirst for wildness that Thoreau had shown in the Ktaadn ascent. Yet here he stands reverently holding the secret of new life in his hand. Thoreau's regard for these small creatures signified a dedication to the protection of the living world and an affirmation of the availability of creative energy within our reach. My tattered paperback copy of Walter Harding's edition of *Walden* has a cover illustration of Thoreau with an owl on his shoulder and a monarch butterfly on the tip of his outstretched finger. This tender friend of nature is an inspirational figure we must never lose.

The music of nature and its panoramic beauties became the key subjects of Thoreau's continuing saunters in early May 1852. His efforts to identify the surrounding birds led to a close attention to the details of their songs and eventually to meditations on the nature of sound itself as a natural phenomenon. In a dawn excursion, he first heard the "Chipping sparrow" whose "rapid tchi-tchi-tchi-tchi-tchi-tchi" fascinated him (*PJ* 5:14). Thoreau attempted to reproduce the sound with his onomatopoetic series of tchi's, capturing both the character and length of the song as an aid to his memory. He connected birdsong with human language, suggesting the close kinship of bird and human, who both utter communicative sounds in response to the natural world. This kind of thinking and experimentation broke through the boundaries between living species of animals, linking the human hearer of the birdsong to the bird itself. This connection expanded for Thoreau the human understanding of expressive communication through sound.

Thoreau continued this experiment in a moonlight excursion to Fair-haven Hill, where he listened closely to what he named "the dream frog" (*PJ* 5:21), the hypnotic night sound created when all the frog cries merge. It was "a trembling note—some higher some lower along the edge of the earth—an all pervading sound," he wrote (*PJ* 5:22). There was no night silence in the woods. This wavering music saturated the entire landscape, a call and refrain endlessly proclaiming new life. The frog chorale was answered dramatically by the striking of a clock that brought "a grand rich musical echo trembling on the air long after the clock had ceased to strike." Thoreau called it "a vast organ filling the air with a trembling music like a flower of sound." The bell bloomed into life as its tolls merged delicately into the melodious night. Admiring the way that the village bell merged with the frog's night singing, Thoreau declared, "Nature adopts it. Beautiful is sound" (*PJ* 5:23).

The visual presence of the light of the moon enriched Thoreau's evocation of the beauty of the night sounds. He had noted the "great brassy moon going down" (*PJ* 5:19) as he began his earlier morning excursion. When he returned that evening, he found that "the moon is full" and "the air is filled with a certain luminous liquid white light" (*PJ* 5:21) that gave the surrounding night a shimmering glow. It was as if he were entering a holy or enchanted place. Thoreau marveled over the unusual quality of the moonlight, which seemed as if "it were reflected from the atmosphere which some might mistake for a haze." He termed it "a glow of mellow light" and continued with a remarkable portrait of the moonlight around him. It is "as if the air were a very thin but transparent liquid." This luminous transparency, which "has depth—& not merely distance (the sky)," imbues the entire scene with a rare and absorbing quality. Thoreau evoked here the transparency that Emerson had so notably connected with transcendence. It was, however, Emerson himself who felt transparent in that famous passage from *Nature*, continuing to "see all" even as he proclaimed, "I am nothing" (*CW* 1:10). In contrast, Thoreau's description of the "liquid" moonlight suggests a feeling of gently puzzled wonderment and a welcoming immersion into the place he has found. For Thoreau, each such place becomes a holy place, one where he may "discover that God is" (*Corr* 2:55).

Such early spring saunters also brought moments of scenic transport when Thoreau sought hilltop vistas to expand his appreciation of the surrounding landscape. These hills were neither as high nor as fierce as Ktaadn but were more generous in their scenic revelation. In the morning that preceded the moonlight walk on May 3, Thoreau had gone straight to the cliffs at dawn, being transfixed by what he saw. "How cheering & glorious any landscape viewed from an eminence! for every one has its horizon & sky" (*PJ* 5:19). From his perspective, each configuration of the sky and landscape was a new reality. His doctrine that every return to a place makes it new was closely aligned with his belief that every spring was the act of original creation. Looking from his perch on the cliffs, he saw the unique arrangement of the moment before him as an affirmation of his gospel of the eternal new. "The landscape is as if seen in a mirage," he wrote of the early sunlight. "The cliff being in shadow & that in the fresh & dewy sun shine (not much dew yet.) Cool sunlight— The landscape lies in a fresh morning light—the earth & water smell fresh & new—the water is marked by a few smooth streaks" (*PJ* 5:20). These brushstrokes, Journal entries that Thoreau derived from his jotted notations in the fields, remind today's readers of imagist poems with their treatment of the thing itself as sufficient. However, as these fascinating entries gather, they become Thoreau's witness to the sacred energies that define the natural world.

Notes

1. For an annotated collection of Thoreau's letters to Blake with an informative introduction, see Henry David Thoreau, *Letters to a Spiritual Seeker*, ed. Bradley P. Dean (New York: W. W. Norton, 2004). For the definitive work on Thoreau's spirituality, focusing on his interest in Asian religions, see Alan D. Hodder, *Thoreau's Ecstatic Witness* (New Haven, CT: Yale University Press, 2001).

2. For a more critical commentary on Thoreau's experience on Ktaadn, see Ronald Wesley Hoag, "The Mark on the Wilderness: Thoreau's Contact with Ktaadn," *Texas Studies in Literature & Language* 24 (Spring 1992): 23–46; Robert Milder, *Reimagining Thoreau* (New York: Cambridge University Press, 1995), 38–40; Laura Dassow Walls, *Seeing New Worlds: Henry David Thoreau and Nineteenth-Century Science* (Madison, WI: University of Wisconsin Press, 1995), 112–15; Randall Roorda, *Dramas of Solitude: Narratives of Retreat in American Nature Writing* (Albany, NY: State University of New York Press, 1998), 21–56; David M. Robinson, *Natural Life: Thoreau's Worldly Transcendentalism* (Ithaca, NY: Cornell University Press, 2004), 130–43; and James S. Finley, "Who Are We? Where Are We? Contact and Literary Navigation in *The Maine Woods*," *Interdisciplinary Studies in Literature and Environment* 20 (Spring 2012): 336–55. In focusing on Thoreau's religious sensibility in this essay, I have given more attention to the often overlooked questioning and disorientation that Thoreau reveals in his

Ktaadn essay, especially the questions that follow his "*Contact!*" proclamation, and to Stanley Cavell's discussion of Thoreau's work as a form of scripture.

3. Walls, *Seeing New Worlds*, 113.

4. For the connections between the ordinary and the uncanny, see Stanley Cavell, "The Uncanniness of the Ordinary," Tanner Lectures on Human Values, delivered at Stanford University, April 3 and 8, 1986, https://tannerlectures.utah.edu/_documents/a-to -z/c/cavell88.pdf.

5. For an excellent account of Cavell's discovery of Thoreau and Emerson, see Barbara Packer, "Turning to Emerson," *Common Knowledge* 5 (Fall 1996): 51–60. For a lucid exposition of Cavell's conception of the ordinary, see Sandra Laugier, "The Ordinary, Romanticism, and Democracy," *MLN* 130 (2015): 1040–54.

6. Stanley Cavell, *The Claim of Reason: Wittgenstein, Skepticism, Morality, and Tragedy* (New York: Oxford University Press, 1979), 463.

7. Stanley Cavell, *The Senses of Walden: An Expanded Edition* (Chicago: University of Chicago Press, 1992), 10.

8. Cavell, *Senses of Walden*, 59.

9. Cavell, 61.

10. Cavell, xv.

11. Cavell, 14–15.

12. Cavell, 36–41, 103–10.

13. For key studies of what is becoming an ocean of writings on Thoreau and the sciences of his age, see William Rossi, "Poetry and Progress: Thoreau, Lyell, and the Geological Principles of *A Week*," *American Literature* 66 (June 1994): 275–300; Michel Benjamin Berger, *Thoreau's Late Career and "The Dispersion of Seeds": The Saunterer's Synoptic Vision* (Rochester, NY: Camden House, 2000); and Robert M. Thorson, *Walden's Shore: Henry David Thoreau and Nineteenth-Century Science* (Cambridge, MA: Harvard University Press, 2014).

14. For an excellent analysis and demonstration of Thoreau's Journal as a literary document, see François Specq's "Thoreau's Journal or the Workshop of Being," *Criticism: A Quarterly for Literature and the Arts* 58 (Summer 2016): 375–408.

15. Richard B. Primack, *Walden Warming: Climate Change Comes to Thoreau's Woods* (Chicago: University of Chicago Press, 2014).

14

COUNTER FRICTIONS

THOREAU AND THE INTEGRAL COMMONS

Laura Dassow Walls

Anniversaries can be occasions to bury as well as revive, and Thoreau's 200th was no exception: many critics still find good reason to draw borders around Thoreau, confining him to a past with little relevance to the twenty-first century. After all, didn't he take his laundry home to mother and steal pies from her windowsill? Wasn't he the town crank, the village atheist, sitting alone on his Walden throne hectoring everyone with a job, a family, and a mortgage? Shouldn't we listen when the environmental historian Richard White tells us "that if we want to understand what we have done and how we have acted in nature," we should spend *less* time, not more, thinking about Thoreau? Didn't Hannah Arendt herself call him out as a narcissist? Aren't we up to date with the *New Yorker*, where we are admonished to ditch Mr. "Pond Scum," that sanctimonious hypocrite, that amoral monster of misanthropy and misogyny?[1]

I, too, am sick of that Thoreau—all the more so because he never existed. The first step toward a Thoreau beyond borders is to ditch the notion that Walden was an escape from civilization to a pure, wild Nature-with-a-capital-N, by some lonely and possibly not-OK white guy who nailed up a "Keep Out" sign. The man Concord knew, who comes alive even today in town records and historical archives as well as his own words, was far more interesting: this Thoreau trembled not for the precious integrity of his individual conscience, as Arendt mistakenly asserted, but for the collective conscience of his beloved country.[2] What he defended was not mere individualism but the common humanity that makes every human person an individual to be cherished, and what he beheld at Walden wasn't simply "nature" divorced from humanity but the natural commons, even unto the Earth itself, the absolute planetary precondition for all life. Friends, if loving nature means hating humanity, we are all in trouble. Thoreau, that cross-lots thinker, witnessed both the social and the natural commons under attack, and he bent his life toward becoming "a counter friction," as he called it, powerful enough to arrest the industrial machine already grinding life into profit.

Frictions

Even to his friends, Thoreau was a paradox: a sworn realist, he was born on a farm to a family barely scraping by, whose fortunes improved thanks to their chance discovery of a graphite mine, their ingenuity in converting that graphite into pencils, and their willingness to scrimp and save to send Henry to Harvard. Affluence came only after he applied that Harvard education to the family pencil business, inventing both a better pencil and the machinery to make it. Keeping it all afloat took hard work from everyone and unremitting Yankee thrift, the kind that balances account books to the halfpenny. Yet there was also something strange about Henry Thoreau, a brooding, restless desire to see into the heart of the cosmos. Nathaniel Hawthorne said that when he lifted his eyes, "there would be a kind of perplexity, a dissatisfied, wild look in them, as if, of his speculations, he found no end."[3] Even as he relished good conversation and presided daily over the family dinner table, he fiercely guarded his hours of solitude. Thoreau's creative process was driven by this tension: he absolutely had to go every day into the wild—his "skylight," he called it—where he walked with a "grand, serene, immortal . . . companion" who steadied his nerves and kept him sane (*J* IX:209). Henry Thoreau became that most terrifying of beings, a self-reflective moral seeker whose quest had changed his life, so he looks you in the eye and asks, What are *you* seeking? Why have you not changed *your* life?

Thoreau did leave Concord once, in the spring of 1843, on a mission to become a New York City writer. He got through a long, hot New York summer by writing beautifully about the bitter cold Concord winters—a balm to his New England soul; but his rural wares did not tempt urban buyers. By Christmas the New York dream was over and Thoreau was back home, just a Concord writer after all, perambulating between farmers and philosophers. But New York did give him something crucial: a close, hard look at the explosion of modern capitalist technologies. Inspired by revulsion, he wrote a snappy take-down titled "Paradise (To Be) Regained," in which he lambasted the visionaries who think all our problems can be solved simply by reengineering "the globe itself" (*RP* 20): with just a turn of a crank, mankind could plane away Earth's troublesome hills and valleys, drain and fill those stinking swamps, plant, harvest, and distribute crops all around the globe, engineer roads from anywhere to everywhere, fill the air with music, and betake ourselves in "large and commodious vehicles" whenever we please to whatever climate we like. As Thoreau snipes, why not just "run the earth off its track into a new orbit, some summer, and so change the tedious vicissitude of the seasons?"—or while we're at it, why not migrate from Earth altogether, "to settle some vacant and more western planet"? (*RP* 34–35). But Thoreau was no Luddite. It was as an engineer himself, whose inventions were making his family wealthy, that he objected to such geoengineering schemes: in the real world, machines "require time, men, and money." Real labor cannot be done by a fantasy turn of a crank, but only by hand, by hard work, and by, as he said, "the constant and accumulated force, which stands behind every spade in the field" (*RP* 40). By this force of farmers' arms, Thoreau meant *moral* force, which alone could overcome the machine—by revealing the Earth as the paradise it already is.[4]

Back home from New York, Thoreau plunged gratefully into life on Earth, but in his absence something dreadful had happened. In 1843, the town fathers, hoping to revive a Concord still reeling from the Panic of 1837, had arranged for the railroad to swerve through on its way from Boston to New Hampshire. No one was prepared for what happened next: instantly Concord was transformed from a regional center of commerce and industry, a place people came *to*, into a space people sped *through* on their way to somewhere else—a flyover town, a whistle stop on the global network. The homesick Thoreau discovered that while he'd been away, globalization, embodied by the railroad, had slashed through woods and farmlands, opening a great gash in the hillside and cutting across Walden's prettiest cove.

The railroad also exposed Walden Pond to purchase and enclosure by land speculators. Late in September 1844, Ralph Waldo Emerson happened across several men bidding on a prime piece of Walden property, and anxious to preserve the pond, he outbid them on the spot. Once Emerson gave Thoreau permission to build on his land, Thoreau had the means to realize the dream he had cherished since childhood, but the very conditions that made that dream possible also undermined it. Instead of a retreat from modernity, Walden Pond became an experiment in confronting it. Passenger and freight trains passed his door twenty times a day; people hurled taunts at him from the main road; he built with boards recycled from an Irish shantytown just yards away, and he was visited as he worked by Irish railroad workers; he put fugitive slaves onto that same railroad, north to freedom. Concord, too, like New York, was being swept into industrial capitalism. But in New York, humans and natures and technologies were so entangled that nothing could be seen clearly. Out on the edge of town, Thoreau could untangle the mess, study what was happening, sift out the truly essential.

Ironically, then, and quite by chance, Walden Pond turned out to be the perfect place to study the expansionist, consumerist energies that were tearing down and rebuilding the planet. Thoreau took notes as the locomotive screamed past his door, its wheels striking sparks that now and again set the Walden woods afire. Streaking up from Boston's Long Wharf (where his French Huguenot grandfather had once outfitted ships) came scrap iron and salt cod, torn sails bound for the paper mills, Panama hats, Manila hemp, Chinese silks and Southern cotton, lumber from Maine, Caribbean molasses, French brandy, and Spanish cowhides, their tails whipping in the wind. Whizzing down from the uplands came huge pine logs for ships' masts "shot like arrows through the township," cranberries raked up from the meadows, newly made cottons and woolens, sheep and oxen and "cattle of a thousand hills." "The air is filled with the bleating of calves and sheep," Thoreau wrote, "and the hustling of oxen, as if a pastoral valley were going by" (*W* 119–22).

Indeed, the railroad was causing the collapse of Concord's rural economy, a 200-year-old system of sustainable husbandry washed away by the global marketplace. To build those rails and fuel those engines, Concord farmers cut down their ancient woodlots, which they planted in English hay to feed the new breeds of cattle they grazed on Concord's hilltops for slaughter and export to the West Indies. They speculated in new crops, desperate to find something, anything, that would make money on the global marketplace: asparagus, dairy cows, Concord grapes, whatever might pay the big new mortgages they needed to fund their new, improved modern way of life. Farmers who could not keep up lost their land; Thoreau documented, sadly, the depopulation of the rural countryside, while the increasingly affluent townsfolk filled their closets with Paris fashions and their pantries with China tea, prairie wheat flour, tropical oranges, and slave-grown sugar. "So," Thoreau wrote—driving the last nail into the coffin of romantic escapism—"So is your pastoral life whirled past and away" (*W* 122). He knew down to the bones of his being that he was being sucked into the vortex, witnessing a pivotal turn in the nexus of ecological and political violence. This was the drama of his life and the point of everything he wrote. To think otherwise is obstruction of justice.

Counter Frictions

In 1852, Concord's farmers, including many of Thoreau's closest friends, organized the Concord Farmers' Club to meet weekly and discuss how to survive in this new modern regime—how to survive it, and how to *resist* it as well. Concord survives as a place today despite being bisected by a freeway, penetrated by Hanscom Air Force Base, riven by a tourist economy, and besieged by rampant property speculation largely because of their combined efforts; they turned to each other for advice and information, and many of Thoreau's pages, if they were laid into their archives, would fit right in. By the time Thoreau lay dying, even as the Civil War was ramping up, his farmer friends were putting his proposals into practice, protecting whatever they could salvage of their shared natural, political, and cultural commons.

In 1846, Thoreau had gone to jail rather than pay his poll tax. In 1848, at a public lecture, he explained why: to protest slavery, the Mexican War, and the removal of Native Americans, three injustices committed by American civil government that violated the community's ethical standards. To his townspeople, Thoreau offered a blunt and realistic assessment of their joint situation: Unjust laws exist. We therefore have three choices: we may obey them, we may amend them and obey in the meantime, or we may transgress them at once. To make his reasoning concrete, Thoreau turns social justice into an engineering problem: violations of ethical standards have become the foundation of civil society only because citizens (meaning both himself and his audience) not only accept those violations but perpetuate them as well, agreeing to be cogs who serve the State "as machines, with their bodies" (*RP* 72–73). But *humans* must serve the State "with their consciences also" (*RP* 66). This might mean resisting it.

This dilemma posed the question of how and under what conditions resistance might be appropriate. "All machines have their friction," Thoreau pointed out, speaking to his audience as the designer of a machine, a mill, that used friction to grind graphite—friction that might, in time, wear it out (*RP* 67). That is, Thoreau's theory of resistance was enabled by his technological savvy: "If the injustice is part of the necessary friction of the machine of government," he suggested, "let it go, let it go"—let it wear out on its own. But if the machine is *designed* to make *you* a cog in its mechanism, designed, that is, to make you the necessary agent of injustice to another, "then, I say, break the law. Let your life be a counter friction to stop the machine" (*RP* 73–74). In short, it is because Thoreau builds and repairs machines himself that he knows how machines fail—and more, he knows how to *make* them fail: by returning those human cogs to consciousness, dissolving the mystified, monolithic Machine back into the multitude of human/machine couplings required to keep it in working order. In the civil machinery of democracy, this involves, by definition, rethinking all the constant and daily decisions made by every one of us, we whose actions keep it, too, in working order. Thoreau's engineering mind does not quail before the machine but analyzes it into its component wheels and screws; the factory hand who builds the engine knows not only how to make it go but also how to make it stop.

Such a mind, with such a hand, also knows how to build a new kind of engine. For friction does not only make things *stop* but also makes things *go*. Friction is where the rubber hits the road—or, where the foot hits the footpath.[5] That is, Thoreau's theory of counter friction points *both* ways. Sometimes, he says, justice demands throwing in a little sand, or maybe a monkey wrench, to gum up the works. Looking around at his neighbors (few of whom were heroes), he also said, more gently, that not everyone can or must invite martyrdom by throwing their body into its innards. But some will. They are our saints, and they need our support: he cites Socrates, Christ, Copernicus, and Luther. Soon he will defend John Brown as another of these saints, even as the civil government and all the national media were crying him down as a madman and a terrorist.

But there are other paths than martyrdom, which takes us back to the railroad. As Thoreau warned, "We do not ride on the railroad; it rides upon us" (*W* 92). That is, it takes more than a single locomotive to make a railroad: it takes an entire infrastructure and superstructure to make a railroad possible—worse, to make it *necessary*. Sure, some are the richer for it; but, asks Thoreau, "are we certain that what is one man's gain is not another's loss, and that the stable-boy has equal cause with his master to be satisfied?" (*W* 56). Any ethical deliberation must count not just the technologies themselves but also those who build and use them and who are used by them. Thoreau's critique thus embraces the Irish railroad workers over whose bodies the tracks were being laid, the southern slaves and northern factory workers whose lives were consumed to manufacture clothing at the highest profit, even the fishes whose small lives were destroyed by the dams erected to power the cotton mills. "Who hears the fishes when they cry?" he asks; "who knows what may avail a crow-bar against that Billerica dam?" (*Wk* 37).

But even as Thoreau wrote, he knew the railroad, with all its infrastructure, had woven itself inextricably into the very fabric of daily life. In *Walden* he noted how it was changing time itself—literally, because keeping the new "railroad time" required standardizing all the local clocks, hitherto set to planetary time measured by the sun, to global time synchronized with England's Greenwich Mean according to electronic signals sent pulsing from Cambridge through the telegraph wires that, in 1851, teams of workers were stringing up along the railroad tracks. Thoreau, naturally, tagged along to watch (*PJ* 4:16). He noticed how the railroad electrified the very atmosphere around it—and good thing, too, for in this new world we must stay tuned to every signal, alert to every warning: "There is no stopping to read the riot act, no firing over the heads of the mob, in this case. We have constructed a fate, an *Atropos*, that never turns aside. (Let that be the name of your engine.)" (*W* 117–18).

Friction, where the rubber meets the road, wears the road into a rut, wears the globe itself into a single, smoothed-over global space, that false geoengineered paradise networked with tracks we pretend will take us from anywhere to everywhere, friction free. By pointing to the friction, Thoreau points to his other form of "counter friction": get off the damn tracks. Make your own tracks: "Every path but your own is the path of fate" (*W* 118). So after letting the engine of *Atropos* hurtle straight at us until we shiver at our inevitable technological doom, Thoreau concludes with a swerve: he simply steps out of the way. "I cross it like a cart-path in the woods" (122). In short, counter friction also means creating "counter paths," like the path that took him away from New York to Walden and, after the paths he'd worn at Walden had deepened into ruts, that took him away from Walden back to town, where he spent the rest of his life devising counter frictions that would speak to his friends and neighbors. Thoreau knew he could not stop the machine in its totality, but he could hope to call the cogs to consciousness.

Commons

It is a mistake to assume such paths lead only to "Nature." Had the term *ecology* existed, Thoreau would surely have used it, for he spent his life inventing it. The term he had instead was commons. This is why it's so important that Walden was not, after all, untrammeled wilderness; it was a historic common, useless for crops but good for fishing and firewood, hence open to the use of all so long as they obeyed law and custom. It had been a rural slum (as Thoreau documents in *Walden*) because out there on the margins, in the woods and briars, one might eke out a living. That is, outcasts wound up at Walden because it was a place no one valued much; by placing himself there, Thoreau hoped to found a new system of value, recentering the "wild" margins as, literally, "the preservation of the world" (*Exc* 202). Once stripped to the core, aren't we all in the same condition, out on the far side of the tracks with the immigrant workers and freed slaves, inventing a new, squatters', underground kind of life—a tent camp, a refugee community, a commune?—the very seedbed of resistance, of *resilience*. In fact, though Thoreau left Walden, he never left the lifestyle, just moved it into the attic of the communal household on Main Street run by his mother and sisters and aunts.

Thoreau said the point of *Walden* was to wake his neighbors up. What he wanted to wake them up *to* was the accelerating loss of the commons: shared spaces that, by including everyone, bring us together around a place we all work to create.[6] Concord had long understood itself as just such a commons, being New England's first inland settlement, founded as a traditional sixteenth-century English common village. For two centuries its economy had depended on managing essential resources over which no one could claim sole ownership: swamplands for muck to fertilize the sandy soil, water drainages for power and irrigation, woodlands for firewood and timber, hillsides for berry picking, the river for fishing and hunting ducks and muskrats.[7]

The keystone of this entire human/natural ecosystem was the Great Meadow, the Concord River floodplain where farmers harvested the wild native grasses that fed the cattle whose manure fed the fields. But as Thoreau watched, the entire complex collapsed. Expanding to meet the demands of the new global marketplace meant draining the swamps and clear-cutting the uplands, which caused erosion and flooding, which destroyed the river-bottom hay meadows, which led to further clear-cutting to plant domestic hay. In 1859, Concord's farmers, in a panic as the vicious circle closed in on their most valuable lands, hired Thoreau as an expert witness to survey the river and document its stream flow, evidence they used in their lawsuit against the Billerica Dam, which they blamed for flooding their rich bottomlands and destroying their agricultural economy. Eventually the farmers won the lawsuit, but they lost the war: by then it was too late. The damage could not be repaired. Today the Great Meadow is deep under water, the old dikes repurposed into pathways for bird-watchers.[8]

"Who knows what may avail a crow-bar against that Billerica dam?" Thoreau had asked in his most Edward Abbey moment. He was defending the migratory fishes whose small lives had been destroyed by the dams erected to power the Lowell cotton mills; his question—"Who hears the fishes when they cry?"—extends his defense of our common humanity into the natural world, anticipating Aldo Leopold's land ethic. It's also a defense of the human commons, for destroying the annual shad and ale-wife runs had ruined one of Concord's major food sources. Deforestation was doing the same for the woodlands: Thoreau's first call for preservation came early in 1852, when he discovered that landowners had logged off the hills around White Pond, the town jewel. By 1854, when *Walden* was published, Walden Pond, the woodland lake of his childhood, was also treeless. Thoreau knew all too well that his career as Concord's leading land surveyor meant that he himself was complicit in all this: the boundaries he drew on open lands first became the borders he so insouciantly crossed and then the fences closing off yards, completing the loss of another neighbor-hood common. In response, Thoreau became a close student of the process, carefully documenting both the land practices of his neighbors, as they clear-cut one woodlot after another, and the regrowth of forest trees. In 1860, he stood up at the county fair and offered a lecture, "The Succession of Forest Trees," to share what he'd learned with his farmer friends so they could manage their lands for resilience and beauty as well as profit.

Wild huckleberries were another commons that held the town together; every August, the grand event was the annual huckleberry party. Children and servants would pile into Thoreau's borrowed hayrick, while the adults trotted behind in carriages. Each year Thoreau scouted out the best spots in advance, until the summer of 1858, when he found the best huckleberry fields staked off with "No Trespassing" signs or let out for picking at a price. The whole countryside, he fumed, "becomes, as it were, a town or beaten common," leaving nothing but a few hips and haws for the pickers; "What sort of a country is that where the huckleberry fields are private property?" (*J* XI:78–79). Infuriated, Thoreau drafted a new lecture, "Huckleberries," a spirited defense of the commons: whereas the Indians kept "the earth and all its productions . . . common and free to all the tribe, like the air and water," we who have supplanted the Indians "retain only a small yard or common in the middle of the village, with perhaps a grave-yard beside it, and the right of way, by sufferance," a right of way shrinking every year. Most civilized men, he snorted, would sell their share of nature's beauty for a pittance; "Thank God they cannot yet fly and lay waste the sky as well as the earth."[9] Yet.

One day in October 1859, while on a hilltop overlooking the disappearing Great Meadow, Thoreau had an idea: "Each town should have a park, or rather a primitive forest, of five hundred or a thousand acres, where a stick should never be cut for fuel, a common possession forever, for instruction and recreation." As he surveyed all that was gone, his tone turns to regret: "All Walden Wood might have been preserved for our park forever, with Walden in its midst" (*J* XI:387). Yet it was not yet entirely too late: in *Wild Fruits*, Thoreau drafted this idea as a formal proposal, adding that each town should have "a committee appointed to see that the beauty of the town received no detriment," to reserve its rivers and forests, hilltops and cliffs, for a higher use than "dollars and cents," that is, for "public use." His regret for what was already lost points to his solution, offered to an expanding nation: Concord's own town planners, for instance, "should have made the river available as a common possession forever," opening the riverbanks as public walkways and parks instead of lotting them off into private hands (*WF* 236–38). As Lance Newman shows, even as Thoreau was campaigning for social justice, he was amassing the data

and developing the arguments "for the preservation of public green space
and biological reserves" that he doubtless would have pressed further had
he lived a bit longer.[10]

In 1862, as Thoreau lay dying, one of his neighbors offered Thoreau's
proposal (slightly downsized) to a meeting of the Concord Farmers' Club:
"Why should not every village have its public park of from 50 or 100 acres
supported at public expense? . . . Suppose we had such a park in Concord
of 100 acres, comprising hill and dale and water scenery, beautifully laid
out in walks and drives . . . Would it not be the resort of the whole town;
would it not have its silent influence upon everyone, making us more
social and genial; bringing out all the finer traits which are inert in the
human character?"[11] Just as neighbors turned to Thoreau for knowledge
and advice, so did he turn to them to help enact his words. Here was a
form of resistance they could all get behind, a symbiosis buried in the town
records. Starting here, Thoreau's words left traces in every American public
park—places protected as a "common possession forever," so that the commons might survive.

But Thoreau's thinking hardly stopped at the town boundaries, that
artificial border dividing nature from society. His life and writings also
amount to an extended defense of the community's shared practices of
knowledge, inquiry, and discussion: town meetings, where he spoke up,
and public schools, which he materially supported to the end of his life;
libraries and reading rooms to which he donated books and funds; the
Lyceum lecture series, which he helped run and where he lectured regularly. As he said, "We are all schoolmasters, and our schoolhouse is the
universe" (*WF* 238). And as Jedediah Purdy adds, "The world we make tells
us how to live in it, makes us know our place," meaning that every public
decision institutes a choice about how our world will teach us to live in it.[12]
What holds this entire system together is, then, the political commons, the
democratic infrastructure that makes everything else possible. This was the
point of Thoreau's machine metaphor in "Civil Disobedience," which asks
each of us to weigh how our own actions might be degrading that commons, as we lend ourselves, without thinking, to political injustices and
economic inequalities. As Thoreau declares in *Walden*, "To act collectively
is according to the spirit of our institutions" (*W* 110).

Thoreau even considered technology as a commons, a view not unusual
back when machines were still hands-on, offering a creative means of

overcoming divisions by revealing the material connections that make work possible.[13] As Thoreau wrote, "What right has a man to ride in the cars who does not know by what means he is moved?" Everyone should understand the workings of the steam engine, cotton and woolen mills, the locomotive, the steamboat, the telegraph. He made a point of spending time at Boston's largest locomotive factory, making sure he understood the use "of every wheel & screw, so that I can build an engine myself when I am ready" (*Corr* 2:3). When the owner of a cotton mill invited him to lecture in Clinton, Massachusetts, Thoreau asked for a tour of the mill's 578 looms and countless spindles, tracing the process from raw cotton to finished cloth. The workers (nearly all of them women), who knew and counted every thread, awed him with their precision. "The arts teach us a thousand lessons," he concluded with a telling pun: "Not a yard of cloth can be woven without the most *thorough* fidelity in the weaver" (*PJ* 3:170–77; emphasis added). In *Walden*, Thoreau expanded on the notion: "Give me a hammer, and let me feel for the furrowing . . . Drive a nail home and clinch it so faithfully that you can wake up in the night and think of your work with satisfaction,—a work at which you would not be ashamed to invoke the Muse. So will help you God, and so only. Every nail driven should be as another rivet in the machine of the universe, you carrying on the work" (*W* 330). We are all, Thoreau tells us, weavers and mechanics, dreamers and builders, carrying on the work of building a proper world, one that unceasingly teaches us that we create it, together, so that it might hold us together.

Thoreau once observed, in a thoughtful moment, that "it would be a wretched bargain to accept the proudest Paris in exchange for my native village." Even Paris could be, at best, only "a school in which to learn to live here, a stepping-stone to Concord, a school in which to fit for this university," in which Concord's "commonest events," everyday walks, conversations with his neighbors, "may inspire me, and I may dream of no heaven but that which lies about me" (*J* VIII:204). Thanks for nothing, a critic might counter; we can't all live in Concord. True, replied Thoreau, which is why, on his travels to New York and New Jersey, Maine, Canada, and the far West, he was glad to discover "the materials out of which a million Concords can be made" (*PJ* 3:97). His travels to the Maine wilderness taught him what those materials are. High on the drear and inhuman slopes of Mt. Katahdin, he reached the one border he could not cross, the absolute limit of what bonds us together: "Think of our life in nature,—daily to be shown matter, to come in contact with it,—rocks, trees, wind on our cheeks! the *solid* earth! the *actual* world! the *common sense! Contact! Contact! Who* are we? *where* are we?" (*MW* 70–71). His answer was that we are all of us creatures of contact, who build out of this "hard matter in its home" a home for ourselves as well. Yet while returning to Walden, he further realized that our most perfect parks and groves are not those we build at all but those we leave alone: our local wild places, our ordinary swamps and woods and fields, "the common which each village possesses, its true paradise" (*PJ* 7:139). "Or," he adds sadly, "such *were* our groves twenty years ago" (*MW* 156).

We, too, often forget that Thoreau, like us, lived in a broken world. His environmentalism arose from the pain of loss and grief for all that had disappeared, across the temporal fracture we now think of as the onset of the modern world; his nostalgia for that lost world, the wooded Walden of his childhood, is not a retreat from the present but a way of reclaiming the past, all the pasts, renewing them as visible layers of the present that measure the work needed for regeneration.[14] Similarly, Thoreau's political thought arose from rage at America's leaders who were trashing the legacy of the Revolution—a rage that was personal, given that Concord ignited that revolution—while laying the rails for the *Atropos* of the Civil War, then the Gilded Age, and now the Anthropocene, the future we refuse to face. Thoreau, too, is a part of the past that we must not lose but renew, to measure the work that we must engage in if we are to offer those who come after any hope of regeneration. After Thoreau saw his own world turn to ashes, he spent his last years working to build a Concord resilient enough to plant in those ashes the seeds of a better world to come—or better, build a million Concords, plant a billion seeds. As he said all along, we do live in paradise already, heaven under our feet. Wake up! The force we need is the moral force behind "every spade in the field," the force that can plant those billion seeds and nourish them into a common world forever, our true paradise.

Coda: Integral Ecology

For Thoreau to survive to his tricentennial, we need to redraw the borders. We must make a distinction where we now make a false conflation, and an integration where we now make a false distinction. The false conflation is between global and planetary, two concepts that are related but not identical. Thoreau was deeply concerned with the ways in which global thinking was materializing into technological networks: the railroad became his unifying figure for a whole range of technological embodiments that we must bring to consciousness by bringing into *contact*. That is, Thoreau critiques the geoengineers of his era for confusing the globe with the planet, thus concocting a false paradise in which nothing actually touches anything. By contrast, Thoreau the engineer insists that each apparently "global" element is really a point of planetary coupling, or contact: wind to cheek, hand to spade to earth, engine to wheels to rails to ground. As Bruno Latour urges us to recall, these intimate couplings are what we lose sight of when we smooth the Earth into a Globe "without paying the slightest attention to the way in which that Globe might be built, tended, maintained, and inhabited."[15] When Thoreau counters by stepping off the tracks, he is stepping off the globe onto the planet, asserting himself as a terrestrial being who offers, as counter friction to the well-oiled machine of modernity, the stickiness of place-consciousness—in place of our apocalyptic millennialism, a new, *terrennial* consciousness.[16]

To elaborate this insight, Thoreau distributed his own consciousness so fully across Concord that the place became a kind of cognitive assembly—a landscape, thinking. His method was simple and widely applicable: follow all the networks of affection that nurture a place into being, whether small and fast as the mouse he fed at Walden or big and slow as the coming of democracy. Each coupling, each loop, adds to the connective fabric of the whole, growing the connections until the planet has grown into existence, an Earth big and deep and diverse enough to slow us down. This is why Thoreau is so immersive, tactile, sensual; it is also why he is so concerned to save the features that keep the commons alive, for he wants to make sure we keep stumbling over singularities, hoping we'll all realize, at some point, that we walk not on some abstracted globe but "on some star's surface," heaven under our feet.[17] Each coupling, each contact or loop, knits the human/natural landscape into an open-ended but integrated array of knowledges and ontologies, a planetary ecology grounded in geohistory, capacious enough to embrace beings both human and parahuman, and loaded onto a literary lightning bolt aimed, like *Atropos*, right at us. Thoreau is trying to help us, too, to survive—to *resist*.

Now for the false distinction: We will never advance in our art so long as we keep gluing together humans and nature, social and environmental justice, like two halves of a broken bowl. Yes, we have lost the commons that, in Thoreau's day, fused them together; we tried to compensate by setting garden against machine. But now the Anthropocene tells us the garden is the machine; there is no border. Or, it is all border: as Thoreau hinted, the margins turn out to be all the places where we actually *live*, the only places where meaning can actually be produced, or at least any meaning that can succeed in weaving past and future, "humans" and "nature," together into an ecological commonwealth in which all beings might thrive. When will we remember that the flourishing of each is the condition for the flourishing of all? How many ties of affection, how many couplings of dependency, must be acknowledged before the radical hope for a future is made tangible? "*Contact, contact!*" cried Thoreau from the mountaintop: con-tact, touching in common, when what we touch is touching back. For while we can do almost anything on the globe, what we cannot do is touch the face of the planet—nor the face of anyone we love. This is Thoreau's counter friction: distinguishing globe from planet while binding humans and nature together into an integral ecology.[18] Integral is a good term to think with. It is calm, and sturdy, and comes from useful roots: integrate, integrity, tangible, tact—and, yes, contact.

Notes

1. Richard White, *The Organic Machine* (New York: Hill and Wang, 1995), xi; Katie Fitzpatrick, "Change the World, not Yourself, or How Arendt Called out Thoreau," *Aeon*, August 22, 2018, https://aeon.co/ideas/change-the-world-not-yourself-or-how-arendt-called-out-thoreau; Kathryn Schulz, "Pond Scum," *New Yorker*, October 19, 2015, 40–45.
2. Hannah Arendt, "Reflections: Civil Disobedience," *New Yorker*, September 12, 1970, 70–105. In this important essay, Arendt repeats the common misunderstanding of Thoreau according to which "individual conscience" means a "subjective," or private, conscience, one that validates whatever feels right. In Thoreau's post-Puritan New England, the concept of individual conscience was still firmly grounded in a community ethos rooted in shared Christian ethics; it helps to know that Thoreau's family was entirely orthodox and that the two most immediate sources for his moral reasoning in "Civil Disobedience" were the Unitarian ministers William Ellery Channing and Orestes Brownson. Finally, as has been well established, Emerson himself equated self-reliance with reliance on God and on higher law. This means that Thoreau's concept of civil resistance was not individualist in today's sense but communitarian; his sources, his audience, and Thoreau himself would have found our modern liberal concept of selfish or "subjective" individualism incoherent.

3. Nathaniel Hawthorne, "Septimius Felton," in *The Elixir of Life Manuscripts*, vol. 13 of *The Works of Nathaniel Hawthorne*, centenary ed. (Columbus: Ohio State University Press, 1977), 6.

4. See also Laura Dassow Walls, "Technology," in *Henry David Thoreau in Context*, ed. James S. Finley (Cambridge: Cambridge University Press, 2017), 165–74.

5. Anna Lowenhaupt Tsing, *Friction: An Ethnography of Global Connection* (Princeton, NJ: Princeton University Press, 2005), 5–6. This sense of friction as resistance is invoked by Thoreau's original 1849 title for the essay posthumously titled "Civil Disobedience": "Resistance to Civil Government."

6. There is a huge literature on this subject. Good starting points are Lance Newman's discussion of Thoreau and the commons in *The Literary Heritage of the Environmental Justice Movement: Landscapes of Revolution in Transatlantic Romanticism* (London: Palgrave Macmillan of Springer Nature Switzerland AG, 2019), 194–219, and Rob Nixon, "Neoliberalism, Genre, and 'The Tragedy of the Commons,'" *PMLA* 127, no. 3 (May 2012): 593–99.

7. On Concord as a medieval English common village, see Brian Donahue, *The Great Meadow: Farmers and the Land in Colonial Concord* (New Haven, CT: Yale University Press, 2004), 61, 69, 111–12. Deer, which had once sustained the Native American commons, were locally extinct in Thoreau's day. On the destruction by European settlers of the Native economic/ecological base, effectively replacing one ecological relationship with another, see William Cronon, *Changes in the Land: Indians, Colonists, and the Ecology of New England* (New York: Hill and Wang, 1983), chap. 3.

8. Laura Dassow Walls, *Henry David Thoreau: A Life* (Chicago: University of Chicago Press, 2017), 443–44. Brian Donahue has documented this collapse in "Henry David Thoreau and the Environment of Concord," in *Thoreau's World and Ours: A Natural Legacy*, ed. Edmund A. Schofield and Robert C. Baron (Golden, CO: North American Press, 1993), 181–89. See also Robert Thorson, *The Boatman: Henry David Thoreau's River Years* (Cambridge, MA: Harvard University Press, 2017).

9. *WF* 57; Henry David Thoreau, "Huckleberries," in *Collected Essays and Poems*, ed. Elizabeth Hall Witherell (New York: Library of America, 2001): 468–501, 493, 497.

10. Newman, *Literary Heritage*, 212. See Erik Reardon, "Fishing and the Rural Economy: Farmer-Fishermen and the Merrimack River, 1800–1846," *New England Quarterly* 84, no. 1 (March 2016): 54–83, and Brian Donahue, *Reclaiming the Commons: Community Farms and Forests in a New England Town* (New Haven, CT: Yale University Press, 1999).

11. Walls, *Henry David Thoreau*, 444. Thoreau's neighbor who offered this proposal was Albert Stacy, the town printer and bookseller.

12. Jedediah Purdy, *This Land Is Our Land: The Struggle for a New Commonwealth* (Princeton, NJ: Princeton University Press, 2019), 86.

13. See John Tresch, *The Romantic Machine: Utopian Science and Technology after Napoleon* (Chicago: University of Chicago Press, 2012), 308–11.

14. My thanks to graduate student Sarah Coogan for pointing this out so eloquently in her award-winning chapter, "Fragments of a Mythos: Nostalgia and Anamnesis in David Jones' *The Anathemata*," in "Chosen Homelands: Nostalgia and National Identity in the British and Irish Modernist Epic" (PhD diss., University of Notre Dame, 2020).

15. Bruno Latour, *Facing Gaia: Eight Lectures on the New Climatic Regime*, trans. Catherine Porter (Cambridge: Polity, 2017), 123.

16. The coinage is my own, inspired by Bruno Latour: "For the Terrestrial is bound to the earth and to land, but it is also *a way of worlding*, in that it aligns with no borders, transcends all identities." Latour, *Down to Earth: Politics in the New Climatic Regime* (Cambridge: Polity, 2018), 54; emphasis in original.

17. *MW* 71; "Heaven is under our feet as well as over our heads" (*W* 283).

18. The phrase "integral ecology" originates with Pope Francis's 2015 encyclical *Laudato Si'*, published in a secular edition as *Encyclical on Climate Change and Inequality: On Care for Our Common Home*, with an introduction by Naomi Oreskes (Brooklyn, NY: Melville House, 2015), 85–99.

CONTRIBUTORS

Kristen Case is associate professor of English at the University of Maine at Farmington. Her first scholarly book, *American Poetry and Poetic Practice* (Camden House, 2011), was reissued in paperback in 2017. She is also the author of two books of poems, *Little Arias* (New Issues Press, 2015) and *Principles of Economics* (Switchback Books, 2019). In addition to peer-reviewed articles on Ezra Pound, Robert Frost, Wallace Stevens, William James, and Henry David Thoreau, Case has written essays on the value of the public humanities for the *Chronicle of Higher Education* and *Maine Policy Review*. She is the author of the introduction of the Penguin Classics bicentennial edition of Henry David Thoreau's *Walden and Civil Disobedience*, director of *Thoreau's Kalendar: An Online Archive of the Phenological Manuscripts of Henry David Thoreau*, and coeditor of *Thoreau at 200: Essays and Reassessments* (Cambridge University Press, 2016).

Danielle Follett is associate professor (maître de conférences) in American literature at the Université Sorbonne Nouvelle, Paris. She specializes in transcendentalism, pragmatism, music, and aesthetics and has published numerous articles on Coleridge, Emerson, Thoreau, Peirce, and Cage. She is coeditor of *The Aesthetics of the Total Artwork: On Borders and Fragments* (Johns Hopkins University Press, 2011).

Rochelle L. Johnson is professor of English and environmental studies at the College of Idaho. Her work focuses on nineteenth-century landscape aesthetics, and she has published on Ralph Waldo Emerson, Susan Fenimore

Cooper, and Thoreau, among other early naturalists. She is coeditor of three volumes by or about S. F. Cooper and author of *Passions for Nature: Nineteenth-Century America's Aesthetics of Alienation* (University of Georgia Press, 2009). Her current project, a critical biography of S. F. Cooper, has been supported by grants from the Idaho Humanities Council, the Beinecke Library, and the National Endowment for the Humanities. She is currently serving as president of the Thoreau Society.

John J. Kucich is professor of English at Bridgewater State University. He serves as the editor of *The Concord Saunterer*, the journal of the Thoreau Society. He is the author of *Ghostly Communion: Cross-Cultural Spiritualism in Nineteenth-Century American Literature* (Dartmouth, 2004) and several recent essays on the intersections between Native and European American cultures in the eighteenth and nineteenth centuries. Most recently he edited the collection of essays, *Rediscovering the Maine Woods: Thoreau's Legacy in an Unsettled Land*, also published by University of Massachusetts Press (2019).

Daniel S. Malachuk is professor of English at Western Illinois University. He is the author of *Two Cities: The Political Thought of American Transcendentalism* (University Press of Kansas, 2016) and *Perfection, the State, and Victorian Liberalism* (Palgrave Macmillan, 2005) as well as the editor (with Alan Levine) of *A Political Companion to Ralph Waldo Emerson* (University Press of Kansas, 2011), and has served as president of the Ralph Waldo Emerson Society.

Julien Nègre is associate professor of American literature and culture at the École Normale Supérieure de Lyon, France, and a researcher affiliated with IHRIM (in the Centre National de la Recherche Scientifique). His work in spatial literary studies focuses on the place of maps and mapping in American texts from the eighteenth to the twenty-first century. Nègre received his PhD from Université Paris Diderot in 2014 with a dissertation on the place of cartography in Henry David Thoreau's writings. He is the author of a book on Thoreau's maps, *L'arpenteur vagabond: Cartes et cartographies dans l'œuvre de Henry David Thoreau*, published in 2019 by ENS Éditions (the university press of the École Normale Supérieure de Lyon), as well as several articles on William Byrd of Westover, James Fenimore Cooper, Herman Melville, Henry David Thoreau, and Jack Kerouac.

Henrik Otterberg is an independent scholar and economist at the Johanneberg Science Park in Gothenburg, Sweden, where he received his PhD in 2014 from the University of Gothenburg; his doctoral thesis, *Alma Natura, Ars Severa: Expanses & Limits of Craft in Henry David Thoreau*, was awarded the Lundberg Prize by the Swedish Academy. In 2008, he published *Bernströms Bestiarium*, a compilation on the Nordic cultural history of animals in premodern times. Otterberg publishes regularly on Thoreau and has written on pastoral aesthetics and ecocriticism ranging from the eighteenth-century Swedish poet and musician Carl Michael Bellman to twentieth-century British-Canadian novelist Malcolm Lowry. He currently serves on the Thoreau Society Board of Directors and is resident bibliographer for the *Thoreau Society Bulletin*; in 2017 he was awarded the Marjorie Harding Memorial Fellowship by the Thoreau Society, and in May 2018 he organized an international symposium titled Uses and Abuses of Thoreau at 200, held at the Wallenberg Center in Gothenburg, Sweden.

Benjamin Pickford is maître-assistant (assistant professor) in American literature and culture at the Université de Lausanne, Switzerland. His work focuses on the economic imagination, cultural labor, and poetic theory in nineteenth- and early twentieth-century American literature. His articles have appeared in *Nineteenth-Century Literature* and the *Open Library of Humanities*. He sits on the steering committee of the British Association of Nineteenth-Century Americanists.

Sandra Harbert Petrulionis is Distinguished Professor of English and American Studies at Penn State University, Altoona. Her books include *To Set This World Right: The Antislavery Movement in Thoreau's Concord* (Cornell University Press, 2006) and *Thoreau in His Own Time* (University of Iowa Press, 2012). She is also the editor of *Journal*, vol. 8, *1854*, in The Writings of Henry D. Thoreau (Princeton University Press, 2002), and coeditor of *More Day to Dawn: Thoreau's* Walden *in the Twenty-first Century* (University of Massachusetts Press, 2007); *The Oxford Handbook of Transcendentalism* (Oxford University Press, 2010); and *Intercontinental Crosscurrents: Women's Networks across Europe and the Americas* (Universitaetsverlag Winter, 2016). Her current projects include coediting (with Noelle A. Baker) *The Almanacks of Mary Moody Emerson: A Scholarly Digital Edition* and writing a biography of nineteenth-century reformer and author Thomas Wentworth Higginson.

David M. Robinson is Distinguished Professor Emeritus of American Literature and director emeritus of the Center for the Humanities at Oregon State University. He has held fellowships from the National Endowment for the Humanities and the American Council of Learned Societies and served as a Fulbright professor at the University of Heidelberg. In 2010 he was elected a fellow of the Massachusetts Historical Society. From 1988 to 2008, Robinson authored the chapter "Emerson, Thoreau, Fuller, and Transcendentalism" for the Duke University Press annual *American Literary Scholarship*. His publications include *Natural Life: Thoreau's Worldly Transcendentalism* (Cornell University Press, 2004); *Emerson and the Conduct of Life* (Cambridge University Press, 1993); *World of Relations: The Achievement of Peter Taylor* (University Press of Kentucky, 1998); *The Unitarians and the Universalists* (Greenwood Press, 1985); *Apostle of Culture: Emerson as Preacher and Lecturer* (University of Pennsylvania Press, 1982); and the edited collections *The Spiritual Emerson* (Beacon Press, 2003) and *The Political Emerson* (Beacon Press, 2004). His current projects include studies of Margaret Fuller's political identity, Stanley Cavell and Transcendentalism, and Thoreau's sacred places.

François Specq is professor of American literature and culture at the École Normale Supérieure de Lyon, France, and a researcher affiliated with IHRIM (in the Centre National de la Recherche Scientifique). His scholarly activities focus on American literature from the colonial era to the early twentieth century and on ecocriticism and environmental humanities. He has published critical studies and translations of works by Thomas Jefferson, Henry David Thoreau, Ralph Waldo Emerson, Herman Melville, Frederick Douglass, Margaret Fuller, Mary Austin, and Jack London. He has also edited or coedited collections of essays on Thoreau (*Thoreauvian Modernities: Transatlantic Conversations on an American Icon*, University of Georgia Press, 2013); on the representations and philosophy of walking in literature and the arts (*Walking and the Aesthetics of Modernity*, Palgrave Macmillan, 2016); and in the field of ecocriticism (*Environmental Awareness and the Design of Literature*, Brill, 2016).

Christa Holm Vogelius has taught at the University of Alabama and the University of Copenhagen. She works on literature and visual culture in the long nineteenth century, including ekphrasis and photography in relation to such writers as Emily Dickinson and Margaret Fuller. She is currently completing a monograph on mid-nineteenth-century women writers that frames forms of literary and visual copywork as key practices for understanding discussions of gender, originality, and nationalism. Her next project focuses on early documentary and reform photography through the work of photojournalist Jacob Riis.

Laura Dassow Walls is the William P. and Hazel B. White Professor of English at the University of Notre Dame and a fellow in the History and Philosophy of Science Program. Her research centers on Thoreau, Emerson, and American Transcendentalism, with a continuing interest in British, French, and German science. Her latest book, *Henry David Thoreau: A Life* (University of Chicago Press, 2017) won the Phi Beta Kappa Christian Gauss Award and the *Los Angeles Times* Book Prize for Biography. Her other books include *The Passage to Cosmos: Alexander von Humboldt and the Shaping of America* (University of Chicago Press, 2009); *Seeing New Worlds: Henry David Thoreau and Nineteenth-Century Natural Science* (University of Wisconsin Press, 1995); and *Emerson's Life in Science: The Culture of Truth* (Cornell University Press, 2003); she coedited (with Joel Myerson and Sandra Harbert Petrulionis) *The Oxford Handbook of Transcendentalism* (Oxford University Press, 2010). Walls has received numerous awards, including the Thoreau Society Medal for Distinguished Achievement (2019), two NEH fellowships, and a Guggenheim Fellowship (2010–11).

Michael C. Weisenburg is reference and instruction librarian for the Irvin Department of Rare Books and Special Collections at the University of South Carolina. He received his PhD from the University of South Carolina in 2017. Weisenburg has published articles in the *New England Quarterly* and *Emerson Society Papers* and has work forthcoming in the *Rhetoric Society Quarterly*.

INDEX

Page references in *italics* indicate figures.